W9-CPF-459

# The ONE YEAR® *Sacred* OBSESSION

## BECKY TIRABASSI

## DEVOTIONAL

TYNDALE HOUSE PUBLISHERS, INC., CAROL STREAM, ILLINOIS

Visit Tyndale's exciting Web site at www.tyndale.com

Check out the latest about Becky Tirabassi at www.changeyourlifedaily.com

*TYNDALE* and Tyndale's quill logo are registered trademarks of Tyndale House Publishers, Inc.

*The One Year* is a registered trademark of Tyndale House Publishers, Inc.

*The One Year Sacred Obsession Devotional*

Copyright © 2007 by Becky Tirabassi. All rights reserved.

15 Skills for Effective Listening in the June 15 reading copyright © 1998 Roger Tirabassi, Spiritual Growth Ministries.

Three-step anger management system in the July 6 reading copyright © 1996 Roger Tirabassi, Spiritual Growth Ministries.

Cover photo copyright © by Laura Benedict/Getty Images. All rights reserved.

Author photo copyright © 2006 by A. Niesing Photographer. All rights reserved.

Designed by Stephen Vosloo

Edited by Linda Washington

Scripture quotations are taken from the *Holy Bible*, New Living Translation, copyright © 1996, 2004. Used by permission of Tyndale House Publishers, Inc., Carol Stream, Illinois 60188. All rights reserved.

---

**Library of Congress Cataloging-in-Publication Data**

Tirabassi, Becky, date.
  The one year sacred obsession devotional / Becky Tirabassi.
    p. cm.
  Includes bibliographical references.
  ISBN-13: 978-1-4143-1223-1 (sc)
  ISBN-10: 1-4143-1223-7 (sc)
    1. Vices—Prayer-books and devotions—English. 2. Sins—Prayer-books and devotions—English. 3. Devotional calendars. I. Title.
  BV4625.T57 2007
  242'.2—dc22                                        2006034346

---

Printed in the United States of America

12  11  10  09  08  07
7   6   5   4   3   2   1

## Dedication

To men and women of every age and every generation . . .
if you will read God's Word daily, you will receive indescribable
hope, supernatural power, and wise instruction for living.

*The word of God is alive and powerful.*   HEBREWS 4:12

*Commit yourselves wholeheartedly to these commands that I am giving
you today. Repeat them again and again to your children. Talk about them
when you are at home and when you are on the road, when you are going
to bed and when you are getting up.*   DEUTERONOMY 6:6-7

*Oh, the joys of those who do not follow the advice of the wicked, or stand
around with sinners, or join in with mockers. But they delight in the law of
the LORD, meditating on it day and night.*   PSALM 1:1-2

# Foreword

I have spent over twenty years praying and reading the Bible daily. I believe that these two nonnegotiable activities have changed—and continue to change—every area of my life. Therefore, I encourage *you* to get into God's Word every day, because I am convinced it will guide you right into the heart, hands, and mind of God Himself!

Anyone can master this daily discipline—and you don't even have to be disciplined! My secret to having read the Bible every day for over twenty years is as simple as having a plan.

The *Change Your Life Daily Bible* (a special edition of *The One Year Bible*) is my secret. Every day, I open the Bible to that day's entry and read excerpts from the Old Testament, New Testament, Psalms, and Proverbs. I highlight and underline any verse in the day's reading that speaks to my heart. Then I record my further thoughts and impressions, as I listen to God speak to me, by journaling in the corresponding sections of *My Partner Prayer Notebook*.

The book you now hold in your hands, *The One Year Sacred Obsession Devotional*, is one more way for me to encourage you to connect with God on a daily basis. It was inspired by my book *Sacred Obsession*, which was written to:

• cause you to chase after God with such unfettered passion that your heart explodes, and
• inspire you to live life with such abandon that your love for God cannot be contained!

If *Sacred Obsession* lit a fire in your heart, *The One Year Sacred Obsession Devotional* will keep the fire burning.

If *Sacred Obsession* changed the way you live, *The One Year Sacred Obsession Devotional* will help you sustain the change.

If *Sacred Obsession* inspired you to read the classics, *The One Year Sacred Obsession Devotional* will give you even more of their depth and insights.

If *Sacred Obsession* created a new passion for Jesus in your heart, *The One Year Sacred Obsession Devotional* will increase your passion!

Be encouraged,
Becky

## Your Choice

*Oh, the joys of those who do not follow the advice of the wicked, or stand around with sinners, or join in with mockers. But they delight in the law of the LORD, meditating on it day and night.* PSALM 1:1-2

I t is your choice to follow after, stand around with, or join in with those who chase after the holy or unholy. *But of this I am sure, whatever you chase after, you will become....*

You undoubtedly have seen a person's life fall apart or seen someone who has become entangled with the wrong friends, a secret tryst, or a devious plan to acquire some illegal, unhealthy, or immoral possession. It never ends well. Loss of family, job, reputation . . . for what? An immediate pleasure that steals from self and humiliates God?

The psalmist gives you such a simple picture of what, how, and whom to chase—if you want to know *real* joy.

In fact, the secret is in the chase. Chase the holy—the Word of God—and you'll find safe counsel, honorable companions, and unending courage. Chase the unholy—the wicked who mock the Lord and love to sin—and you'll become just like them. It is your choice.

## The Chase

*"Why are you so angry?" the LORD asked Cain. "Why do you look so dejected? You will be accepted if you do what is right. But if you refuse to do what is right, then watch out! Sin is crouching at the door, eager to control you. But you must subdue it and be its master."* GENESIS 4:6-7

**M**aybe we forget. But the Scriptures make it clear from the earliest passages. . . .

Sin will actively pursue us *all* of our lives. We will never be free from sin and its eagerness to control us. Yes, sin chases us, every one of us—from the most professional minister to the newest believer—all of our lives.

Therefore, the simple command in the passage is to "do what is right." If you refuse to do what is right, watch out! Rather than let sin control you—*you* must become its master. You will either be the one who is controlled or the one who controls.

I have many, many friends who call themselves Christian who are *subdued*—overwhelmed, overcome—by sexual sin (same-sex attraction, pornography, sexual immorality, even adultery). They lose the fight daily to the sin, rather than become master over it. . . .

To hate sin, run from it.

## Don't Go

*My child, if sinners entice you, turn your back on them! . . .*
*My child, don't go along with them! Stay far away from their paths.*

PROVERBS 1:10, 15

During a recent tour of twenty-three college campuses over a forty-day period, I found myself speaking to students more often as a parent than as a youth worker. The compromised lives they were leading and the resentments that many divulged toward their parents and pastors were not surprising in light of the statistics: Over 43 percent of their parents are divorced.

Rather than blame these students for following after their worldly peers, I wanted to strangle some parents and pastors out there who have suggested by their moral failures that moral blamelessness—fidelity in marriage, sobriety, and holiness—is impossible!

Perhaps in the twenty-first century, we must admit that our peers, parents, or pastors should not set the spiritual standards for our lives—the Word of God alone must be our source of counsel and guidance.

## Follow Jesus

*Jesus traveled throughout the region of Galilee, teaching in the synagogues
and announcing the Good News about the Kingdom. And he healed
every kind of disease and illness. News about him spread as far as Syria,
and people soon began bringing to him all who were sick. And whatever
their sickness or disease, or if they were demon possessed or epileptic or
paralyzed—he healed them all.*   MATTHEW 4:23-24

I love the stories that tell how often, how quickly, how
dramatically, and how completely Jesus healed people when
He walked the earth. One who has been healed—physically,
emotionally, or mentally—will never be convinced that Jesus
won't, can't, or doesn't heal today.

Having been an alcoholic and drug addict for almost five
years, I identify myself as having had a disease, possibly even being
demon-possessed. Yet the unexplainable power of my conversion
experience is that *within twenty-four hours* of asking Christ to come
into my life, to forgive my many sins, and to fill me with His Holy
Spirit, I quit drinking and doing drugs. With over thirty years of
sobriety, I contend that my healing was miraculous.

Having shared this story in a variety of venues for over three
decades, I was not surprised when a neurosurgeon from Johns
Hopkins humbly told me that what happened in my brain on the
day of conversion that "flipped the switch" from chronic addiction
to instant sobriety . . . was indeed a miracle.

I believe in miracles—I am a miracle. . . . Maybe that is why
I can't stop telling my Good News story.

## Hear Me!

*O LORD, hear me as I pray; pay attention to my groaning. Listen to my cry for help, my King and my God, for I pray to no one but you. Listen to my voice in the morning, LORD. Each morning I bring my requests to you and wait expectantly.* PSALM 5:1-3

Through this psalm, King David taught much about the expectant attitude of a powerful pray-er.

He begins his prayer as if he is putting his hands on each cheekbone of the face of his God and saying, "Please pay attention to my pain and anguish. No one else who listens to my complaints has the power to change my circumstances as You do, O Lord, for You are the God above all gods. You are all-knowing, always present, and all-powerful."

The truth taught in every psalm is this: *God alone is Sovereign.* The psalmists were convinced that they could petition the King of kings with the smallest or deepest angst of their hearts—He was neither too great nor too busy nor too powerful to care about the singular needs of His followers. And David wasn't going to wait until day's end to speak with Him. No, the earliest hour of his day was barely soon enough.

Plan your appointment with the King one day in advance. Put it on your calendar as the first uninterrupted hour of your day.

## Worn Out?

*O Lord, don't rebuke me in your anger or discipline me in your rage.*
*Have compassion on me, Lord, for I am weak. Heal me, Lord,*
*for my bones are in agony. I am sick at heart. How long, O Lord,*
*until you restore me? Return, O Lord, and rescue me. Save me because*
*of your unfailing love. For the dead do not remember you.*
*Who can praise you from the grave?*  PSALM 6:1-5

For many centuries, the book of Psalms was the tool used by the church to teach believers how to pray. I find that most of us, in general, are swayed by misconceptions of prayer that we learned as children or heard as adults that "sounded" right. But I encourage you to read the Psalms *daily*, and make them your personal prayers. Rewrite and paraphrase them, knowing they are the written prayers of those who knew and loved God deeply. Pour out your heart . . . and record God's answers.

If or whenever you feel afraid, attacked, or apart from God, stop everything and tell Him exactly how you are feeling and what you are thinking. Ask or even beg Him to immediately help, forgive, restore, or rescue you physically, emotionally, spiritually, and mentally. Don't stop praying until you feel His presence.

## Alone Time

*When you pray, go away by yourself, shut the door behind you,*
*and pray to your Father in private. Then your Father, who sees everything,*
*will reward you.* MATTHEW 6:6

There is nothing like having the undivided attention of someone you love or respect. There is no price we wouldn't pay to have a private meeting with someone who holds an esteemed title or a powerful position, or has access to a network we'd like to reach.

That is why it is so incredible how little effort, interest, or commitment we place on making and keeping an appointment with the King of kings.

To have an audience with the King of kings is the privilege of every child of God . . . but most of us—and this is not an exaggeration—are either too busy, too tired, or too lazy to pray. We resist setting aside time to be alone with God. Why? It is not convenient. Also we've lost the awe-inspiring image of a personal, powerful God who waits for us. . . .

We miss *so much* power, passion, and purpose when we do not make time daily to hear His voice and respond to Him with immediate acts of love and obedience.

Corrie ten Boom, Holocaust survivor, said, "Have an appointment with the Lord and keep it. A man is powerful on his knees."[1] Will you make an appointment with the King today—and every day for the rest of your life? If so, put it on your calendar. If not, you must ask yourself, *Why not?*

## Lonely Road

*You can enter God's Kingdom only through the narrow gate.*
*The highway to hell is broad, and its gate is wide for the many who choose*
*that way. But the gateway to life is very narrow and the road is difficult,*
*and only a few ever find it.* MATTHEW 7:13-14

On a recent tour of college campuses I spoke with more students who were struggling to live a vibrant life of faith than those who were excited about their relationship with God. Those who were "on fire" for God—sold out to prayer, set apart in purity, and sent out with purpose—faced significant opposition in comparison to those who nonchalantly led immoral, compromising lives.

I'm just telling you what I saw and heard—when I put my ear to the ground, I heard the cries of the lonely.

Frankly, I can identify with this lonely lifestyle. Most likely you won't be the most popular person in the crowd if you stand for biblical principles, say no to common practices, or speak against culturally acceptable trends. In fact you might be accused of being narrow or legalistic.

My husband, Roger, a pastoral counselor, often says, "I'm sick of the word *legalism*. Instead, how about we use the word *disciplined* to describe one's willingness to stay married, live sober, and be morally blameless?"

If you choose this way of life, the road will often be lonely. But that doesn't mean this life isn't the one to choose.

## Sing Praise

*I will praise you, LORD, with all my heart; I will tell of all the marvelous things you have done. I will be filled with joy because of you. I will sing praises to your name, O Most High.* PSALM 9:1-2

If you find yourself alone, broken, discouraged, or even desperate, there is an antidote for your pain. Sing praise!

Praise is a powerful way to express your admiration to the living, loving God. It is a practical way to move your emotions from low to high.

Singing songs to worship the God who loves us by telling Him how wonderful, how marvelous He is will instantly or eventually jog your spirit to connect with His. Songs will stir a fond memory or a sweet sensation of when He comforted you or when you trusted Him. They lift you to Him.

Do you need joy, *real* joy, in your life? Are you *regularly* filled with the presence and power of God? If not, then sing praise! Not just when prompted during a meeting, but at all times: in your car, in your home, on your walk. Sing to the Lord—with your full passion—tell Him how great He is! And I guarantee you, it won't be long before you'll be telling others, "How great is my God!"

# Wedding Bells

*Laban and Bethuel replied, "The LORD has obviously brought you here,*
*so there is nothing we can say. Here is Rebekah; take her and go.*
*Yes, let her be the wife of your master's son, as the LORD has directed."*

GENESIS 24:50-51

Most of us either want to get married or can remember well what it felt like to be a single person who wondered just how and when and where we were going to meet "Mr. or Miss Right."

Rebekah's story seems somewhat unusual . . . yet it is a picture of how God made clear that He had chosen her from afar to be Isaac's mate—using a servant, a water jug, and silver and gold jewelry to confirm the union.

Two thousand years later, I believe God is still in the matchmaking business!

After a tumultuous dating life, I gave my life to Christ at age twenty-one and returned home to Cleveland, Ohio. For the following year, I worked under an executive director who trained a troop of us—single, young Christian leaders—in a high school ministry called Campus Life/Youth for Christ.

All the girls liked Roger, but God chose me for him through a number of very interesting circumstances and events including the loss of a pair of eyeglasses and the annual student-staff Mud Bowl! When he finally asked me to marry him, we had never kissed or dated. I said, "Yes!" We've been married almost thirty years! (And for the record, my birth name is Rebecca. . . .)

Always be alert to the unorthodox methods God might use to direct your steps.

## Fear Factor

*Don't be impressed with your own wisdom. Instead, fear the LORD and turn away from evil. Then you will have healing for your body and strength for your bones.* PROVERBS 3:7-8

From the first hour Christ entered my life in a simple prayer and the Holy Spirit of God sealed me with God's imprint of possession in my life, I've been afraid. . . .

I've been afraid to shame His name. I've been afraid to hurt Him. I've been afraid to lose His love and favor . . . because His love and favor are like nothing I've ever felt before! I've been afraid to disappoint Him. I've been afraid to take Him to places where He wouldn't want to go.

And the result of fearing the Lord has been healing in my body and strength for my bones! I had so many problems—physical and emotional—on the day I came to Christ. Believing that He lived inside of me gave me courage and conviction to overcome so many of them very, very quickly.

And I had to turn. I had to turn from the very *evil* things I used to love and run from them, even hate them. To fear God . . . you *must* hate evil.

## Follow Me!

*As Jesus was walking along, he saw a man named Matthew sitting at
his tax collector's booth. "Follow me and be my disciple," Jesus said to
him. So Matthew got up and followed him. Later, Matthew invited Jesus
and his disciples to his home as dinner guests, along with many tax
collectors and other disreputable sinners.* MATTHEW 9:9-10

I find this passage so indicative of Christ's influence on a person. This is how I first felt when I met Christ. I heard Him say, "Follow Me," and the next thing I knew, everything about me had changed: friends, jobs, even states! I turned and followed and brought everyone with me who would listen to the Good News story!

It happens to so many who meet Jesus—whose lives are disreputable. He comes with an offer to leave your old life and begin anew, to leave everything and follow Him. Your response of obedience to His call determines how quickly your life will change!

When *you* hear Jesus ask you to "Follow Me," don't hesitate; only one response will *immediately* impact your life.

## Be Encouraged!

*Just then a woman who had suffered for twelve years with constant bleeding came up behind him. She touched the fringe of his robe, for she thought, "If I can just touch his robe, I will be healed." Jesus turned around, and when he saw her he said, "Daughter, be encouraged! Your faith has made you well." And the woman was healed at that moment.*

MATTHEW 9:20-22

In the Gospels, a consistent theme marks Jesus' ministry—healing. Much of Jesus' life and work focused on healing the sick and demon-possessed, and even bringing the dead back to life! And every story was different. Some people were healed instantly, and others were healed without having to be in His presence.

In this account, a woman believed she simply needed to get near Jesus—to touch Him, not even tell Him her need. She believed Jesus was full of as much power as she needed to be healed! And Jesus encouraged her faith. I believe He encourages our faith as well.

But when we come to Him, we must *first* believe He is all-powerful to hear and answer our prayers. Though we cannot tell God how to answer our prayers, we must believe that we can come to Him with our requests. And as George Müller taught through his life experiences and teaching on prayer: *If you don't believe, don't pray*.

## Right Words

*When you are arrested, don't worry about how to respond or what to say. God will give you the right words at the right time. For it is not you who will be speaking—it will be the Spirit of your Father speaking through you.*  MATTHEW 10:19-20

Dietrich Bonhoeffer, a renowned minister and seminary professor, was imprisoned and ultimately executed by the Nazis in 1945 for his resistance to Hitler. Tucked away in the preface of his book *Life Together* is a description of his life by another imprisoned English officer.

> *He was one of the very few persons I have ever met for whom God was real and always near. . . . On Sunday, April 8, 1945, Pastor Bonhoeffer conducted a little service of worship and spoke to us in a way that went to the heart of all of us. He found just the right words to express the spirit of our imprisonment, the thoughts and the resolutions it had brought us. He had hardly ended his last prayer when the door opened and two civilians entered. They said, "Prisoner Bonhoeffer, come with us." That had only one meaning for all prisoners—the gallows. We said good-by to him. He took me aside: "This is the end, but for me it is the beginning of life." The next day he was hanged in Flossenburg.*[2]

I sobbed when I read this account for the first time. I felt as if I was there . . . hearing, watching, feeling a man allow God to speak and minister joy, light, and eternal life in the worst of situations.

Consider your life and words instruments for God to use at any time in any situation.

## Written Prayer

*O Lord, how long will you forget me? Forever? How long will you look the
other way? How long must I struggle with anguish in my soul, with sorrow
in my heart every day? How long will my enemy have the upper hand? Turn
and answer me, O Lord my God! Restore the sparkle to my eyes,
or I will die. Don't let my enemies gloat, saying, "We have defeated him!"
Don't let them rejoice at my downfall. But I trust in your unfailing
love. I will rejoice because you have rescued me. I will sing to the Lord
because he is good to me.* PSALM 13:1-6

One of the greatest advantages of reading the Psalms every
day is to receive "permission" from the psalmists to
pour your heart out to the Lord, recording everything
from your deepest despair to your most exhilarating moments of
rescue. David, who recorded the high and low points of his life
through this and many other psalms, brilliantly shows us how to be
absolutely transparent in our prayers to God.

Written prayer, though obviously not a new idea, became my
pattern for prayer over two decades ago (February 1984), when
I determined to spend one hour a day with God in prayer and
Bible reading—every day—for the rest of my life. This two-way
conversational pattern immediately helped me talk to God about
*everything*—and to record what I heard Him speaking back to me
as I read His Word daily. I encourage you to try this. Begin by
paraphrasing this passage into your own heartfelt psalm, and then
listen to God as He speaks to you through the verses.

## Come Near

*Jesus said, "Come to me, all of you who are weary and carry heavy burdens, and I will give you rest. Take my yoke upon you. Let me teach you, because I am humble and gentle at heart, and you will find rest for your souls. For my yoke is easy to bear, and the burden I give you is light."* MATTHEW 11:28-30

Most of us will struggle to establish a daily appointment with God until something happens in our lives to convince us that there is nothing else we can do to find peace, help, hope, answers, or courage than to come to God in prayer. Unfortunately, prayer becomes a last resort, rather than our initial response.

I've spent over two decades teaching people to pray, and frankly, I've heard every imaginable excuse why people don't pray . . . but what people most often fail to understand is what they are *missing* when they neglect to pray: power to overcome, comfort to sustain loss, courage to stand against temptation, faith that is invincible, and the ability to perceive the supernatural. These are the very real benefits of spending time with God.

Prayer will no longer be a passionless duty or a monotonous discipline if you get a glimpse of the moment-by-moment power and intervention of God available to you. When you hear God calling you to come near to Him, you must expect that He wants to give you more peace, power, and rest—look for it, ask for it, don't leave your time without it.

Rosalind Rinker, one of InterVarsity's first staff workers and author of *Prayer: Conversing with God*, called prayer "a dialogue between two persons who love each other."[3]

I can just hear Jesus saying, "Come to Me. I know your needs. I truly love you. Do not be afraid. Come, rest in Me."

# Unspoken Rules

*Who may worship in your sanctuary, LORD? . . . Those who despise flagrant sinners, and honor the faithful followers of the LORD, and keep their promises even when it hurts.* PSALM 15:1, 4

I hate to say it, but maybe *somebody* should just get it out in the open.

I don't think our words mean so much anymore, even the little ones such as "I'll be there," or "I won't tell anyone," or "I'll send the check in the mail today," much less the more weighted words such as "I do."

I find it is only hard to keep a promise if it is also hard to keep your word! You and I both know people who *always* do what they say they will do—they are consistent, dependable, and disciplined. They are admirable, aren't they?

I recently spoke at a college in which each student who attended that institution agreed in writing to follow certain rules. But it was also an "unspoken" rule that many students *never* intended to follow those rules.

Interestingly, a student from a different institution (whose school required students to sign a similar statement) brought the subject up in front of a large group after reading a recent campus news article discussing the contradiction. He said (I'm paraphrasing), "I kind of think the rules are stupid too, but if you are going to sign the statement, then it is your integrity that is at stake. If you sign the document but have no compulsion to follow the rules or be a person of your word, it is a worse offense than the rules themselves."

Hmmm. . . . What a novel idea.

## Now Here

*I know the LORD is always with me. I will not be shaken,*
*for he is right beside me.* PSALM 16:8

Do *you* know that God is right beside you? That He is near? As a child, I was taken to church every Sunday from birth until I left home at seventeen. Around the age of four, my very old Sunday school teacher taught with a flannelgraph board every week. I've never forgotten one lesson. She carefully placed the following letters on the board, each one right next to the other:

*NOWHERE*

Then she told us how, though we cannot see God, He is right beside us. Then she put a small space between the very same letters and spelled

*NOW HERE*

Though we cannot see Him, the Holy Spirit prays through the believer to enable him or her to say, "I know the Lord is always with me. I will not be shaken, for He is right beside me."

Today and every day, no matter what circumstance you face or where you find yourself . . .

allow your hope,

strength,

confidence, and

peace to come from God alone, who sees and hears, and is ever near to you.

## Nonnegotiable Prayer

*I am praying to you because I know you will answer, O God.*
*Bend down and listen as I pray.* PSALM 17:6

Y ou must resolve this issue.

Do you believe that God answers your prayers?

Do you even believe that God listens to you when you talk to Him?

Most of us have misconceptions about prayer. Some of us have been taught that God only listens to very important requests or to very important people. Some of us have been told not to bother God with repeated requests. Many of us are very haphazard in how often we pray or what we really believe about prayer—*so we don't pray effectively, passionately, consistently, or with power.*

My Christian life dramatically improved when I searched for all the verses in the Bible that contained the words *ask*, *believe*, and *pray*. I realized that if I acted like I believed half of what the Bible said about prayer—I'd be living on the edge of excitement and adventure!

I discovered that Jesus was all about, all over, prayer! He often went alone to talk to the Father to be restored and refreshed, as well as to receive counsel before making decisions. He taught His disciples how to talk and listen to the Father. Prayer was simply nonnegotiable in His life—is it in yours?

## Sold Out

*The Kingdom of Heaven is like a merchant on the lookout for choice pearls.*
*When he discovered a pearl of great value, he sold everything he owned*
*and bought it!* MATTHEW 13:45-46

It is so evident when someone is "sold out."

Those who have given up something of value for something they consider irresistible or of greater value are usually a bit eccentric! They are visibly ecstatic, noticeably infatuated, over the top in love, unashamedly outspoken, and often relentlessly persuasive!

They start up organizations with limitless energy and passion. They quit their secure positions in order to give their lives to a cause. They abruptly and positively change their behavior in order to show their true love to another.

It is not usually a gradual decision; it is a prompt, impassioned pursuit that drives them to *sell out* of what was comfortable but passionless.

It is no different for those who are sold out to Jesus. . . . They often look and act eccentric—visibly ecstatic, noticeably infatuated, over the top in love, unashamedly outspoken, and often relentlessly persuasive!

Makes sense though. . . .

Once you meet the One who died for you, you know you have found what you've been searching for all your life—unending love and eternal life. What greater treasure is to be found?

## Refuse It

*They scoffed, "He's just the carpenter's son, and we know Mary, his mother, and his brothers—James, Joseph, Simon, and Judas. All his sisters live right here among us. Where did he learn all these things?" And they were deeply offended and refused to believe in him. Then Jesus told them, "A prophet is honored everywhere except in his own hometown and among his own family." And so he did only a few miracles there because of their unbelief.* MATTHEW 13:55-58

For centuries, one of the greatest sins discussed by notable authors and theologians and considered as most destructive to the work of God and to one's walk with God has been the sin of unbelief.

Those who fall into the category of either spreading unbelief or struggling with unbelief must pay attention. Unbelief is incredibly harmful to your own faith and to others. What does it look and sound like? Criticism. Negative comments. Doubt.

Hannah Whitall Smith, author of *The Christian's Secret of a Happy Life*, identified how to rid herself of the continual struggle with the sin of unbelief. She wrote, "Like any other sin, the stronghold is in the will, and the will to doubt must be surrendered exactly as you surrender the will to yield to any other temptation. . . . Remember, we cannot give up doubting gradually. We must give it up all at once and must completely rely on the Lord for deliverance when we are tempted. . . . We must refuse to entertain the doubt a single moment."[4]

What is the secret of victory over any sin? Refuse to entertain it. Even for a moment.

## God's Purpose

*"Please, come closer,"[Joseph] said to them. So they came closer. And he said*
*again,"I am Joseph, your brother, whom you sold into slavery in Egypt.*
*But don't be upset, and don't be angry with yourselves for selling*
*me to this place. It was God who sent me here ahead of you to*
*preserve your lives."* GENESIS 45:4-5

P ushed aside and forgotten by "brothers" or "sisters," friends
or family members who simply didn't appreciate your
vision, personality, or ideas—has it ever happened to you?
In Joseph's case, this wasn't the only time he was overlooked,
mistreated, or misunderstood! This was a pattern in his life!

Many of you have been in a similar situation at least once.
But Joseph's response is so unusual—he was not bitter. He did
not refuse to help his brothers who found themselves in great
trouble due to the vast famine in their region. He did not demean
or disapprove of his brothers. Instead he consoled them! He found
God's good purpose in the situation.

The book *Dream Big: The Henrietta Mears Story* tells how Henrietta
Mears—teacher and mentor to hundreds of college students in
the mid-1900s—developed her own Ten Commandments. One
impressed me so greatly from the moment I read it that I determined
to implement it as a goal for my life. She vowed never to let a person
know he or she disappointed her—no matter who that person was or
what he or she did.[5]

The implication and application of her "commandment"
are also found in Joseph's response to his brothers. . . . How
will our relationships and work proceed if each of us views the
situation from God's perspective, rather than reacting out of
disappointment?

## True Christianity

*These people honor me with their lips, but their hearts are far from me. Their worship is a farce, for they teach man-made ideas as commands from God.* MATTHEW 15:8-9

While writing to Christians, seventeenth- and eighteenth-century authors John Owen, William Wilberforce, and Jonathan Edwards began to coin phrases such as *true Christianity* and *real Christianity.* They were outspoken about the sorry state of religion in their generation and the chasm between those who give lip service to God and those whose hearts are "for" Him as evidenced by their lives.

In the nineteenth and twentieth centuries, respectively, Charles Finney and A. W. Tozer addressed the same apathetic trends among those of their generations who called themselves Christians. They called for—prayed for—revival and became part of it.

I find the same conversations and chasms in the twenty-first century. And I hear the same call to prayer and revival! As Finney suggested, "A Revival of true Christianity arouses, quickens, and reclaims the backslidden church and awakens all classes, insuring attention to the claims of God. Revival presupposes that the church is mired in a backslidden state."[6]

Do you think the twenty-first century church needs a revival of true Christianity? Can I get a witness?

## Pay Attention

*My child, pay attention to what I say. Listen carefully to my words.*
*Don't lose sight of them. Let them penetrate deep into your heart,*
*for they bring life to those who find them, and healing to their*
*whole body. Guard your heart above all else, for it determines the*
*course of your life.* PROVERBS 4:20-23

Those of us who have children *love* this passage. We want desperately for our kids—young or old—to grasp the wealth of our knowledge that comes from wisdom, age, natural protectiveness, and even from our mistakes.

But I think it would do each of us—single, married, young, or old—great good to read these verses out loud slowly, as if our heavenly Father called us aside (to our favorite spot) to be alone with Him.

Hear the Father speak these words just to you. . . .

*My child . . . spend time with Me. I know everything you need. Get*
*your counsel from My Word. Let Me bring life and healing to your*
*body. Most of all, let My Words guard your heart—your affections—*
*for this will determine your direction. I love you.*

# Crooked Trail

*The lips of an immoral woman are as sweet as honey, and her mouth is smoother than oil. But in the end she is as bitter as poison, as dangerous as a double-edged sword. Her feet go down to death; her steps lead straight to the grave. For she cares nothing about the path to life. She staggers down a crooked trail and doesn't realize it.* PROVERBS 5:3-6

In my recent travels, I concentrated on visiting twenty-three college campuses over a forty-day period, calling college students (and those who work with them) to be sold out to prayer, set apart in purity, and sent out with a purpose. I originally thought I was going to fuel the fire of a national prayer movement that would gain momentum across the country. I ended up in a battle against sexual immorality.

At the beginning of my visits, I was caught off guard—actually shocked—by the number of Christians who were struggling with sexual sin of every kind—pornography, adultery, same-sex attraction, and masturbation. By the middle of my trip, I was convinced that college students in America were losing the battle *and* their will to be a morally blameless people of the living, loving God.

Why are they losing? The lure to sexual fantasy, as depicted in the proverb, says it all: It is sweet and smooth. And before they realize it, it is deadly: Immorality steals intimacy with God and others . . . every single time. . . .

## Utter Ruin

*So now, my sons, listen to me. Never stray from what I am about to say: Stay away from her! Don't go near the door of her house! If you do, you will lose your honor and will lose to merciless people all you have achieved. Strangers will consume your wealth, and someone else will enjoy the fruit of your labor. In the end you will groan in anguish when disease consumes your body. You will say, "How I hated discipline! If only I had not ignored all the warnings!"* PROVERBS 5:7-12

I have so many Christian friends who struggle with addiction to pornography, you wouldn't believe it! In fact, maybe you (or someone you know) struggle with it too. Today's proverb gives explicit counsel on how to win this battle. Make a copy of these verses. Post them on your computer. Write them fifty times. Memorize them.

As often as you or someone you know must seek outside counsel and need accountability *that stings* to stay the course against sexual seduction, you must *as often* access the power in the Word of God in the battle against sin. The Word of God is meant to warn you! These verses imply that you will lose your honor and groan in anguish if you stray from purity and holiness and venture into a life of the illicit and immoral. And if you keep on that destructive path, though it promises tantalizing sensations, you *will* face utter ruin and public humiliation. I've seen it happen. It's ugly. Don't go *near* there.

If you are looking for an even more explicit, radical sexual boundary, try this one: *I will not look at or touch another's private parts, except those of my spouse when I'm married.*

## Set Free

*Jesus called a little child to him and put the child among them.*
*Then he said, "I tell you the truth, unless you turn from your sins and*
*become like little children, you will never get into the Kingdom of Heaven.*
*So anyone who becomes as humble as this little child is the greatest*
*in the Kingdom of Heaven."* MATTHEW 18:2-4

Have you experienced the power released in confession? For many years, whenever I've been given the opportunity to speak to any size audience, I almost always share my story of being a twenty-one-year-old, suicidal alcoholic and how praying with a stranger, the janitor of a church, changed my life. The dynamics of that prayer—then and now—convince me that the key to my immediate and dramatic turn from my immoral, addicted life was my detailed prayer of confession.

The janitor guided me in a prayer of confession, asking me if there were any sins in my life that I could think of and would I be willing to renounce them—to give them up? He made it clear that we weren't talking about bad habits, but sin—those things that I knew in my heart were wrong. Oddly, I hadn't been to church, read a Bible, or heard a sermon in years, but I knew what sins I had committed. In humiliation, I named them one by one. And as the janitor listened to my lengthy, tearful, honest confession, I immediately began to feel different—clean and free. He told me that the Bible says God forgives the sins of those who confess and turn from them. He said this prayer would bring healing into my life. And I believed him. I quit drinking that day. I moved out of my boyfriend's apartment that day. I quit cursing that day.

Hating or humbly turning from and confessing sin in your life *will* set you free!

## My Shepherd

*The LORD is my shepherd; I have all that I need. . . . Even when I walk through the darkest valley, I will not be afraid, for you are close beside me. Your rod and your staff protect and comfort me.* PSALM 23:1, 4

On the toughest days (and in the scheme of things, there are far more difficulties in life to face than I have experienced), I have found that . . .

When I can't see the light at the end of the tunnel,
When I can't understand why something happens,
When I can't fix some mess someone I know and love is in,
When I can't explain my own fears, loneliness, or
    discouragement . . .

I know that God's name is a strong tower, and I literally force myself to write a prayer of gratitude for *all God is and has done* to meet my needs. I even pray out loud to remind myself how near He is to me.

In moments, hours, or even days of desperation, do not hesitate to whisper or even shout out the Lord's name. Tell Him, "You are all I need."

# God's Voice

*The LORD said to Moses, "Get up early in the morning and stand before Pharaoh. Tell him, 'This is what the LORD, the God of the Hebrews, says: Let my people go, so they can worship me.'"* EXODUS 9:13

Τhe more time I spend in prayer and in the Word, the more I feel sure of God's voice. That is why I am not afraid when I feel that God wants me to speak a specific word to certain people on His behalf!

Now, few of us will be sent to leaders of countries on God's behalf like Moses. But that does not mean we should hesitate sharing or receiving a word from the Lord.

You and I don't have to use the phrase "God told me to tell you this" in order to have credibility with a person. But you can say, "This morning I was praying for you and this thought came to mind. I would encourage you to seek the Lord's heart and mind on this." Other times, you may feel very strongly that the Lord has given you a warning for someone—a child or a spouse—on His behalf. In those situations, I think you should speak up! Even then, you can say, "I feel as if God is pressing something on my heart to share with you."

Loving and well-meaning parents, friends, and even spouses can be misguided. So a word from someone on God's behalf should be confirmed over time through the Word of God, by the Holy Spirit's conviction in that person's heart and mind, *and* by those in authority over the person. But when all those components are in agreement, a word from the Lord through another person can serve as very strong confirmation that God is speaking to us.

## Servant Leader

*Among you it will be different. Whoever wants to be a leader among you must be your servant, and whoever wants to be first among you must become your slave. For even the Son of Man came not to be served but to serve others and to give his life as a ransom for many.* MATTHEW 20:26-28

In his book *Spiritual Leadership*, author J. Oswald Sanders discussed the teaching of Jesus' closest disciples as leadership done "on the way." He said, "Jesus did not ask the twelve to sit down and take notes in a formal classroom. Jesus' classrooms were the highways of life; His principles and values came across in the midst of daily experience. Jesus placed disciples into internships . . . that enabled them to learn through failure and success. . . . He delegated authority and responsibility to them as they were able to bear it. Jesus' wonderful teaching in John 13–16 was their graduation address."[7]

What did the disciples learn from Jesus in chapters 13–16 of the Gospel of John? Jesus washed the disciples' feet! They shared bread and wine together, not fully understanding the meaning of His broken body and spilled blood. And that was just the beginning of the humble lives they would lead. . . .

Your challenge and mine as followers of Christ is to be His servant-leaders, walking with Him just as His disciples did, with the same call upon our lives to fulfill the Great Commission.

Daily you must see yourself enrolled in Christ's school of leadership.

## Good Advice

*What are worthless and wicked people like? They are constant liars, signaling their deceit with a wink of the eye, a nudge of the foot, or the wiggle of fingers. Their perverted hearts plot evil, and they constantly stir up trouble. But they will be destroyed suddenly, broken in an instant beyond all hope of healing.*  PROVERBS 6:12-15

The alluring message of any culture will often sound like "good advice," but it is quite frequently different from God's call for those who know and follow Him.

Every generation is barraged with messages, images, and concepts that are based on cultural mores, but that subtly pervert truth and promote lies.

That is why it is imperative that you discern truth and base your standards for living on the Word of God, not on what others *suggest* as good advice.

I sincerely mean this. Our rules and roles in life are not to be defined by what we see on television or read in magazines, or even by what our parents, professors, peers, or pastors might suggest. (Consider the divorce rate, the number of leaders with public, moral failure.) No one is flawless, sinless, or completely without bias. And though most people do their "very best" when counseling others, the only One whose Words and ways are to be followed is the God of the Bible.

Determine today to let the Word of God be your source of truth and counsel. Read it daily; read through it yearly.

## Not Elusive

*The LORD went ahead of them. He guided them during the day with*
*a pillar of cloud, and he provided light at night with a pillar of fire.*
*This allowed them to travel by day or by night.* EXODUS 13:21

God's presence and guidance are no less visible today than
when the Lord went ahead of the Israelites (by cloud and
fire) in the wilderness.

Psalm 25:14 reads, "The LORD is a friend to those who fear
him. He teaches them his covenant." His Word is clear. His voice
can be heard day or night in any generation. Will we follow?

Every culture vies to issue a set of freshly formed acceptable
standards. Our companions also have unwritten rules we must
follow to be included. Our educational institutions, religious
denominations, and ethnic traditions all have mission, vision, and
value statements which beg us to follow them wholeheartedly.

Yet God asks us to follow *Him*. And He hasn't changed—He
*still* leads by day and night. He is not elusive, distant, or unwilling.
He is the same yesterday and today. His Word—the Bible—lights
our paths, convicts our hearts, imparts wisdom, and pricks our
consciences—if we let it. His Word is available daily to comfort
and counsel us, to reveal truth if we will diligently and daily read
it, meditate on it . . . love it.

Martin Luther has been quoted as saying, "The Bible is alive.
It speaks to me; it has feet. It runs after me. It has hands; it takes
hold of me. . . ."

## Regrets Only

*Jesus also told them other parables. He said, "The Kingdom of Heaven can be illustrated by the story of a king who prepared a great wedding feast for his son. When the banquet was ready, he sent his servants to notify those who were invited. But they all refused to come!"* MATTHEW 22:1-3

I recently attended one of the *most fabulous* weddings I can remember—including my own! Because I knew the bride well, I knew she had dreamed of and planned for this celebration for many years—even before the couple met—and it showed! Every detail of the ceremony and reception had been carefully considered. But what surprised me most was that every guest felt as if we were an integral part of the wedding—not simply an outsider or observer! We felt as if *we* were honored guests!

From the moment we walked through the church door until the second we left the reception, there was something to sing, do, eat, or enjoy. There was a guest book that included our photos! There was more food than we could eat—from stuffed mushrooms to filet mignon to chocolate-covered strawberries to root beer floats. On a romantically lit parquet floor under a spectacular moon, the dancing and entertainment never stopped as tambourines were passed into the crowd! And as each guest reluctantly departed, we were greeted at the door with take-home gifts from the bride and groom.

Every person who got an invitation and chose not to attend missed a *most* unforgettable night! Why did they refuse to come? Too busy, too jealous, or too jaded? God sees the same regrettable traits in those whom He willingly invites to the banquet of His Son. . . . Those who refuse the invitation miss the finest celebration they will ever experience.

Have you accepted His invitation?

## Patient Waiting

*Wait patiently for the LORD. Be brave and courageous.*
*Yes, wait patiently for the LORD.* PSALM 27:14

I've been told many times that I model perseverance and endurance. And there is a reason. It is not because I have overcome some great obstacle or achieved some great feat. Instead, those comments stem from those who know I have been waiting on God *over thirty years*, expecting Him to do something that has not happened yet—and I just won't give up! That is my claim to fame!

If you've been waiting for God to do something in your life for many years, then you are not alone! Oswald Chambers, author of one of the most beloved devotionals of all time, *My Utmost for His Highest*, said, "One of the greatest stresses in life is the stress of waiting for God."[1]

Waiting on God is a nonnegotiable aspect of faith. Waiting is the action step a believer takes in faith that shows he believes what he cannot see.

The psalmist, in an effort to encourage all who wait on God, suggests that waiting must not be done anxiously or impatiently. He generously gives us instruction on how to wait. In a sense he says, "Wait with a brave heart and a courageous spirit." (It appears that you need the skills of a warrior to wait patiently!)

If you are waiting on God to introduce you to your future spouse, to sell your house, to open a door to a new opportunity, or to confirm your call . . . you just can't give up. You must wait . . . patiently.

Patient waiting is, perhaps, the true character of one who trusts another.

## Only Me

*I am the LORD your God, who rescued you from the land of Egypt, the place of your slavery. You must not have any other god but me.*  EXODUS 20:2-3

I don't know anyone who doesn't struggle with some issue from which he or she needs to be rescued—whether it is abuse or a failure from the past, a gnawing disappointment, or a lingering character flaw.

Yet most of us can't admit we need to be rescued. We run, hide, rationalize, or numb ourselves. But if we were painfully honest, we might be able to identify one shared emotion between us: pride.

Pride keeps us from surrendering to God. Pride keeps us from confession. Pride keeps us from renouncing all those people and things that hinder us from worshipping, loving, or following the Holy One.

Today, in your heart, identify the god that has more of your time, energy, and passion than the Lord your God. Is it a person or position where compromise is recurring? Is it a forbidden addiction? Is it a dominating desire of which you will not let go? Is it a prestigious ambition that hurts your most intimate relationships? Does something or someone from your past have a bitter hold over you? Are you stuck in a shameful place?

Ask the Lord to be your rescue. Let Him be your only God.

## The Window

*I saw some naive young men, and one in particular who lacked common sense. He was crossing the street near the house of an immoral woman, strolling down the path by her house. It was at twilight, in the evening, as deep darkness fell. . . . So she seduced him with her pretty speech and enticed him with her flattery. He followed her at once, like an ox going to the slaughter. He was like a stag caught in a trap, awaiting the arrow that would pierce its heart.* PROVERBS 7:7-9, 21-23

This antiquated proverb is an incredibly apt description of how pornography captures men and women in the twenty-first century.

This pervasive habit begins naively and always lacks common sense. The warning signs are everywhere—internally and externally.

Yet those trapped in the addiction will tell you that they give in to their lust most often at night—in the dark—when others are sleeping, when no one is watching. They admit that the flat screen is as seductive as if someone of "flesh and blood" were in the room, seductively calling out to them. Rarely are words even spoken.

The lure of the trap is swift. It pounces, then pierces the heart and soul of the foolish, naive one who fell or flew into its snare. Its goal is possession.

I've spoken to hundreds of men and women—married, single, young, old, and even in ministry—who are addicted to pornography. Not one of them believed he or she would fall prey to such an immoral addiction. But all did . . . and quickly. And it always cost them something very, very precious—their intimacy with God and others!

## A Warning

*Listen to me, my sons, and pay attention to my words. Don't let your hearts stray away toward her. Don't wander down her wayward path. For she has been the ruin of many; many men have been her victims. Her house is the road to the grave. Her bedroom is the den of death.* PROVERBS 7:24-27

The days of fidelity and purity as a lifestyle are dangerously near extinction.

Perhaps we've quit listening to anyone who issues strong, sincere warnings of the humiliation, pain, or devastation inevitably wrapped up in illicit sex. Perhaps we've formed our own opinions about sex.

Perhaps we've stopped warning people about the "den of death" because we've wandered down the "road to the grave" ourselves.

Perhaps pastors, preachers, teachers, parents . . . have grown silent because many have become the victims of immorality.

But we have to talk about it. We also have to do something about it. It does no good to pretend it doesn't exist. Pornography addiction and other forms of sexual immorality among twenty-first-century Christians are ridiculously rampant.

From what I have observed, living a pure life for the honor of God just isn't sexy enough for some. They believe that living a pure life isn't required when others seem to have no conscience or consequence for their immoral ways. We just don't believe sexual immorality will lead to ruin . . . and so we wander.

We must stop believing the lie that says, "It's impossible to live a pure and holy life!" It's not impossible with God's help.

## Expectant Prayer

*Turn your ear to listen to me; rescue me quickly. Be my rock of protection, a fortress where I will be safe.* PSALM 31:2

David had God's ear. David had God's heart.

I know when I am praying with people who have God's ear and heart. They are sure of God's power and protection. They expect God to move and work in their lives. They do not ever doubt Him. They talk to Him as their Commander and King. And if they do not see or hear Him immediately, they do not give up asking of Him, looking for His answers, waiting on Him.

They have expectation! They expect that He withholds no good thing from them. They expect that He is just and fair and always on time. They expect that He is who He says He is, that He will do what He says He will do.

They have His ear and His heart.

Do *you* pray so boldly, so confidently? Can you cry out, "Listen, Lord! Come, Lord! Save me, Lord!" Do you have His heart and His ear?

Your power in prayer will rise to new heights when you understand that God is *your* rock, *your* tower, *your* hope, *your* confidence, *your* courageous protector.

# Written Prayer

*Have mercy on me, LORD, for I am in distress. Tears blur my eyes.*
*My body and soul are withering away.* PSALM 31:9

Author and pastor Eugene Peterson describes the book of Psalms as the place where Christians for many centuries have learned to pray.

I had been writing my prayers daily for over a decade when I realized that written prayer was not a new idea with me, but was a discipline maintained since before the time of King David as recorded in the Psalms. Each psalm, in essence, is a prayer formed in the hearts of God's greatest warriors, leaders, and singers. They uncover a very real, emotional, and conversational path to God.

The psalmists held nothing back. They were often desperate, broken, and overwhelmed with fear. As they professed their love for God, they gave their whole hearts to God in prayer.

They knew He cared for them as if they were the only one alive! He was their friend. He was their Father. He was their King. He was their provider, protector, and healer. They cried tears of sadness, pain, and disappointment. They cried out for comfort. They withheld no confession from Him. . . .

In Psalm 31, David was not reluctant or afraid to remind God of his pain and frailty. He asked for mercy. . . .

I encourage you to personalize the psalms by paraphrasing them in your own words. Over the next month and year, learn to pray by praying the Psalms.

## One Hour . . .

*Jesus went with them to the olive grove called Gethsemane, and he said, "Sit here while I go over there to pray." He took Peter and Zebedee's two sons, James and John, and he became anguished and distressed. He told them, "My soul is crushed with grief to the point of death. Stay here and keep watch with me." . . . Then he returned to the disciples and found them asleep. He said to Peter, "Couldn't you watch with me even one hour? Keep watch and pray, so that you will not give in to temptation. For the spirit is willing, but the body is weak!"* MATTHEW 26:36-38, 40-41

Jesus went away to pray. He spent time alone with God in places that offered Him privacy and solace.

Jesus prayed when He was deeply distressed. Prayer was the method by which He could regain strength and receive counsel from God. It was not His last resort.

Jesus asked others to pray for Him—intercession meant *more* power. He was neither ashamed nor afraid to enlist the prayers of others. He found prayer necessary, especially in His most desperate hour.

Jesus knew that true prayer was a difficult discipline—it was a "watch." It would take focus and effort. He begged the disciples to understand that prayer required all their faculties—heart, mind, body, and soul—to be alert. Otherwise fatigue, distraction, or even temptation would take over.

And He asks us to pray.

Will *you* watch with Him for even one hour?

## Confess *All*

*Finally, I confessed all my sins to you and stopped trying to hide my guilt.
I said to myself, "I will confess my rebellion to the LORD." And you forgave
me! All my guilt is gone.* PSALM 32:5

Recently, I stumbled upon the incredible power released when a believer confesses any known sin. After reading the life stories of D. L. Moody, Charles Finney, and Hudson Taylor, I couldn't help but see a common thread in each of their revival ministries—it was confession. Their revival meetings and messages always included a call for those who knew God— who professed Christ to be their Lord—to come clean from any sin and resist any temptation that possessed their hearts and minds.

The power in the revival meetings was released when the lies of Satan were exposed and renounced through confession! Using this formula at my meetings, I began to methodically offer believers an opportunity to honestly admit any addictions (pornography, sexual immorality, drugs, alcohol, and eating disorders) that have trapped people in our twenty-first-century culture. And I saw results incredibly similar to the revival accounts from earlier centuries.

Immediately upon confession, revival broke loose! Believers were broken, their hearts and minds no longer filled with guilt and shame over hidden sin. As hot tears of remorse were shed, relief and hope overwhelmed them. They understood how powerful it was to chase sin out of their lives with confession. With clean hearts, they were free to walk with others and enjoy peace with God on an hour-to-hour basis.

In *any* century, confession of all known sin leads to revival.

## Instant Obedience

*Suddenly, Jesus' words flashed through Peter's mind:"Before the rooster crows, you will deny three times that you even know me."And he went away, weeping bitterly.* MATTHEW 26:75

God speaks to us. He warns us and calls out to us all day long. He uses verses in the Bible to impress us, to give us direction. He allows circumstances, even strangers, to be part of His messenger system. He wants to spare us hurt and pain. He desires us to be right with Him and others. He has a plan for our lives every single day.

We don't necessarily hear audible words. Most often His Holy Spirit gives us direct but simple thoughts which we initially debate in our heads. Very often, we push them (and God) away—perhaps not intending to ignore them (or His advice) forever, but just for the moment. . . .

Peter's denial experience is so common to all of us. We hear a thought—*Don't go there; don't say that; don't forget; make that call* . . . and we brush it off, laugh it off, rationalize, procrastinate, or choose some other direction. Then, like Peter, we die the death of shame and remorse. We heard God talk to us and we didn't believe . . . we didn't obey.

Why don't we listen to God? Why don't we heed the warning? Why don't we run when He says go? Why do we stay?

It is a choice—made in an instant—to obey or disobey His voice.

I am absolutely convinced that when we quickly respond to God's promptings—those thoughts that require the immediate action of our mind, body, or soul—in *those moments*, we powerfully experience God! Faith becomes sight.

A supernatural encounter with God unfolds whenever we obey—rather than ignore—His voice.

## He's Everything . . .

*The L‍ORD looks down from heaven and sees the whole human race. From his throne he observes all who live on the earth. He made their hearts, so he understands everything they do.*   PSALM 33:13-15

If we lived like we believed even half of what the Bible says about the Lord our God, we would be far more radical, powerful agents of change, warriors of faith, and leaders of a revolution!

If we truly believed He watches us, we'd be more discerning. We'd see both the angels surrounding our premises and the demons gnawing at our heels! We'd understand that our earthly lives are incredibly short compared to the limitless expanse of eternity. We'd believe, reach for, and expect God to do the impossible, instead of doubting Him. We'd ask His counsel on the small and great challenges of our daily lives, instead of asking everyone else what he or she thinks!

> We'd look up more often.
> We'd look outside of our little worlds . . . much more often.
> We'd give without fear of being taken for granted.
> We'd trust Him not only to fight but to win our battles.
> We'd lead rather than follow.
> We would not be reluctant, but willing to consult Him constantly.

But most importantly, we'd understand how precious we are to the One who created us. We'd live for Him. We'd love Him back. And we'd be unable to stop telling others about the One who made their heart and understands everything they do!

## Design Master

*Moses told the people of Israel, "The LORD has specifically chosen Bezalel son of Uri, grandson of Hur, of the tribe of Judah. The LORD has filled Bezalel with the Spirit of God, giving him great wisdom, ability, and expertise in all kinds of crafts. . . . And the LORD has given both him and Oholiab son of Ahisamach, of the tribe of Dan, the ability to teach their skills to others."* EXODUS 35:30-31, 34

This passage is especially meaningful to those who create, design, or build!

God chooses you! Then He imparts great—not just good, but awesome—abilities to do what others simply cannot do: to make something out of nothing, to turn raw materials into beautiful finished products, or to become a master teacher of your craft.

Perhaps Moses told the people that God filled these men with His Holy Spirit—giving them extraordinary skills, excellence in their trade, and wisdom from above to build and decorate the house of the Lord—so that no one would get confused about the source of his God-given talents!

When others notice and comment on your exceptional talents and abilities, that is your signal that God's Holy Spirit is working powerfully in and through you! Give Him honor. And in those dry spells, when creative ideas don't easily flow, do not hesitate to ask God for more of His Holy Spirit to invade your thoughts and give you a new idea from the reservoir of His design center!

# Burning Hearts

*Jesus came and told his disciples, "I have been given all authority in heaven and on earth. Therefore, go and make disciples of all the nations, baptizing them in the name of the Father and the Son and the Holy Spirit. Teach these new disciples to obey all the commands I have given you. And be sure of this: I am with you always, even to the end of the age."* MATTHEW 28:18-20

In the twentieth century, among many heroes of faith there was one who impacted millions by making these verses his rally cry. Dr. Bill Bright gave his life to the work of evangelism and discipleship. By the time he died, shortly after the turn of the twenty-first century, over fifty million people had given their lives to Christ through the organization he founded in the early 1950s—Campus Crusade for Christ!

How did one man impact so many lives for the Lord Jesus Christ?

It began with the Fellowship of the Burning Heart. Bill's commitment to worldwide evangelism can be traced to a simple document that he signed along with three others in a cabin after a passionate night of prayer in a Southern California campground in 1947. They committed themselves to four Christian principles of discipleship that included (1) one hour in prayer and the Word, (2) sobriety, (3) fidelity/chastity, and (4) "to seek every possible opportunity to witness, and to the end that I may be responsible for bringing at least one to Christ every 12 months."[2]

The Fellowship—Bill Bright, Henrietta Mears, Richard Halverson, and Louis Evans—charged themselves with a lifelong responsibility to fulfill the Great Commission. And each of them left a lasting legacy with his or her life through decades of effective ministry.

It only takes a spark to get a fire going. . . .

## Beloved Son

*One day Jesus came from Nazareth in Galilee, and John baptized him in*
*the Jordan River. As Jesus came up out of the water, he saw the heavens*
*splitting apart and the Holy Spirit descending on him like a dove.*
*And a voice from heaven said, "You are my dearly loved Son, and you bring*
*me great joy." The Spirit then compelled Jesus to go into the wilderness,*
*where he was tempted by Satan for forty days. He was out among the*
*wild animals, and angels took care of him.* MARK 1:9-13

The description of Jesus' baptism causes you to wonder what all the observers were thinking and feeling when they heard a voice from heaven and saw the Holy Spirit descending upon Jesus like a dove! From Mark's eyewitness account, we are given vivid sights and sounds that explain Jesus' relationship to His heavenly Father.

So verse 12 ("The Spirit then compelled Jesus to go into the wilderness") seems to be an abrupt turn from a beautiful, if not surreal encounter with God to forty days of severe temptation by His archenemy. In four short verses, any false impression that God's anointed Son would—or should—never face trials is obliterated.

God's one and only, highly favored, deeply loved Son upon His baptism and anointing by the Holy Spirit was seriously tested. And so are we—God's beloved children—tested after every encounter with God. Our hearts, minds, and bodies always have to choose allegiance. The mountain highs are given to us to build reservoirs of strength, hope, and power for the inevitable valley lows or dangerously dry deserts in our lives.

Always drink deeply of the Word and Spirit of God.

# The Healer

*That evening after sunset, many sick and demon-possessed people were
brought to Jesus. The whole town gathered at the door to watch. So Jesus
healed many people who were sick with various diseases, and he cast out
many demons. But because the demons knew who he was, he did not allow
them to speak. Before daybreak the next morning, Jesus got up and went
out to an isolated place to pray.* MARK 1:32-35

Over and over in the Gospels, the eyewitnesses told incredible stories of Jesus' healing ministry—miraculous, powerful, and unexplainable healing of the masses. Many came to Him for healing; more were brought to Him by those who loved them. So many people were oppressed, depressed, and possessed. Yet He never appeared too busy or too tired to relieve their pain,

to cast out the demons that tortured them,

to heal their diseases, or

to treat them with compassion.

In addition to the miracle healings, there was another noticeable pattern in Jesus' ministry—private, personal prayer with the Father was His regular, sacred habit. Though He was physically and emotionally exhausted, after time in prayer with His Father, He had increased motivation, resolve, discernment, power, and authority.

To be effective, Jesus knew His body, mind, and spirit had to be under the influence of His Father. And that took time. Time alone; time away with Him. How can we manage on anything less?

## Sin Whispers

*Sin whispers to the wicked, deep within their hearts. They have no fear of God at all. In their blind conceit, they cannot see how wicked they really are. Everything they say is crooked and deceitful. They refuse to act wisely or do good. They lie awake at night, hatching sinful plots. Their actions are never good. They make no attempt to turn from evil.* PSALM 36:1-4

Do you believe that sin *never* stops chasing you—before or after you become a Christian?

No matter how young or old you are, you must always recognize the subtle whispers of sin. Sin will *always* chase you—most often through the habits, voices, and opinions of those near to you who have become its ally.

I've seen and heard the proof of these verses in the stories of children who've been abused by their own parents, of pastors who gave in to some lust and lost everything, or of spouses who divorced—oblivious of the destruction the divorce caused their families and friends.

Sin has a voice, an influence. It lures you from that which is good, right, true, and pure toward that which is crooked, deceitful, and wicked.

Sin chases, pounces, steals, and destroys. And so very often it starts with a whisper that enters your heart, tells you lies, pretends it is your friend, then chases you wholeheartedly until it consumes and numbs you.

The psalmist warns us that the destruction of sin never happens without warning. It doesn't happen while we are asleep or nestled away in some *dream*. It happens one whisper, one act, one hatched plot at a time.

Don't be fooled. Guard your heart. Be alert.

## Anger Management

*Stop being angry! Turn from your rage! Do not lose your temper—*
*it only leads to harm.* PSALM 37:8

Some of us need to post this verse on our car's rearview mirror, our bedside table, or even on the refrigerator! For me, anger is not a bad habit—*it is a harmful sin!* Maybe you struggle with uncontrolled anger, too?

*Awareness* that you have a problem with anger is the first step in getting its grip off of you! Usually an embarrassing, if not destructive, situation exposes the truth about your anger, and you are finally willing to change the way you act. The second step to change—and this is where the power to change is released— happens when you humbly *admit* to God (and others) that you have a problem, need help, and are sorry for hurting Him or them. I reiterate—the key word is *humble.* . . .

Change is practically achieved in the third step—when you willingly follow a daily, written *action plan* that is both practical and monitored! For this step to take hold in your life, it must become a lifestyle, not just a good intention.

The fourth and final step to sustaining any change in behavior is in *accountability*. This step happens only with the help of others—a prayer partner, counselor, or small group regularly asking tough questions.

If God is speaking to you about the sin of anger, don't hesitate to move toward these four steps—today.

## Good Soil

*The seed that fell on good soil represents those who hear and accept
God's word and produce a harvest of thirty, sixty, or even a hundred times
as much as had been planted!* MARK 4:20

The parable of the seeds and soil shows how different people allow God's Word to impact their lives! Jesus' descriptions of the four types of soil have great relevancy when you talk with students or your own children about God.

The first seed "represents those who hear the message, only to have Satan come at once and take it away" (Mark 4:15). I've worked with so many of these students. Their families are broken and have been broken for most of their lives. They have no Bible knowledge, no Christian friends, and no loving support system. They have little chance to grow in Christ without help.

The second seed represents those who "fall away as soon as they have problems or are persecuted for believing God's word" (verse 17). In today's culture, students who have problems or are persecuted are the *majority* of the population! It takes a very prayerful, discerning youth worker (or parent) to breathe courage into his or her students or children.

The third seed falls among thorns, and "all too quickly the message is crowded out by the worries of this life, the lure of wealth, and the desire for other things, so no fruit is produced" (verse 19). College students especially are overwhelmed with daily decisions that steal valuable time away from getting to know God through the study of His Word . . . and the Word of God goes unread.

The fourth seed represents someone determined, even compelled—to hear and accept the Word of God as nourishment. This person feeds on it and feeds others with it.

Farmers, take every opportunity to prepare the soil around you. . . .

## Sacred Position

*You must distinguish between what is sacred and what is common,*
*between what is ceremonially unclean and what is clean. And you*
*must teach the Israelites all the decrees that the LORD has given*
*them through Moses.* LEVITICUS 10:10-11

The Lord was speaking to Aaron regarding the laws of the priesthood.

In all they did, priests represented the holy God and His standards for working inside and living outside of the Tabernacle.

When Christ came to earth, the priesthood became a role and responsibility of everyone who believes in the Son of God. Those who know Jesus Christ are His anointed priests on earth. We are the ones who display His glory and tell His story.

I find few who disagree with the assertion that the anointed priesthood (those who call themselves Christ-followers in the twenty-first century) struggles greatly to discern what is sacred and what is common in God's eyes in our culture. There isn't even much of a discussion anymore. . . . Our culture has consumed us with its standards, the cry against legalism has replaced common spiritual disciplines, and impurity is far, far more rampant among those who call themselves believers than are sobriety and sexual purity.

How can believers reverse the trends of culture upon them— illicit Internet voyeurism, adultery, divorce, and self-absorption— and regain their sacred position as a holy priesthood? We must return to a day when children and adults simply know the difference between what is clean or unclean, right or wrong in God's eyes and choose that way. One child, one family of God at a time. . . .

For when God's people are holy, He is all over us! He lights us up! We become His lamps to light the hill. We are *His* anointed priests, teachers, healers, lovers, and leaders.

## Be Holy

*For I, the LORD, am the one who brought you up from the land of Egypt,*
*that I might be your God. Therefore, you must be holy because I am holy.*

LEVITICUS 11:45

On the afternoon that I asked Christ to come into my life,
I was a known addict who lived with my boyfriend, used
very foul language, and lacked integrity in most areas of
my life and relationships.

In an unorthodox "salvation service for one," I confessed my
sins, was filled with God's Holy Spirit, and was sent out the door
to be an ambassador of the living, loving God. (See 2 Corinthians
5:17-20.) The man who led me to Christ, a janitor who was working at a church, articulated the Word of God to me with such
authority *that I believed him*!

*I believed* I was forgiven, clean, given the gift of eternal life,
and filled with the Holy Spirit of the living God. And with that
understanding, I had a sense of a divine calling and a deep responsibility to reflect the Holy God who loved and saved me.

One immediate result of the "salvation service" was the
knowledge that the *Holy* Spirit lived in me. I felt different. I even
had power to act differently! Everyone who had known me for
years knew I was not holy one minute before I confessed my sins
to God. But from the moment *after* He forgave me and His Holy
Spirit entered my heart—I was absolutely changed! I was given
a new, indomitable courage and an unexplainable supernatural
commissioning to be holy like He is holy!

Within twenty-four hours of my "janitor prayer," I moved out
of the apartment I shared with my boyfriend, quit using drugs and
alcohol, and stopped swearing.

Over three decades later, I know that the living God filled me
with His Holy Spirit *then*—and *still* fills me daily—that I might
*continually* be more like Him!

# Moral Courage

*People who wink at wrong cause trouble, but a bold reproof
promotes peace.* PROVERBS 10:10

I can't tell you how many Christian coeds tell me they are actively involved in something they know is wrong, but can't turn from it or their friends. Why? They don't want to be left out because of speaking out. They confess that they lack confidence to follow their hearts or live by the truth they know is in the Bible.

It takes guts to speak boldly to your peers when you see or feel that something isn't right. And the "right" view is not usually the popular viewpoint or the crowd favorite! Either speaking against or going along with trouble creates pressure.

In the early twentieth century, Charles Spurgeon found the same struggle among Christians. In one sermon, he challenged and equipped believers with these words: "May you also possess the grand moral characteristic of courage. By this we do not mean impertinence, impudence, or self-conceit, but real courage to do and say calmly the right thing, and to go straight on at all hazards, though there should be none to give you a good word. I am astonished at the number of Christians who are afraid to speak the truth to their brethren."[3]

You must not silently look the other way when your Christian friends are involved in activities you know are clearly wrong.

Your bold reproof and sincere offer to help them to turn from sin might be just what they need—even want—to hear. By speaking out, you might save their reputation, relationships, even their lives.

To be quiet shows a lack of courage. So don't judge them. Pray that you would possess the grand moral characteristic of courage and speak up!

## Alone Time

*Immediately after this, Jesus insisted that his disciples get back
into the boat and head across the lake to Bethsaida, while he sent
the people home. After telling everyone good-bye, he went up into
the hills by himself to pray.* MARK 6:45-46

Quiet time, prayer time, alone time, devotional time . . .
whatever you call it, prayer always takes time.
Spending time alone with God—talking and
listening to Him—is not something that just happens.
The busyness and cares of daily life will always vie for, if not crowd
out, your time with God. When I considered my time alone with
God as important as meeting with a special and honored person,
and placed it as an appointment on my calendar—*everything* shifted
in importance in my life.

I've found the secret to "alone time" with God is not to pray
*only* when I feel like it! A nonnegotiable decision twenty-three
years ago to meet with God has shaped and empowered every area
of my life. And after all these years, I need my alone time with
God more than I did the day, month, or year before!

In fact, I've read numerous books written over a span of three
centuries by prayer experts (Andrew Murray, George Müller,
Wesley Duewel, Henri Nouwen, Richard Foster) which give the
same advice. If you want to develop spiritual muscle and memories with God, you must steal away. Jealously guard and plan in
advance a regular meeting with Him that is quiet, private, and
uninterrupted.

# Changed Hearts

*Jesus called to the crowd to come and hear. "All of you listen," he said, "and try to understand. It's not what goes into your body that defiles you; you are defiled by what comes from your heart." MARK 7:14-15*

J esus said you possess the greatest principle for successful living when you understand that your heart is where evil *is found and will flourish* unless tamed by the Holy Spirit of the living God. If you learn to guard your heart, you will live an absolutely different life from those who do not!

Steve Sherbondy suggests that a child's attitude is more important than his or her behavior. He writes, "If parents don't correct negative, critical, rebellious, rude attitudes, then they are condoning their children's disrespect and condemning them to a life of misery."[4] He is adamant that parents handle carefully and prayerfully the shaping of their children's character. Interestingly, he admonishes parents to discipline their children out of a "mature love."

The most basic statistic that shows "mature love" to children is a lasting marriage relationship. Yet the divorce rate among couples who call themselves Christian is almost equal to those who do not profess the Christian faith.

I've spoken to hundreds of college students in the past few years whose hearts are broken. Many of them are angry, disappointed children whose parents never learned how to master their own hearts. Instead they followed lustful desires, envy, pride, greed, and foolishness to the destruction of their entire family.

Changed hearts start in the home; so do broken hearts. Guard yours.

FEBRUARY 25

## Find Life!

*The LORD said to Moses,"Give the following instructions to the people of Israel. I am the LORD your God. . . . If you obey my decrees and my regulations, you will find life through them. I am the LORD."*

LEVITICUS 18:1-2, 5

In these verses are both a stern warning and a promise! I'm wondering if you caught the phrase, "you will find *life* through them"?

God is like a parent standing at the door before the kids leave for a Friday night to go out with their friends. He begs us not to imitate the ways of those who do not love and honor Him. He warns us to be careful.

I don't know about you, but the last thing I remember hearing my father say on weekend nights as I was heading out the door was, "Don't forget you represent the Hunters [my maiden name]." And I always forgot what he'd asked by the time I hit the driveway . . . or I didn't care. I thought only of myself and how quickly I might find my "high."

Looking back on those years has always been sad for me. I lost out on so much—numerous friendships, family respect, athletic opportunities, scholarships—and I embarrassed my family over and over.

For me, it took the bottom to fall out before I would look up, grab God's hand, and let Him lift me out of the mud and mess, clean me up, and give me another chance to follow His way.

Don't miss the promise in today's verses: "You will find life through them." If you are like I was—chasing after or imitating ways that lead to death—don't be trapped, fooled, or stupid any longer. Instead . . . stop, drop, and turn. Chase hard after the life God offers those who will obey and follow His ways.

# No Shame

*Calling the crowd to join his disciples, he said, "If any of you wants to be my follower, you must turn from your selfish ways, take up your cross, and follow me."* MARK 8:34

Simply put, the call of Christ to each of us . . . is to turn from self: self-interest, self-accomplishment, self-promotion, self-love. Deny self. Let go. Lay down your life for the sake of the Good News. In this way, you will save your life and make the Father proud of you.

It's a tough call in any century. But we can't refute statistics . . . not much has changed in two thousand years. We live in "adulterous and sinful days" (Mark 8:38).

So how can we turn, take up our cross, and follow . . . to live and act unashamed of Jesus?

Your life and your call will be very specific to you. Where do you live, go to school, or work? Who are the people your life touches every day of every week? What do you hear Christ asking you to give up for the Good News?

Christ calls you to walk with Him. He has a specific plan for your life!

How many children have led their parents to Christ? How many handicapped people have shown the love of God to their caretakers? How many elderly people have shown a neighborhood of parentless children the way to the Cross? How many students have forsaken the ease of their upbringing or education to become missionaries on foreign soil? How many teenagers have stood by a pole to pray, showing their peers that they honor the living, loving God? How many single parents have raised their children to know and love God despite hardship and even unjust circumstances?

What is your cross?

## Set Apart

*You must be holy because I, the LORD, am holy. I have set you apart from all other people to be my very own.* LEVITICUS 20:26

I rarely meet a single woman who doesn't want to get married! She looks forward to the day when she will be chosen and set apart for just one man.

So why does it so often feel like an imposition for us as believers to be set apart and remain holy for the One who has chosen us?

It must be in our attitude! For surely, if we thought about our relationship with God in the same way single people long to be taken in marriage, we'd be much more content to live holy, set-apart lives.

*The Pulpit Commentary*, edited by H. D. M. Spence and Joseph S. Exell, addresses the "divine call" of holiness as found in Leviticus: "The holiness which God requires is *personal holiness*—holiness in life, manners, habits, food, everything which concerns the man himself." And "holiness must be the characteristic of *God's people as a community*."[5]

What does it look like for me to be set apart for God? Because I am married, I don't flirt or date others, I wear my wedding ring at all times, and I don't pretend I'm not married. As believers, we can show the same faithful love to God by honoring His name by the way we live and love. Set apart and holy—in our relationships with God and all others in our lives—is the standard God asks of His followers.

Perhaps you need to let go of some unholy passion? I encourage you to spend time in humble confession to God regarding your resistance to or acceptance of His "divine call" to holiness, and do *whatever it takes* to recommit your heart, mind, and body to Him today in fidelity and purity.

## Pure Life

*Do not bring shame on my holy name, for I will display my holiness among the people of Israel. I am the LORD who makes you holy.* LEVITICUS 22:32

I recently read in a business journal that people are far more motivated to achieve something difficult when there is positive incentive to succeed rather than a negative result if they don't. . . .

The call to holiness causes many of us to react negatively. We resist, resent, or run from it because we fear unhappiness, constraint, or being forced to sacrifice. And in the process of self-preservation, we not only delay our call in life, we bring shame on God's name!

Second Timothy 2:21 says, "If you keep yourself pure, you will be a special utensil for honorable use. Your life will be clean, and you will be ready for the Master to use you for every good work."

When you consider God's mandate to be holy, in light of Timothy's excitement over being ready for God's use, you have a very motivating and positive incentive for staying pure and holy!

God has put a call on your life. He has set it deep in your heart. He created you for a special purpose. The longing in your heart to fulfill the purpose for which you were created will never go away. Paul exhorts and even begs you to keep yourself clean (or holy) *because God wants to use you* to do something only you can do!

So don't miss your call. Get ready and stay ready to be used by God—your time is coming.

A set-apart life displays God's holiness. (If you need a working definition of holiness, start with Jerry Bridges's simple description from his book *The Pursuit of Holiness*: "To be holy is to be morally blameless.")[6]

## Lamp Tending

*The LORD said to Moses, "Command the people of Israel to bring you pure oil of pressed olives for the light, to keep the lamps burning continually."* LEVITICUS 24:1-2

The idea of keeping a lamp continually lit became a reality and responsibility for me while traveling to twenty-three colleges over forty days in the winter of 2006. There was one purpose for each school: to keep the lamps of prayer burning for twenty-four to seventy-two hours, culminating in 960 consecutive hours of prayer on college campuses for revival in America!

In advance of each campus's watch, a student or staff coordinator was asked to find one or more students, faculty members, or administrators who would "tend the fire" by praying in the prayer room for one or more hours until the next hour was covered—night and day for forty days. It was no small effort to find willing, prayerful, reliable people to travel to the prayer room at all hours to pray. But I visited each campus and found the fire was tended for every hour . . . sometimes by one, often by a dozen people at a time!

Every campus prepared a "tabernacle" or prayer room. One school purchased beams and colored cloths and draped the walls of a large meeting room, changing its appearance from ordinary into something sacred. Another campus remodeled a fifty-year-old prayer chapel into a contemporary "furnace of prayer" on their campus. Some of the state schools transformed libraries, dining halls, or classrooms into temporary twenty-four-hour prayer rooms. But every campus honored the request to have someone covering a prayer shift, attending the prayer room, petitioning the Lord for personal and corporate revival.

I will *never* forget the experience of lamp tending. . . .

What might it look like for you to "keep the lamp burning" in your prayer life?

## Servant Tour

*Jesus called [the disciples] together and said, "You know that the rulers in this world lord it over their people, and officials flaunt their authority over those under them. But among you it will be different. Whoever wants to be a leader among you must be your servant, and whoever wants to be first among you must be the slave of everyone else."* MARK 10:42-44

Before heading out on the 40 Days of Prayer for Revival on College Campuses tour in January 2006, I spent time in prayer regarding the upcoming trip. I prayed daily about the people I would meet on each of the campuses and asked God what He required of me.

One of my first thoughts was, *Be a servant.* My previous campus visits had always been as a speaker on a promotional or chapel tour where I was escorted to a campus and carefully housed in speaker's quarters, fed well, and often invited to meet the campus leaders and staff.

During the 2006 tour, I was an itinerant prayer coordinator. Most of the time, a student I had never met before picked me up in a barely working vehicle! I often slept in someone's house, apartment, or extra bedroom.

At the very first prayer room an hour before one prayer for revival was uttered, it was apparent that someone needed to vacuum the chapel floor! My first thought was, *Be a servant.* Without hesitation, I carefully vacuumed the floor for the hundreds of students who would kneel or lie face down on the carpet over the next forty-eight hours, bringing their truest petitions to the King.

What would it look like—this week, right where you are—to serve others in the name of the Lord Jesus Christ?

# No Doubt

*Jesus said to the disciples, "Have faith in God. I tell you the truth, you can say to this mountain, 'May you be lifted up and thrown into the sea,' and it will happen. But you must really believe it will happen and have no doubt in your heart."* MARK 11:22-23

Hannah Whitall Smith is a favorite author of mine. In the classic *The Christian's Secret of a Happy Life*, she confesses her most grievous and destructive sin: doubt! She laments over the pain that it has caused her, identifying its power over her as equal to any other temptation. She contends that doubting must not be given up gradually, but all at once!

Complete surrender—what a novel idea! Actually, this method of surrender over temptation is the only way I have found victory in troubling areas of weakness—anger, alcohol, sexual immorality. Dabbling with them or denying their power never seems to get rid of it!

Smith was adamant that doubt is the most basic and subtle of temptations in a believer's life. It deceives believers, delays their progress, denies the truth of God, and substitutes it with lies.

As a practical way to resist doubt—or any temptation—she writes, "The soul must rest absolutely upon the Lord for deliverance in each time of temptation. It must lift up the shield of faith the moment the assault comes. It must hand the very suggestion of doubt over to the Lord and must tell Satan to settle the matter with Him. It must refuse to listen to doubt a single moment."[1]

The secret? Moment by moment surrender!

When doubts (or any tempting thoughts) enter your mind . . . stop them. Speak back to them. Hannah Whitall Smith suggests saying, "Jesus save me." I always say, "In the name of Jesus, get out of here!"

Win the battle over temptation—one thought, one moment at a time.

## Firm Foundation

*When the storms of life come, the wicked are whirled away, but the godly have a lasting foundation.* PROVERBS 10:25

I know you have faithful, believing friends, just like I do, who are living in the midst of a storm. Their worlds have been shattered by disease or misfortune, the untimely death of a loved one, or the intrusion of some unexpected, undeserved situation.

Yet they stand on a firm foundation. They somehow hunker down and stay the course. Though their tragedy is real and overwhelming, they possess an unexplainable yet indomitable trust in the unseen God.

As Christians we hope that we might not face tragedy. But there is no guarantee. We can't follow a formula in order to receive a life untouched by trauma or evil. In every book of the Bible, in every church, in every community, godly people are struck by a storm.

In fact, *when* is more probable than *if* regarding the storms of life. So what is the constant hope of the godly? We have an eternal relationship with a just and loving Father who knows our pain.

We cannot assume that the godly will never experience storms. Instead, we must be prepared for them. It begins with knowing our God and His character. We must teach our children and live our lives with the knowledge that God has given us His Holy Spirit to guide us through every earthly circumstance we will face.

# God's Word

*Jesus replied, "Your mistake is that you don't know the Scriptures, and you don't know the power of God."* MARK 12:24

In his 2005 book *Revolution*, researcher George Barna suggests, "One of the greatest frustrations of my life has been the disconnection between what our research consistently shows about churched Christians and what the Bible calls us to be."[2]

Barna claims there are seventy-seven million American adults who call themselves Christian. Imagine the impact we would have if we lived radical lives as set forth in the Bible—where faith moves mountains.

There is a very simple way to turn this all around. . . . Make a decision to read the Bible daily—until you hear God speak to you—and spend time *daily* talking to Him about every decision, detail, and dream in your life. Allow the Word of God to influence you, guard your heart, and fill you with contagious courage to live a compelling and different life.

I know this simple action step to be life changing. Though neither a scholar nor a theologian, over twenty-three years ago I determined to know God's Word and His power by spending one hour a day talking to Him through written prayer and listening to Him by reading a one-year Bible. And every day He has given me more insight, courage, and direction than the day before. I encourage you to take this same challenge.

## Speak Life

*The LORD said to Moses, "Tell Aaron and his sons to bless the people of Israel with this special blessing: 'May the LORD bless you and protect you. May the LORD smile on you and be gracious to you. May the LORD show you his favor and give you his peace.' Whenever Aaron and his sons bless the people of Israel in my name, I myself will bless them."* NUMBERS 6:22-27

Henrietta Mears was a well-known teacher and author during the second half of the twentieth century. She mentored college students for almost five decades, influencing Dr. Bill Bright, Richard Halverson, and Louis Evans—all young men who later became spiritual giants in American history.

Henrietta lived by a personal philosophy; in fact she called her rules "My Own Ten Commandments." One of them included never letting someone know she was disappointed in him or her.

I was humiliated when I read that commandment, and I immediately determined to make it mine! But this commandment was not Mears's idea. She was really following after the ways of the Lord. . . .

The Lord's counsel to Moses and Aaron for the Israelites is as appropriate for any of us who are leaders, mentors, and parents as it was for them. We must see ourselves as having the responsibility of regularly offering words of blessing and encouragement to others on the Lord's behalf! And we must be intentional.

I challenge you today to allow your words to be affirmations to those around you. Encourage the dream God placed in their hearts. Let them know you are praying for them. Then do it—spend time daily with God, lifting their names and plans to Him. Ask for His protection and favor to be over them. Make a prayer list—and refresh it often.

## Stay Alert

*No one knows the day or hour when these things will happen, not even the angels in heaven or the Son himself. Only the Father knows. And since you don't know when that time will come, be on guard! Stay alert!*

MARK 13:32-33

**M**ost of us never think our lives will be touched by early death or tragedy. So we put off until tomorrow (or beyond) what seems inconvenient or insignificant. We often ignore the warning bells in our heads, rather than allowing them to remind us of impending danger. And so often, when lightbulbs flash in our memories, reminding us to do something we promised another, we resist it rather than run toward it.

But just as Jesus warned His followers when He walked the earth, you and I must be alert to the Lord's strong counsel: "Be on guard! Stay alert!"

What does that mean for you and me?

We must wake up each day believing that every day, every hour we have on earth matters.

We must *not only* look for the opportunities that God sends our way, but respond immediately to them. (This is such a key to possessing a fiery faith!) We must step away from self-centered lives and be conscious—expectant—of a nod of interest in spiritual things from a coworker, a cry for help from a stranger, a check in our spirit to avoid a certain path.

We must live in tune with the Holy Spirit. He must be our favorite counselor. His Word must be our standard. And our hearts must be willing to obey and *not debate* when God impresses some small or large request upon us.

Be on guard. Stay alert. These phrases spoken by Jesus sound more like urgent commands than good ideas for us to consider. Don't you agree?

## Outrageous Love

*While he was eating, a woman came in with a beautiful alabaster jar*
*of expensive perfume and poured it over his head. The disciples were*
*indignant when they saw this. "What a waste!" they said. "It could*
*have been sold for a high price and the money given to the poor." But*
*Jesus, aware of this, replied, "Why criticize this woman for doing such*
*a good thing to me?"* MATTHEW 26:7-10

J esus promised that this woman's deed would always be
remembered and discussed. (See Mark 14:9.) And it has been.
Many, many sermons have been preached about the meaning
behind this message. But for me, it is a simple visual reminder
of what one who loved Jesus could do if he or she had the opportunity to spend time with Him.

This woman's actions were not grandiose or wasteful from
a loyal follower's viewpoint! They were evidence of her gratitude
and respect for the One who spent time with her family and
changed their lives!

As a woman who received an abundant measure of forgive-
ness in exchange for an extensive list of sins, I often put myself
in the shoes of those whom Jesus touched and loved radically.
In fact, I see myself as one who would have dropped everything
I was doing to travel the countryside with Him, to be His follower.
And in essence, that is what I did.

I was never the same after I met Jesus. My friends changed.
My interests changed. My habits changed. My love for others
changed. And if I saw the first-century Jesus today, I'd cry and
laugh and thank Him profusely, then find some outrageous way
to express my love for Him.

Friend, how about you? If Jesus walked into the room right
now . . . what would you do or say?

# Fog Control

*This was their report to Moses:"We entered the land you sent us to explore, and it is indeed a bountiful country—a land flowing with milk and honey. Here is the kind of fruit it produces. But the people living there are powerful, and their towns are large and fortified.We even saw giants there, the descendants of Anak!"... But Caleb tried to quiet the people as they stood before Moses."Let's go at once to take the land,"he said. "We can certainly conquer it!"* NUMBERS 13:27-28, 30

Though Caleb and the other explorers had seen the very same giants and the very same bountiful country, their responses were completely opposite! The account is clear: They disagreed on the ability of the Israelites to conquer either the land or the giants!

My favorite story about the famous nineteenth-century English evangelist George Müller has a similar tone to it.

While aboard a ship on his way from England to Quebec for a speaking engagement, Müller was told that the ship had encountered a very dense fog and he would not make it on time to his destination. Equally unwilling to see the fog as an impenetrable obstacle or to accept the captain's assessment, Müller looked firmly into his face and said, "Captain, my eye is not on the density of the fog, but on the living God who controls every circumstance of my life." After a short session in prayer, the fog was gone, and Müller was in Quebec in time for his speaking engagement.

Do you face giants or fog? I encourage you to repeat the words of the man called a "believing pray-er," over and over, until you believe them: "My eye is not on the density of the fog, but on the living God who controls every circumstance of my life!"

## Absolutely Obsessed

*They will never even see the land I swore to give their ancestors. None of those who have treated me with contempt will ever see it. But my servant Caleb has a different attitude than the others have. He has remained loyal to me, so I will bring him into the land he explored. His descendants will possess their full share of that land.* NUMBERS 14:23-24

At this juncture, the Lord is speaking to Moses and is completely frustrated with the disbelieving Israelites *except for Caleb and Joshua* (noted later)! From previous accounts, Caleb did not receive the same tongue-lashing from God as the others, because he refused to exhibit their lack of faith or agree with their fearful findings even under pressure. He considered it more important to remain loyal to his powerful God than to agree with the politically correct majority! In the end, he was not only vindicated but publicly commended and rewarded with land for his faith!

How often, though, do we call those Caleb-esque spiritual standouts "fanatics" or "overly obsessed"?

Oswald Chambers addressed the topic of spiritual obsession in his daily devotional, *My Utmost for His Highest*. He wrote convincingly, "The total being of our life inside and out is to be absolutely obsessed by the presence of God. . . . If we are obsessed by God, nothing else can get into our lives—not concerns, nor tribulation, nor worries. . . . How can we dare to be so absolutely unbelieving when God totally surrounds us? To be obsessed by God is to have an effective barricade against all the assaults of the enemy."[3]

Based on Chambers's explanation, Caleb was absolutely obsessed with God! He allowed God to chase away all enemies, doubts, and fears. He simply possessed an attitude of loyalty toward God and His Word that remained higher than all other loyalties.

Are you absolutely obsessed with God?

## Rescue Praying

*Come with great power, O God, and rescue me! Defend me with your might.*
*Listen to my prayer, O God. Pay attention to my plea. For strangers are*
*attacking me; violent people are trying to kill me. They care nothing for*
*God. But God is my helper. The Lord keeps me alive!*  PSALM 54:1-4

David's written prayer is a powerful illustration of how to
pray with boldness!

First we must *invite* God to fill us with His great
power, to rescue us and defend us with His might. This is a place
of surrender. Yet without being in a right relationship with God,
we simply will not have David's boldness to ask. Neither would
(or should) we expect Him to pay attention to our pleas if we have
been distant or disobedient to Him. Only a daily, right, transparent relationship with God will give us great courage to approach
God *at any time* with our most urgent needs.

The threat upon David's life by those who cared nothing about
his God is an important component of this prayer—he acknowledged that his enemies were God's enemies! He was in a fierce
battle, not for his own advancement but for the Kingdom of God.
Therefore, he pressed for more of God's help.

David confidently projected an outcome! He expected nothing but victory in the Lord, because he trusted in the power and
name of God!

David's cry for help reveals that he believed prayer was as
integral to gaining victory over his enemy as his sword! Is prayer
*your* greatest and first resource in time of need or is it your last
resort?

## First Fruits

*The LORD also told Moses, "Give these instructions to the Levites: When
you receive from the people of Israel the tithes I have assigned as your
allotment, give a tenth of the tithes you receive—a tithe of the tithe—
to the LORD as a sacred offering. The LORD will consider this offering to
be your harvest offering, as though it were the first grain from your own
threshing floor or wine from your own winepress."* NUMBERS 18:25-27

I attend a church that gives over 10 percent of its income to the
Lord's work. As a young church plant, they determined early
on to regularly set aside a "tithe of the tithe" and call it First
Fruits.

Over the past few years, First Fruits has been responsible for
building an orphanage and training hundreds of pastors in India,
sending hundreds of short-term missionaries across the world,
as well as helping hundreds of local families to stay afloat during
unexpected financial difficulties.

The most interesting aspect of their generous giving plan has
been the fact that they had no church building of their own for the
first seven years of their existence!

Though this growing church attempted repeatedly to secure
a permanent location, they stuffed their growing numbers into a
senior citizen center for four weekend services. In addition, they
had to unload and load their traveling tabernacle into trailers every
weekend, and work out of a house-turned-office-building during
the week. All the while, they were building the Kingdom of God
throughout the world.

Recently I heard an elder of our church comment, "Perhaps
the real reason our church even exists is not for the people here in
Orange County, California, but simply to develop a seminary and
orphanage in India."

The challenge? Consider giving *more* time and money to the
Lord's work than is expected or asked of you!

## Pray Expectantly

*Zechariah said to the angel, "How can I be sure this will happen? I'm an old man now, and my wife is also well along in years." Then the angel said, "I am Gabriel! I stand in the very presence of God. It was he who sent me to bring you this good news! But now, since you didn't believe what I said, you will be silent and unable to speak until the child is born. For my words will certainly be fulfilled at the proper time."* LUKE 1:18-20

L uke began his account with the story of Zechariah the priest, who was visited by an angel of the Lord and given a most incredible, unexpected, and life-altering message! Unfortunately, instead of humbly accepting the exciting news, he asked a question of the angel that expressed his disbelief. His negative response did not bode well *at all* with the angel, who immediately and indignantly sentenced Zechariah to silence until his words were proven true.

What can we learn from Zechariah? Perhaps the most over-looked fact of this account is that the angel began with a confirmation: The prayers of Zechariah and his wife were heard by God and answered!

When you pray, do you expect God to answer your prayers, or are you more like Zechariah—not really expecting God to come in power and do the impossible in your life in answer to your prayers? Do you watch for and consider the small, unusual, or unexpected circumstances or messengers to bring your answer, as part of God's divine orchestration?

The next time you petition God, pray like the psalmist who said, "Listen to my voice in the morning, LORD. Each morning I bring my requests to you and wait expectantly" (Psalm 5:3).

# With God . . .

*For nothing is impossible with God. . . .You are blessed because you believed that the Lord would do what he said.* LUKE 1:37, 45

Young Mary was visited by an angel who proceeded to give her the most unbelievable message any human being would ever be given! Though a virgin, she would give birth to the Son of God. The text reveals that she responded immediately, not with fear or doubt, but in rare humility.

Two of my most favorite verses are contained in this account. The fact that they were spoken to such an uneducated, unlikely young woman should give every one of us confidence and hope!

The first is "For nothing is impossible with God" (verse 37). If you haven't already, one day you will face a problem where the only way out, up, or through is with God's help. This verse—and the story behind it—begs us not to give up or doubt God when He reveals His plans for our lives. Instead, we must actively look for the "impossible" way out and not depend upon anyone other than God to make it happen!

Luke 1:45 is the second verse that continually motivates me to never give up on the dream God has put in my heart. It validates Mary's faith, acknowledging she "believed that the Lord would do what He said." You and I must count on the Lord, trust in His words, and expect Him never to fail us. That is the kind of faith that will be rewarded. Mary proved it.

## Special Call

*And you, my little son, will be called the prophet of the Most High, because
you will prepare the way for the Lord. You will tell his people how to find
salvation through forgiveness of their sins.*  LUKE 1:76-77

In my recent travels, I met a young woman with a most horrific
story. After being abused by her parents when she was a child,
it is truly amazing that she is alive and functioning!

At sixteen, she escaped from the daily physical and emotional
abuse when she was placed in a Christian group home. When I met
her, she was nineteen and trying to start a new life while attending
college and working full-time. After learning more of her story,
I truly understood why she had great mood swings and overt
self-destructive behavior, she expressed repeated doubts about
God, and she fought regularly to overcome an oppressive negative
thought life.

After a short time, we began a regular correspondence. She
would often send desperate, one-sentence questions revealing her
poor self-image and quandary over how God could love someone
like her. Her questions never offended or frustrated me.

From the first day we met, I felt she was going to be used
mightily by God. I could only see in her a woman who would one
day nurture, love, mentor, and bring healing to children who had
also been abused.

When I finally told her what I could see in her future,
I shouldn't have been so surprised when she confided, "One day,
I will have my own orphanage. . . . That's what I want to do."

Friend, please open your eyes, hearts, and homes to the vast
numbers of young men and women who need spiritual moms and
dads to mentor and nurture them. Can you think of anyone today?
Don't hesitate to call and meet with them!

# Spiritual Warfare

*My enemies come out at night, snarling like vicious dogs as they prowl the streets. They scavenge for food but go to sleep unsatisfied.*

PSALM 59:14-15

I walked into the office of an old friend whom I hadn't seen for over five years and was caught off guard when her first question was, "Becky, do you believe in spiritual warfare?"

I quickly replied, "Yes, I do."

But before I could speak another word, she began to tell me of numerous situations that had abruptly or unusually turned upside down, where opposition came from out of nowhere, or where something occurred that resembled more of a sinister attack than a natural phenomenon.

If you have never read the Bible from cover to cover, you might not have a confident response to a similar question, but if you have . . . you only need to read the first and last pages of it—and most in between—to see that God wastes no time in discussing spiritual warfare.

In Genesis, Satan's appearances range from angelic to serpentine and quickly divert God's chosen people from obeying Him. By the final book of Revelation, the end of time is riddled with numerous attacks by a morphing devil.

David, much like every anointed man or woman in the written records of the Word of God, echoes the thoughts of one who encountered evil regularly. David gives evil a face and a feel. It is real, it is ugly, it is vicious. It snarls and prowls and digs and scavenges . . . like a fierce and ultimately famished carnivore stalking its prey.

But David's response to the relentless attacks of his evil enemies—always—was to call on God to be his strength and refuge in time of trouble.

Do you believe in spiritual warfare?

## Keep Coming

*Anna, a prophet, was also there in the Temple. She was the daughter of Phanuel from the tribe of Asher, and she was very old. Her husband died when they had been married only seven years. Then she lived as a widow to the age of eighty-four. She never left the Temple but stayed there day and night, worshiping God with fasting and prayer.* LUKE 2:36-37

Our culture presumes that people are most productive in their younger years—when their physical strength and energy levels are at a peak and their minds are most alert. But Anna's big moment came when she was a very, very old widow.

First, she chose to worship at the Temple day and night, continually fasting and praying. Even one of these spiritual disciplines repeated on a daily basis for decades would be an incredibly rigorous exercise for a person of any age. Yet she never tired of the routine, because she was a prophet waiting for God to rescue Jerusalem.

Herein lies Anna's secret. She had been waiting expectantly for God to rescue Jerusalem and wasn't going to miss His coming! Why didn't she give up after ten years or twenty years or fifty years? I have only one guess. *God* told her to keep coming, to keep waiting, to keep watching. And so she did. . . .

When you hear Him tell you something—whether others agree or disagree—you must keep on trusting Him until you see it happen. And the more you seek Him, the more confident you become in waiting. And no matter how old you are, no matter how long you have waited, if He asks you to keep coming—you will!

That is the secret of faith—being sure of what you hope for and certain of what you do not see!

## Strong Tower

*O God, listen to my cry! Hear my prayer! From the ends of the earth,
I cry to you for help when my heart is overwhelmed. Lead me to the
towering rock of safety, for you are my safe refuge, a fortress where
my enemies cannot reach me.* PSALM 61:1-3

I n this psalm, David, the passionate prayer instructor, reminds us that even God's anointed warrior will experience desperate moments of overwhelming emotion. In those moments, we must gather our frantic selves and surrender every fiber of our beings to God!

Though most of us will never live in the wilderness or physically face armies of enemies, we *all* experience desperate moments when we wish God would just remove us from our present struggle and take us safely aside and minister to us.

I began to capture the essence of a "fortress" at twenty-nine, when I determined to set aside time every day to be alone with God. I escaped to my imaginary refuge daily for one hour—away from the urgent voices calling to me—and asked God to free me from any negative thoughts.

For over twenty-three years, I've gone to my hideaway. It has been the same "fortress" in every house I've lived in. There, I've daily poured out my heart to God in writing, and then opened His Word to listen to His comforting counsel, corrective advice, and strategic directions.

After nearly eight thousand, five hundred days in the "fortress," I've found nothing else that has offered me more safety and strength to face each day. Where is your refuge?

## Unusual Strategy

*I wait quietly before God, for my victory comes from him. . . . Let all that I am wait quietly before God, for my hope is in him.* PSALM 62:1, 5

Oswald Chambers, a nineteenth-century preacher and author, said in *My Utmost for His Highest*, "One of the greatest stresses in life is the stress of waiting for God."[4] I agree! I've found that waiting on God is much harder than doing something, if not *anything*, for God! In fact, I bet most of you consider *any* form of action to be a greater strategy for achieving victory than inaction!

Exhorting politicians to consult God before making decisions, Peter Marshall, former chaplain of the U.S. Senate, wrote of his own struggle in prayer: "Father, I am beginning to know how much I miss when I fail to talk to thee in prayer, and through prayer to receive into my life the strength and the guidance which only thou canst give. Forgive me for the pride and the presumption that make me continue to struggle to manage my own affairs to the exhaustion of my body, the weariness of my mind, the trial of my faith. . . . When I neglect to pray, mine is the loss."[5]

If you react out of impatience or impulse, consider a new strategy. Follow the path of warrior and psalmist King David, who clearly professed that victory was found in waiting on God in prayer. Set aside time daily to discuss your concerns with God. Ask Him for a battle plan. Open your Bible and read intently. Listen. Wait on God to give you a passage that provides strength for the battle and hope for His outcome. And don't move until you receive specific "marching orders" from your Captain!

# Anointed Words

*The Spirit of the LORD is upon me, for he has anointed me to bring Good News to the poor. He has sent me to proclaim that captives will be released, that the blind will see, that the oppressed will be set free, and that the time of the LORD's favor has come.* LUKE 4:18-19

I f you've ever wondered what people who are filled and overflowing with the Holy Spirit look or act like—here is a picture!

- They are anointed—given unusual unction to deliver the Good News message to those who need good news!
- They are sent out—compelled to speak God's healing and hope to those who are blind, held captive, or imprisoned.
- They are empowered to speak freedom to the oppressed, knowing this freedom is unearned and divinely given.

I've asked God to anoint me in the same way. I have paraphrased these words and made them my prayer:

*Lord, anoint me with Your Holy Spirit that I might be sent out to proclaim the Good News of Jesus Christ to a culture that has lost its way. We are broken and confused. We've believed lies about life and love; we've traded lasting love for temporary sex. We're blind and deceived by the enemy, who has glorified what is wrong in Your eyes and made a joke of what is right. Send me to places where You want to reach people who need You, and want You, and are calling to You . . . but You've been kept out. Give me humility to reach the unlovely, and belief and boldness to speak words that will change their lives instantly! Give me all of Your powerful Holy Spirit to set the captives free. . . .*

## Passionate Abandonment

*"Master," Simon replied, "we worked hard all last night and didn't catch a thing. But if you say so, I'll let the nets down again." And this time their nets were so full of fish they began to tear! . . . When Simon Peter realized what had happened, he fell to his knees before Jesus and said, "Oh, Lord, please leave me—I'm too much of a sinner to be around you."*

LUKE 5:5-6, 8

This depiction of Jesus and the first disciples is similar to the experience of many of us who come to Jesus later in our lives.

We first hear Him speak—whether we read His words or someone tells us the Good News about the Son of God—and we are in awe. Then we perceive Jesus asking us to do something that requires us to abandon instinct or our usual method of accomplishing something. We must trust Him.

But without further debate, we step—or leap—into this unknown place of following after an invisible God, and we're amazed by His presence. We can hear Him calling, leading. Then we are immediately struck by our sinfulness in light of His holiness, power, wisdom, and trustworthiness. We don't want what we used to want. We love Him. We want to know Him. We want to follow after Him.

The first disciples left everything to follow Jesus. Oswald Chambers reminds us that the one who desires to know Jesus better must have "an attitude of unrestrained abandon and total surrender about him."[6] That is a fair challenge to give any follower of Jesus! Is your current relationship with Christ as vibrant, humble, and adventurous as it was in the beginning? If not, what will it take to return to passionate abandonment?

## Believe Me

*As Jesus left the town, he saw a tax collector named Levi sitting at his tax collector's booth. "Follow me and be my disciple," Jesus said to him. So Levi got up, left everything, and followed him.* LUKE 5:27-28

A life-changing invitation. An unlikely follower. An immediate response.

*I am a disciple and follower of the Lord Jesus Christ* is a phrase used less often to define Christ's followers than *Christian*. But perhaps it would be more distinctive and personally challenging to call ourselves Jesus' followers and disciples. Those two words have more distinct meanings than *Christian*, don't you think? In fact, the word *Christian* in America has really lost its meaning, or at least its significance.

There are a growing number of resources and messengers who are calling for the distinctive Christian—the "revolutionary"—to stand apart in today's culture. George Barna defines this Christian as "someone who lives only to love, obey, and serve God."[7] The call to be a radical follower—a sold-out disciple of the Lord Jesus Christ—isn't new. But *it is* reemerging in the twenty-first century!

The first life-changing question Jesus asks disciples of any generation is "Will you follow Me?" Following Jesus requires that you relinquish your dreams, your plans, even your identity to follow Him. Many people struggle long over answering this question. A disciple does not.

A second nonnegotiable mark of a disciple is that you buy into, believe, adhere to, promote, even live and die by the teachings of the leader. What does today's Christian believe? Is it evident in his or her knowledge of the Bible, lifestyle choices, or driving ambitions? Making the Word of God your daily bread, your constant study guide, your inspiration in times of trouble is the only way to be a true disciple of Christ.

# Public Confession

*Come and listen, all you who fear God, and I will tell you what he did for*
*me. For I cried out to him for help, praising him as I spoke. If I had not*
*confessed the sin in my heart, the Lord would not have listened.*

PSALM 66:16-18

I stumbled upon the power of confession numerous times in my life.

As a sinner, I was ushered into an unbelievably surreal experience when I confessed my ugliest sins to the Lord in front of a stranger and found myself forgiven. The confession experience was so moving, so freeing that I turned quickly from the powerful sins that had chained me to a self-destructive lifestyle.

But as a believer, I didn't understand that regular—even public—confession of my sins would have the same liberating power over me. I made a habit of concealing sin—anger, jealousy, and unforgiveness. Though I no longer acted like a sinner on the outside—getting drunk, living immorally, or lying to people—I was full of sin in my heart!

Then it occurred to me. If the power of confession could radically change my life and mind *as an unbeliever*, why did I resist confessing my sins to God and others *as a Christian*? Pride. Wanting others to think I was something that I was not kept me quiet.

On the day I began to confess my sins in writing to God on a daily basis—the hiding ended. Besides, people know my sin. And they know yours. You're not hiding anything! Instead, "confess your sins to each other and pray for each other so that you may be healed" (James 5:16).

# All Night

*One day soon afterward Jesus went up on a mountain to pray,
and he prayed to God all night.* LUKE 6:12

Have you ever been to an all-night prayer meeting? Students across the world are setting the stage and pace for prayer like few generations before them! Beginning with the concept of 24-7 prayer, European students set off a bonfire of prayer at the turn of the twenty-first century based on the one-hundred-year nonstop Moravian prayer meetings.

The fire spread across to other nations, including the United States. By 2006, college students across America were turning abandoned buildings, apartment rentals, or decade-old chapels into houses of prayer.

What is all-night prayer like?

First, it is personal. One who prays all night is compelled. No one feels like staying up all night; when you determine to stay up all night *to pray*, you do not plan on being alone. You expect that God will meet you.

Second, it is scriptural. Jesus did it. What better reason to converse with God all night long than because Jesus considered it a great priority in His life?

Third, it is life changing—if not world changing! The power of prayer is indisputable. It is the reason wars were won by inexplicable methods, rains stopped and started, and the dead were brought back to life!

Fourth, it is an expression of passion. If you are desperate to be known and heard, if you ache with confusion, spending all night in prayer with God will be an encounter you will never forget. You will be heard. He will be found.

## Complete Obedience

*Look, I now teach you these decrees and regulations just as the LORD my God commanded me, so that you may obey them in the land you are about to enter and occupy. Obey them completely, and you will display your wisdom and intelligence among the surrounding nations. When they hear all these decrees, they will exclaim, "How wise and prudent are the people of this great nation!"* DEUTERONOMY 4:5-6

You get the feeling that Moses is trying to convince, if not beg, God's people to obey God's rules. Yet history records that obedience was a tough sell to a very rebellious people. Times haven't changed much. But whatever excuses we give, God's mandate hasn't—He is looking for men and women who will display His love and power among all the nations of the world!

Daniel was convinced that if he followed God's ways—even while living in an ungodly culture—he would achieve a level of wisdom and intelligence that others could not match. He proved that . . . and was elevated to the highest place of authority and honor. Over time, all who witnessed his remarkable character and courage had to acknowledge that his God was not only near to him, but heard him when he called! (See Daniel 6.)

Daniel's truest desire, tested over time, was to display to all other men and nations the awesome power of the God he served, so that they, too, might worship Him alone.

Oh, what if we, like Daniel, considered it our great and awesome privilege—rather than such a difficult duty—to *completely* obey the God of the Bible!

# Children's Stories

*In the future your children will ask you, "What is the meaning of these laws, decrees, and regulations that the LORD our God has commanded us to obey?" Then you must tell them, "We were Pharaoh's slaves in Egypt, but the LORD brought us out of Egypt with his strong hand."*

DEUTERONOMY 6:20-21

After almost self-destructing, both my husband and I came to Christ in our twenties. Just as we hit bottom, God saved us, offering us forgiveness and hope for starting over. Upon coming to Christ in the 1970s, we could have been classified as "Jesus Freaks." Roger wore "Jesus" patches on his blue jeans, and I couldn't stop talking about Him to strangers.

Shortly after becoming Christians, we met when we were abruptly catapulted out of our old lives and into full-time youth ministry. One year after we married, we had our only child— a baby boy!

Each week, we would pack up baby Jake and shuttle him to our high school events and youth group meetings. In the summers, from the time he was in preschool until junior high school, we would travel across North America, sharing our love for God with hundreds of students at numerous camps and youth conventions.

One of the greatest joys we have as parents is sharing our love for Jesus with our son. From the time he was a baby until now, in his late twenties, Jake has seen two imperfect people profess a sincere faith in the God of the Bible. In the process of hearing and seeing and knowing God through our lives, Jake chose a path that perfectly fits his personality and passions—he's a soccer missionary!

Yet for those of us who are parents, the job is never finished! Our prayers for our children and our lives before them will speak volumes to them until the day we die.

## Forgiven *Much*

*I tell you, her sins—and they are many—have been forgiven,*
*so she has shown me much love. But a person who is forgiven little*
*shows only little love.* LUKE 7:47

On the way to a formal deposition for a car accident I had been in while under the influence of alcohol, I considered committing suicide. I was twenty-one and completely despondent. Also, I thought I might be pregnant and didn't know by whom. I couldn't have been more desperate for a new life, but I had nowhere to turn, no one to help me.

At the deposition, the lawyer said, "You'll be crucified if you lie on the stand." Those words prompted me to think of the only person I had ever heard of who died by crucifixion—Jesus. So, rather than taking my life, I drove to a church—the kind in which my parents raised me. I thought, *Perhaps I'll find God?* I found a janitor.

As I approached this stranger, I said, "I have to talk."

He replied, "Let's just pray." He led me in a simple prayer: "Dear Jesus . . . come into my heart. . . ." After I repeated the words, he said, "If you can think of any sins, name them and ask God to forgive you."

Some people struggle with calling themselves a sinner. I didn't have that struggle! Without hesitation I prayed, "Forgive me Jesus for . . ." and went on and on and on. The janitor's eyes opened wider and wider with each detail of sin! Yet something happened with every admission—a feeling of forgiveness swept over me and the intense guilt and shame that had enveloped me for months began to *immediately* leave.

If you have never asked Christ to come into your heart, do not hesitate.

# Sacred Obsession

*And now, Israel, what does the LORD your God require of you? He requires only that you fear the LORD your God, and live in a way that pleases him, and love him and serve him with all your heart and soul.*

DEUTERONOMY 10:12

I t is normal to be excited about someone you love.

It is normal to be passionate.

It is abnormal, perhaps even a sign of trouble, if you are passive, bored, or unenthusiastic about your true love.

So why here, on earth, should your holy affection for the living, loving God *ever* fade or remain unexpressed? Who would it benefit for you to be reserved, unenthusiastic, or passionless about the most sacred obsession of your life? In fact, isn't that what everyone is searching and chasing after—endless love, overwhelming joy, undeserved forgiveness, eternal life? . . .

God is not passive in His love toward you. I see no reason whatsoever to be passive in your love toward Him.

I know this to be true. . . .

If you chase after Him, He will not only reveal Himself to you as the object of your deepest longing and heart's desire, but He will fill any emptiness you have up to overflowing! He will fall all over you with His love and presence. He wants to love you deeply. He will light your inner fire; He will warm your heart. He will quench your thirst. He will fill your hunger with Himself. He will immediately infuse you with all you need to exhibit discipline and courage. *He will enable you to do what you could not do before.*

## Tell Everyone

*The man who had been freed from the demons begged to go with him.*
*But Jesus sent him home, saying, "No, go back to your family, and tell*
*them everything God has done for you." So he went all through the town*
*proclaiming the great things Jesus had done for him.* LUKE 8:38-39

Upon coming to Christ, so many aspects of my life changed so abruptly, you couldn't help but notice!

I quit drinking completely! (For an alcoholic—and all those who know an alcoholic's habits—it is truly a remarkable occurrence to stop cold turkey!)

I quit cursing—and for a woman who swore like a sailor, my newfound clean mouth took everyone by surprise!

My life changed so dramatically, I just had to tell everyone about Jesus!

Within three months, neither my friends nor coworkers nor even my boyfriend appreciated the "new" me. So I returned to Cleveland, Ohio, after living in California for two years. Within hours of returning to my parents' home, I not only told them what happened when Jesus came into my life, but I showed them! I was a brand-new person, freed from so much addiction and immorality!

I changed so dramatically that within two months, both of my parents—though involved in church all their lives—asked Christ into their lives with a simple prayer. My brother followed shortly thereafter. When I finished telling my family and friends what God had done in my life, I drove up to the local high school, found my favorite assistant principal, and said, "I've found the answer! I've become a Christian!" He was so shocked, he replied, "You?"

You can have the greatest impact for Christ with those who you knew before you became a Christian. Go back to your old friends, roommates, to each family member—make amends and share the Good News!

# Sent Out

*One day Jesus called together his twelve disciples and gave them power and authority to cast out all demons and to heal all diseases. Then he sent them out to tell everyone about the Kingdom of God and to heal the sick. . . . So they began their circuit of the villages, preaching the Good News and healing the sick.* LUKE 9:1-2, 6

For the past few years, there has been a stirring in me to be involved with student ministry. I can't really explain it— I'm too old for it and have been out of the loop and off the college speaker's circuit.

But no excuse is valid when you feel God is asking you to do something. And He doesn't let up until you do it.

The stirring turned into action. I visited numerous college campuses, extending a call to prayer, purity, and purpose. After a year, I finally determined to do something specific to impact college campuses. I phoned everyone I knew—students or staff— and invited them to be a part of an extended prayer vigil for "revival" during forty days between January 20 and March 1, 2006.

After only four weeks, an itinerary of twenty-three campuses in eleven states came together, and I determined to visit each campus for some part of their prayer "watch." I assumed I would enter each town and join in a very exciting, powerful prayer assembly that would leave us all overjoyed with the experience!

From the first day until the last, I found *more* students and staff who needed prayer for personal—rather than corporate—revival. They needed healing and courage to fulfill their call.

I'm convinced—if we offer to pray for people, they will line up to be prayed for. Please, make prayer for others a priority in your life.

## Daily Word

*When he sits on the throne as king, he must copy for himself this body*
*of instruction on a scroll in the presence of the Levitical priests. He must*
*always keep that copy with him and read it daily as long as he lives.*
*That way he will learn to fear the LORD his God by obeying all the terms*
*of these instructions and decrees.* DEUTERONOMY 17:18-19

From the first day I met my husband, Roger spoke about his commitment to read the Bible for at least five minutes every day for the rest of his life. He came to Christ in his late twenties, and immediately attended a conference where the speaker asked every attendee to make daily Bible reading a lifelong habit. Roger took the challenge.

Over the past thirty-five years, I think Roger has missed only a handful of days of Bible reading. As a single man, he maintained such a level of integrity in his work and social life that no one I met compared with him. As a married man, his life as a pastor, husband, and father has been marked by humility and respect. And for the past thirty years that I have known him, I've never met a man or pastor I respect more.

The Word of God has prevented him from the smallest and largest diversions. Perhaps the truest test is that the people who know him best respect and trust him! And many have been inspired to take on the same daily Bible-reading challenge.

If you've never done so, consider today, March 31, the day you make a nonnegotiable decision to spend at least five minutes in prayer and five minutes in the Word of God—every day— for the rest of your life!

# God Forbid!

*You must be blameless before the LORD your God. The nations you are about to displace consult sorcerers and fortune-tellers, but the LORD your God forbids you to do such things.* DEUTERONOMY 18:13-14

The first hour that I was a Christian it was brought to my attention that God hated such things as Ouija boards, horoscopes, tarot cards, palm reading, and séances.

As part of my introduction to Jesus, the janitor who led me to Christ simply asked if I had engaged in any practices of the occult. I remember thinking, *I am not involved in the occult!* But because I could remember a few times I had played with the Ouija board and could admit that I often read my horoscope in a fashion magazine or newspaper, he asked me to renounce any specific or general activities I could remember.

Did I think it overbearing of him to discuss my involvement with the occult? Honestly, no. But decades later when I look back, my greatest impression is that this was a brilliant strategy.

First, he had the foresight to expose the power of the occult and any demonic oppression that I brought on myself by engaging in those activities. Second, he told me these practices were not acceptable in God's eyes. . . . He wisely advised and protected me the very first hour I was a Christian!

The occult—Wicca, séances, and all forms of horoscope and palm reading—are especially prevalent among students who are searching for an experience with the supernatural. But if you open your heart and mind to it, you're at risk to anger God and invite havoc into your life. Isn't life crazy enough without looking for trouble?

## Harvest Workers

*These were his instructions to them: "The harvest is great, but the workers are few. So pray to the Lord who is in charge of the harvest; ask him to send more workers into his fields."* LUKE 10:2

**B**ecause I have seen myself as a harvester for over thirty years, I completely identify with a poem written by Samuel Shoemaker, early twentieth-century pastor, poet, and Princeton University graduate, called "I Stand by the Door," as it so perfectly articulates the attitude and sensitivity harvest workers must retain all their lives!

*I stand by the door.*
*I neither go too far in, nor stay too far out,*
*The door is the most important door in the world—*
*It is the door through which men walk when they find God.*

*There's no use my going way inside, and staying there,*
*When so many are still outside and they, as much as I,*
*Crave to know where the door is. . . .*

*The most tremendous thing in the world*
*Is for men to find that door—the door to God.*
*The most important thing any man can do*
*Is to take hold of one of the blind, groping hands,*
*And put it on the latch—the latch that only clicks*
*And opens to the man's own touch.*[1]

Shoemaker begs us to never go too far in the door. He asks us to watch diligently for those who are desperate, hurting, or simply struggling . . . to find the door to God.

Think of just one person who has never entered the door. Take hold of his or her hand. Be his or her "janitor"!

## Vow Making

*When you make a vow to the LORD your God, be prompt in fulfilling whatever you promised him. For the LORD your God demands that you promptly fulfill all your vows, or you will be guilty of sin. However, it is not a sin to refrain from making a vow.* DEUTERONOMY 23:21-22

Most people bristle at making a vow or promise to the Lord. I know, because I'm often the one calling people to consider a vow of purity, or to spend one hour a day with God for the rest of their lives! The common response of those who are uncomfortable with a vow is, "I don't want to make a vow to God, then break it. I'd feel terrible, guilty, and ashamed if I failed to keep it."

So I usually reply, "Hmmm. . . . When you sign a contract to buy a car, do you experience fear and leave the car lot, or do you enthusiastically intend to honor your responsibility to pay the monthly payment and drive away with your pretty, new car?"

In our society, people have serious aversions to making significant commitments that require integrity! We call promises that pertain to God legalism, but we'll religiously go to the gym and work out five days a week, pump iron, and run the treadmill—for a monthly fee—and call that discipline.

This passage seems less about making a vow to God—which is up to you—and more about keeping the vows you make!

What is God asking you to do? If it is time to make a vow to Him, then make it and don't look back. Lean into the mandate found in these verses and fulfill it promptly!

## Persevering Prayer

*I tell you, keep on asking, and you will receive what you ask for. Keep on seeking, and you will find. Keep on knocking, and the door will be opened to you. For everyone who asks, receives. Everyone who seeks, finds. And to everyone who knocks, the door will be opened.* LUKE 11:9-10

While reading an e-mail from a person with whom I conduct business, my husband asked, "You just don't take no for an answer, do you? Does he ever get frustrated with you? It seems like you've asked him this question before."

I said, "Well, I don't think he gets frustrated with me. He's known me for twenty years . . . and he seems to understand that I tend to think that his 'no' means 'not now'!"

The principle of persevering prayer is one which many of us struggle to apply to our lives for a variety of reasons. Perhaps we are shy or hesitant by nature, or we feel repeated requests are inappropriate—almost like begging. Maybe we are unaware that Jesus encouraged this type of praying? He is not only giving us permission, but urging us to ask, seek, and knock with shameless persistence!

Asking works for most of us when we are desperate. No matter how shy or uncomfortable we are, when time is running out or someone is in danger if we don't act quickly, we will ask and keep on asking until we get an answer or action begins. Persistent, shameless asking is persuasive and convincing. The premise of persistent prayer is this: The person who never gives up in prayer *is* going to receive what he or she asks for.

For the record, the secret to answered prayer contained in a majority of the classic books on prayer by past leaders (Müller, Murray, Bounds) is . . . perseverance.

# Lights On?

*No one lights a lamp and then hides it or puts it under a basket.*
*Instead, a lamp is placed on a stand, where its light can be seen by all*
*who enter the house.* LUKE 11:33

When my son turned five, I had a very serious conversation with God. It went something like this. He said, "You keep yelling and screaming at your child (in private) and he will grow up to hate you."

I had been a Christian for almost eight years, the mother of a little boy, a youth worker, and married to a youth worker. In public I was an outgoing, fun-loving speaker and coach to high school students. In private, I was an angry, bitter, overworked mother. I was struggling to be the same person at home as I was in public.

It was during the first week of praying for one hour a day that God began to remind me of the many times I had allowed anger to extinguish His light in my home life. He made it clear that I needed to confess my anger as sin and get rid of it—so that His light would shine *brightest* in my home. I responded to God by making immediate changes in the way I talked to and treated my son. . . . Today, I am grateful that I listened to God.

Those of us in ministry who are called to be evangelists, preachers, teachers, and pastors often find it easier to be "lights" in public than in our own homes. In fact, the enemy loves to destroy the families of those who are in full-time ministry or leadership positions. Perhaps Jesus knew that keeping the light of God shining brightly in your home would be your greatest test and the greatest training ground for any future ministry.

If you can keep your fire lit, your cup clean, and your relationships right at home . . . if you are the same person in public that you are in private, your light (and legacy) will never diminish and God will be greatly glorified in you.

## Revolutionary Ways

*Now listen! Today I am giving you a choice between life and death, between prosperity and disaster. For I command you this day to love the LORD your God and to keep his commands, decrees, and regulations by walking in his ways. If you do this, you will live and multiply, and the LORD your God will bless you and the land you are about to enter and occupy.*

DEUTERONOMY 30:15-16

I f you've read the book of Deuteronomy, you are undoubt-edly impressed with the fact that this is not the first time this instruction is given. In fact, Moses varies his words very little! These words are repeated enough times to make one thing clear to his listeners: *Obedience to God is not an option* if you desire to live a long life!

How does this mandate apply to a twenty-first-century believer?

First and foremost, it is a choice. You and I have one choice to make: Either we turn our hearts toward God or allow them to be drawn toward and serve other gods.

This command isn't about following group religion. It is about following wholeheartedly after the one true God.

From my vantage point—the "god" of our American culture is sex. Sexual immorality has captured the hearts of people *much more* than purity or fidelity.

If those of us who call ourselves followers of Jesus would search our hearts in light of God's Word on sex and determine to wholeheartedly follow His Word and His ways, we would begin a sexual revolution. Anyone interested?

# Stop It!

*Can all your worries add a single moment to your life? And if worry can't accomplish a little thing like that, what's the use of worrying over bigger things?* LUKE 12:25-26

Over a decade ago, Juan Carlos Ortiz preached a sermon that I never forgot!

During his thirty-minute presentation, Juan Carlos made one point that everyone from the fourth grader to the senior citizen found relevant: Worry will not

solve your problems,

change your situation,

relieve your stress, or

move heaven and earth!

Worry is a harmful, nonproductive emotional behavior that has no ability to change anything! So stop it!

Philippians 4:6-7 says, "Don't worry about anything; instead, pray about everything. Tell God what you need, and thank him for all he has done. Then you will experience God's peace, which exceeds anything we can understand. His peace will guard your hearts and minds as you live in Christ Jesus."

Let's be honest. Has worry ever changed your situation? Or has it only brought on more anxiety, depression, or pessimistic thinking?

Consider this: Worry and prayer take the same time and effort! So instead of worrying—pray! Prayer diminishes the power of worry over you. Prayer connects you with God and His Holy Spirit. Prayer releases hope, faith, and—action! Finally, in prayer, God gives you thoughts and ideas to move toward a solution or the patience to wait for directions.

## Unconditional Love

*The very hairs on your head are all numbered. So don't be afraid; you are*
*more valuable to God than a whole flock of sparrows.* LUKE 12:7

A young girl recently asked me, "How could God love a person like me? I just can't believe I am worth anything to Him."

One of the devil's greatest lies is to convince a person that he or she has to be good enough to earn God's love. But the Bible gives us the truth to combat the lies. The good news is that "God showed his great love for us by sending Christ to die for us while we were still sinners" (Romans 5:8).

I remember the words that caught my attention when I was at the height of my sinful, unlovable, unworthy life. They were, "God loves you just the way you are. . . ."

I was afraid to believe those words. But they were too good to be true, I thought. They offered hope when no one or nothing else could give me hope. They would come back to my mind whenever I thought things couldn't get any worse. And they were strong enough to pull me toward God when I was most hopeless.

What is the great hope of every human being? God loves you just the way you are. . . .

If you've never understood or accepted God's unconditional love, you don't have to be at a church service or crusade to do so. Right now, simply admit to God that you know you are a sinner, that you have "fallen short." Tell Him you understand how much He loves you—enough to send Jesus to die for your sins. Ask Him to forgive your sins—name any you can think of. Ask Him to fill you with His Holy Spirit. Then live like you believe that He loves you today, tomorrow, and forever!

# Be Encouraged!

*Worry weighs a person down; an encouraging word cheers a person up.*

PROVERBS 12:25

For the past decade, I have signed most of my correspondence with the closing *Be encouraged!*

And very often I receive a response that says either *You be encouraged* or *I am encouraged!* Both replies make me smile. I love to encourage people, probably because I like to be encouraged.

In fact, I like to encourage perfect strangers. If I am on an elevator or passing another woman, I always try to find something quick to say that will encourage her—how beautiful her smile, how cute her shoes, how kind she was to her child.

I want to challenge you today to go out of your way and enthusiastically encourage as many people as possible!

- Tell a student how much you admire his or her hard work.
- Tell a service clerk that you appreciated his or her friendly service.
- Tell a friend how great it was that he or she made you laugh.
- Give your spouse a meaningful affirmation before you part ways.
- Send a note to someone who deserves kudos from you.
- Call a parent or sibling and thank him or her for something small.
- Buy a gift under five dollars for someone who works for you.
- Smile at a stranger. Open a door or carry a package for him or her.
- Bring a smoothie or a cup of coffee to work for the receptionist.

Did you know that the word *enthusiasm* means "God within"? When you encourage others with your words and actions, you are allowing God—who lives within you—to encourage others through you!

## Stay Focused

*Be strong and very courageous. Be careful to obey all the instructions Moses gave you. Do not deviate from them, turning either to the right or to the left. Then you will be successful in everything you do. . . . This is my command—be strong and courageous! Do not be afraid or discouraged. For the LORD your God is with you wherever you go.* JOSHUA 1:7, 9

Most avid Bible readers have memorized—or at least marked and highlighted—these "power" verses in the first chapter of Joshua because they breathe strength and courage into anyone who has to fight a battle.

I recently spoke with a young woman who told me that she was finding it very difficult to stay sexually pure with her Christian boyfriend.

I asked, "Why is that?"

She replied, "He really feels strongly that we will grow closer the more we are sexually intimate."

I said, "Really? Hmm. Where in the last few months have you heard a pastor tell you or read in your Bible that sex outside of marriage would increase your intimacy with your boyfriend?" Of course, no one said it and nowhere in the Bible did she read it. She had deviated. . . .

There are a great many unsuccessful, discouraged, distracted, weakened followers of Christ who struggle to live their lives for and with God because they either do not know what the Bible says or they ignore it.

To be a strong, courageous, successful warrior in God's army you must meditate and study the Bible—seriously consider God's instruction—so that you will be equipped to honor His name—and obey Him.

## Memorial Stones

*Joshua said to the Israelites, "In the future your children will ask,
'What do these stones mean?' Then you can tell them, 'This is where the
Israelites crossed the Jordan on dry ground.'"* JOSHUA 4:21-22

The first memorial stone that my husband and I had to "show and tell" our son was the gravestone! We said, "Son, this is where we died. Our old life was buried with Christ on this day in this place. This stone was erected to remind us of the day we were given new lives. . . ."

The next stones we told our son about were markers of decisions we made that were life-altering. For example, the day my husband made a decision to read his Bible for at least five minutes every day—that stone is now over thirty-five years old. There is my sobriety stone, erected when I decided to never have another drink. . . . It has been standing for over thirty years. It is especially meaningful because of the devastating effect alcoholism had on my life and the two generations before me.

Then there is the stone when my husband and I made a vow in front of four hundred people that we would stay married all our lives—until death parted us. That stone is twenty-nine years old now. We've watched many of our friends' stones crash during these years.

Then there is the stone of prayer. I erected that stone on February 18, 1984—when I decided to pray for one hour a day for the rest of my life, to receive God's counsel and live intentionally for Him.

It is never too late to erect memorial stones in your life . . . and never too early to erect them in the lives of your children!

# Changed Lives

*In the same way, there is more joy in heaven over one lost sinner who
repents and returns to God than over ninety-nine others who are righteous
and haven't strayed away!* LUKE 15:7

When Jesus talked to sinners about their lives, a common statement that He made was, "Go and sin no more." He didn't ask them if they were sorry. He asked them to change . . . to cut it out.

We've all seen (and perhaps experienced) a momentary sorrow for doing or saying something that we regret or that got us into trouble. But repentance isn't simply sorrow for getting caught. It is exhibiting so much sorrow and humiliation for what we've done that we'll do whatever it takes to change our ways—and turn to God.

Most of us are unwilling to repent until we've hit bottom. It doesn't have to be that way—God sends plenty of messengers to show us a way of escape. Yet most of us refuse to either call ourselves sinners or humble ourselves to a point of repentance.

But when the "turning" day comes . . . there is no day like it! Some call it the day of salvation. Others say, "I had a dramatic conversion." Many call their experience being "born again." But repentance is an indelible mark in the life of one who has turned to God, received a new heart, and begun a new life!

John Owen, William Wilberforce, and Jonathan Edwards called this *real* or *true Christianity*. They believed a Christian's life must be marked by a change in character *and* action to be real. That is a cause for joy in heaven—and on earth!

# Little Things

*If you are faithful in little things, you will be faithful in large ones.*
*But if you are dishonest in little things, you won't be honest with*
*greater responsibilities.* LUKE 16:10

Jesus suggests that faithfulness, honesty, and trustworthiness can be taught. And training in those character qualities begins with little things.

While traveling across America to speak on college campuses, I've gained a new name. It is not an image or reputation that I was trying to assume. But I got it. . . .

Some call me "Mama Becky." Others suggest that I am their spiritual mother. Parents tell me that I am their children's California Mom.

When I look back for the reason for these titles, it does make sense. I'm both tough and tender. It is very difficult to look in my eyes and lie to me. I like to give hugs. I am willing to talk about the smallest and largest problems—roommates, food selections, dating lives, apologetics, unanswered prayer, addiction to pornography, parents' divorces, siblings' struggles, or financial concerns. It is uncanny that I call just when they are about to do something wrong. I tell them I love them, especially after a tough fall.

Students are looking for people who will call them to higher standards and who are also willing to be kept to those same standards.

From the number of depressed, disillusioned, abused, angry children of divorced couples that I've met lately, I realize that anyone who will take on the role of parenting this young generation will find a very willing, vulnerable mass of young people looking for love and discipline!

# Impossible Prayers

*On the day the LORD gave the Israelites victory over the Amorites, Joshua prayed to the LORD in front of all the people of Israel. He said, "Let the sun stand still over Gibeon, and the moon over the valley of Aijalon."*
*So the sun stood still and the moon stayed in place until the nation of Israel had defeated its enemies.* JOSHUA 10:12-13

This passage sets a standard for prayer—that even impossible requests must be prayed!

*Prayer releases power.* Though no prayer has been answered before or since where the sun and the moon stopped, many of us have witnessed a healing or miracle or unexplainable answer to prayer. From Joshua's answer, we learn that those who pray impossible prayers must believe that with God all things are possible.

What do you believe about prayer?

*Prayer brings rescue.* If you don't believe God is mighty enough to answer your prayers for rescue, there is no need to pray. George Müller believed God would feed, house, and clothe orphans when he had no money to do so. He asked no man for money, but God alone—and God always supplied. Thousands of orphans were fed, housed, and clothed during his lifetime. Their rescue was impossible without God's intervention.

*Prayer gives answers.* James 4:2 reads, "You don't have what you want because you don't ask God for it." You must ask to receive. And with God, you must not limit yourself to thinking rationally or practically. Answers to prayer are divine, not human. They are orchestrated from heaven. So just ask.

## Good Life

*A single day in your courts is better than a thousand anywhere else!*
*I would rather be a gatekeeper in the house of my God than live the good*
*life in the homes of the wicked.* PSALM 84:10

I lived the "good life" until the morning I woke up in bed with a man I barely knew, possibly pregnant, and pending the result of a court hearing for a car accident I had been in while drinking.

The "good life" had ended in ruin for me. At my lowest point, God forgave my sin, lifted me out of the hole I had dug, and gave me a second chance. I scurried into the "house of my God" and determined never to go back to "homes of the wicked."

A funny thing happened once I began to live and work with those who had lived in the house of God most of their lives. I noticed how longingly and how often they would look at the "good life" as if they were missing out on something! And they got dangerously near to it . . . lusting, dabbling, rationalizing, minimizing, touching. I often tried to warn them, but I always came away feeling stupid.

But when two of my minister friends got too close to the "good life in the homes of the wicked," they left their wives for other women and lost their ministries. . . .

I occasionally think about them.

I wonder how often they repeat the words of the verse above.

## Prayer Principles

*One day Jesus told his disciples a story to show that they should always pray and never give up.* LUKE 18:1

**M**ost of us have misconceptions about prayer. One winter, I looked up every verse in the Bible that had the words *ask, believe,* or *pray* in it. I thought, *If I lived like I believed half of what the Bible said about prayer, I'd be a radical Christian.*

When you will take the time to understand what the Bible, particularly Jesus, said about prayer, you will be absolutely stretched and challenged to pray with expectation, persistence, and boldness.

In my search, I came up with at least six powerful prayer principles:

1. *Asking prayer*—In Matthew 7:7, Jesus said, "Keep on asking, and you will receive what you ask for."
2. *Revealing prayer*—James 1:5 reminds us, "If you need wisdom, ask our generous God, and he will give it to you. He will not rebuke you for asking."
3. *Believing prayer*—In Matthew 21:22, Jesus said, "You can pray for anything, and if you have faith, you will receive it."
4. *Interceding prayer*—Paul, in Colossians 1:9, models how to pray for others: "So we have not stopped praying for you since we first heard about you."
5. *Agreeing prayer*—Jesus taught in Matthew 18:19-20, "I also tell you this: If two of you agree here on earth concerning anything you ask, my Father in heaven will do it for you. For where two or three gather together as my followers, I am there among them."
6. *Persevering prayer*—Luke 18:1-8 is my favorite teaching by Jesus on persistent prayer! Read it and you'll be amazed. . . .

Which of the six powerful prayer principles would stretch you into a radical Christian?

# Pure Heart

*Teach me your ways, O LORD, that I may live according to your truth!*
*Grant me purity of heart, so that I may honor you.* PSALM 86:11

I n the 1970s, being a sexually active, binge-drinking college woman was neither trendy nor popular. It was considered almost too wild.

But by the turn of the twenty-first century, according to an April 2002 study funded by the National Institute on Alcohol Abuse and Alcoholism, "It is estimated that 97,000 students each year are victims of alcohol-related sexual assault or date rape, that almost a third (31 percent) of college students meet the criteria for a diagnosis of alcohol abuse"[2] and "6 percent of college students met criteria for a diagnosis of alcohol dependence."[3]

Over the last thirty years, what was considered too wild or unpopular for students has now become the popular trend even among those who call themselves Christian.

In the fall of 2004, I responded to a burning call from God to return to student ministry. My testimony had become more relevant now than it was three decades ago. Through telling my shameful story of how alcoholism and sexual promiscuity stole so much from me, the Holy Spirit of God is honestly confronting students regarding their lifestyles.

I believe God is passionately, powerfully calling out this generation to live according to His truth; to be pure and holy. And their response has been immediate and humbling. . . . Confession follows every meeting.

The psalmist's prayer is for every person of any age in every generation. Make it your prayer today.

## Speak Up!

*Zelophehad, a descendant of Hepher son of Gilead, son of Makir, son of Manasseh, had no sons. He had only daughters, whose names were Mahlah, Noah, Hoglah, Milcah, and Tirzah. These women came to Eleazar the priest, Joshua son of Nun, and the Israelite leaders and said, "The LORD commanded Moses to give us a grant of land along with the men of our tribe." So Joshua gave them a grant of land along with their uncles, as the LORD had commanded.* JOSHUA 17:3-4

I can just imagine how the daughters of Zelophehad felt approaching the priest and all the leaders of Israel! Surely they must have been intimidated. But this account does not mention their feelings, only their unflinching courage.

Their attitude in asking for what was promised is the same attitude the author of Hebrews suggests God's children should have when we come to God in prayer! (See Hebrews 4:14-16.)

Andrew Murray, a nineteenth-century South African minister, wrote numerous books on prayer—*With Christ in the School of Prayer* being one of his most powerful treatises. In his chapter on "The Secret of Believing Prayer," he taught four promise principles:

1. The power to believe *a promise* depends entirely on faith in *the promiser*. . . .
2. Let faith focus on God more than on the thing promised, because it is His love, His power, His living presence that will awaken and work the faith. . . .
3. Whoever knows and trusts God finds it easy to also trust the promise. . . .
4. The man who walks before the Lord and falls on his face to listen while the living God speaks to him will receive the promise.[4]

Today—and every day—come boldly to the throne of God until you receive your promise.

## Wise Advice

*People who despise advice are asking for trouble; those who respect a command will succeed. The instruction of the wise is like a life-giving fountain; those who accept it avoid the snares of death.* PROVERBS 13:13-14

D id you know that the Proverbs cover topics such as anger, time management, business skills, and other lessons for daily life?

Did you know that the Proverbs speak about sexual immorality—a lot? Reading certain proverbs is like watching a movie—you are given a view of every slippery step a person takes as he or she progresses through the stages of lust before falling into the trap of repeated sexual sin.

Did you know that the Proverbs speak about drunkenness—how alcohol feels good when it is going down the throat and how it "bites" like a snake when you've had too much? (See Proverbs 23:31-32.)

Did you know that the Proverbs speak to children about obeying their parents? (See Proverbs 1:8-9.)

Did you know that wisdom calls out to you? (See Proverbs 8:1.)

You never need to be without wise advice—you have the book of Proverbs available to you!

There are thirty-one chapters in Proverbs. . . . Read a chapter a day, and you'll read the book of Proverbs in a month. Read a chapter a day every month, and you'll read through the Proverbs twelve times a year. Read Proverbs daily for a year, and you will become wiser (at least wiser than you were the year before)!

# Novel Idea

*"Teacher," they said, "we know that you speak and teach what is right and are not influenced by what others think. You teach the way of God truthfully."* LUKE 20:21

When Jesus spoke truth, people listened! And some followed.

The Gospel writers give wonderfully visual descriptions of what it was like to be around Jesus! Jesus made people stop and think. His words pierced every heart. And unlike most, He was fearless and unconcerned about what others thought!

What a novel idea—to know truth and do what is right and not care what others think!

In every century, Christians have struggled to follow Jesus amidst their cultural mores, in light of modernity, and in respect to relevance. Yet I'm always surprised at the things people tell me they believe! I think, *Where did you get that idea?* So I've quit being surprised and I've adopted a new favorite saying, especially to students: "Your standards for living the Christian life cannot be based on what your peers, parents, pastors, or professors tell you is right or wrong, but what the Word of God teaches!"

The sooner a person is introduced to the Bible as God's voice to him or her on every aspect of life, the sooner he or she will begin to base decisions, actions, and beliefs on the Word of God . . . and not on what others think, say, or feel. And the sooner he or she will have the conviction to

know truth,

do what is right, and

not care what others think.

What a novel idea!

# Cling Tightly

*Be very careful to follow everything Moses wrote in the Book of Instruction.*
*Do not deviate from it, turning either to the right or to the left. . . .*
*Rather, cling tightly to the LORD your God as you have done until now.*

J oshua had seen his fair share of scary battles. He'd handled difficult negotiations and won miraculous victories. He had heard the same warning from Moses to the Israelites before Moses died: Be very careful not to deviate from the Word of God, don't partner with the godless, and by no means should you serve or worship other gods.

Joshua and Moses knew from years of experience that without complete obedience to God, God's people were vulnerable.

This message is relevant to every generation.

A fully devoted follower of the living, loving God will not be successful without knowing and clinging to the Word of God. If you do not read the Word, you will be . . .

at risk to be easily misguided by self or others,

more often tempted to chase after other gods,

unprotected and vulnerable to fall.

Joshua, one of God's greatest leaders, held tightly to the Word of God. I urge you, as Joshua did, to cling to the Word of God every day for the rest of your life—not out of duty but because it is His voice to you. God's Word is where you receive confidence, counsel, and courage. Don't miss His voice! Have a copy of the Bible at your office, in your car, and by your bed. Read it in the morning or at night, but read it daily.

## Choose Today

*If you refuse to serve the LORD, then choose today whom you will serve.*
*Would you prefer the gods your ancestors served beyond the Euphrates?*
*Or will it be the gods of the Amorites in whose land you now live?*
*But as for me and my family, we will serve the LORD.* JOSHUA 24:15

J oshua had high standards for himself and his family. He did not hesitate to ask others to choose to follow after the Lord. He didn't suggest that people go home and consider their decision for a week or get into a small group to discuss the "pros and cons" of serving God. He called for a decision now, today!

The day I became a Christian, I told my closest friends how Jesus dramatically changed my life. They could see immediate changes in every area of my life. Yet none of them, especially my boyfriend, were thrilled about the "new" me.

Before coming to Christ, I lived with my boyfriend and drank every night until I got drunk. I became a Christian while he was away on a monthlong vacation. By the time he returned home, I had moved out of our apartment. He was shocked, especially when I suggested that we get married! Though I always felt it was wrong to live together, now I stood for what I believed was right in God's eyes. We broke up. Everything from "before" crumbled "after."

Every day something else came up where I had to choose to serve the Lord, rather than live the life dictated by my peers or culture. It wasn't easy. I was heartbroken and cried a lot.

It wasn't long before I met a great Christian man who didn't even kiss me before asking me to marry him! I said yes, and we've been married—and in ministry—almost thirty years.

# Marching Orders

*Teach us to realize the brevity of life, so that we may grow in wisdom.*

PSALM 90:12

Some of the most practical benefits of spending time with God every day are the numerous ideas that come into your mind while conversing with God. Peter Marshall, former chaplain of the U.S. Senate, frequently commented that during his conversations with God, he would get his marching orders from the Captain.

*My Partner Prayer Notebook*, the tool I have used for over twenty-three years to record my two-way conversations with God, includes a section for a to-do list. Why? Inevitably, a verse or prayer request will bring to mind . . .

- a promise I made to send something to someone
- a card or gift to purchase or mail for someone special
- a household chore that is halfway finished
- a phone call to make; correspondence to complete
- an apology to make
- an errand to run
- a powerful, new idea

Prior to disciplining my spiritual life, I couldn't seem to manage my time, weight, personality, or money. I was consistently out of control in every area—physically, emotionally, mentally, and spiritually. But when I determined to talk to and listen to God for one hour a day, I began to exercise regularly, complete projects, be on time for meetings, maintain a more organized workspace, and most importantly, set goals and achieve them!

Consistent time with God in prayer will change your priorities. In prayer, you will become aware of how important every hour of your day is to God—and to others.

Try it! Keep a to-do list in your Bible or prayer notebook and just see if you don't get a few marching orders every day from the Captain!

# Thank God!

*It is good to give thanks to the LORD, to sing praises to the Most High.*
*It is good to proclaim your unfailing love in the morning,*
*your faithfulness in the evening.*  PSALM 92:1-2

For over two decades, I have paraphrased one to five psalms every day, making them my personal praise prayers. And like the psalmist, not a day goes by when I don't have something awesome to thank the Lord for doing in my life.

Thanking God in writing takes your gratitude for Him to a new level. Not only are you more thoughtfully invested, but more importantly, you are acknowledging that an answer to prayer is not because of luck, chance, or coincidence.

A thank-you note forever changed my husband's life.

Roger was an agnostic. A church attendee only until the age of twelve, he turned to psychology for life's answers. By twenty-six, he was newly divorced, alone, and depressed. He had seen a psychiatrist and a psychologist for help. No one had any lasting answers for him. While lying on a mattress, he began to journal. After expressing his pain on page after page, he concluded, "Thank God!" He wrote his next thought; it was almost a voice saying, "That's right, Roger. Thank God. I'm here. I love you." He stopped writing.

Roger was a public school guidance counselor whose secretary was a praying Christian woman. He had discounted her religious comments for two years. When he walked up to her desk the next morning, he thought, *She'll understand if I tell her what happened.* He told her how God met him in the night, and she invited him to church.

Thank God.

# I'm Slipping . . .

*Unless the LORD had helped me, I would soon have settled in the silence
of the grave. I cried out, "I am slipping!" but your unfailing love,
O LORD, supported me. When doubts filled my mind, your comfort gave
me renewed hope and cheer.*   PSALM 94:17-19

A *Time* magazine article reported on the increased suicide
rates among American college students. If you don't
currently parent a high school or college student or work
closely with students, you might not believe the statistics. But
the article states, "Student suicides—which total some 1,100 a
year nationwide, mak[e] suicide the second leading cause of death
among college students, after motor-vehicle accidents."[5]

College students search for significance at this stage in their
lives. And in addition to their unique family challenges, they are
overwhelmed with a fierce competition among their peers for
grades, relationships, jobs, and status.

Is there "one answer" that fits all? I know only one answer that
saved my life when I was an addicted, suicidal twenty-one-year-old
college dropout . . . a desperate prayer, asking God to help me, set
me on a path that changed my life that very hour. There were many
more prayers—daily prayers, hourly prayers—that followed when
I called on God to help me and change me.

He will do the same for you.

# Real Fleece

*The LORD turned to him and said, "Go with the strength you have, and rescue Israel from the Midianites. I am sending you!" "But Lord," Gideon replied, "how can I rescue Israel? My clan is the weakest.". . . The LORD said to him, "I will be with you. And you will destroy the Midianites as if you were fighting against one man."* JUDGES 6:14-16

Have you ever questioned whether or not God was sending you somewhere or asking you to do something that just seemed too out of the ordinary? Have you felt God prompting you—but were too afraid to step out? So was Gideon! He was fearful, but kept asking God to help him believe. And God kept showing Gideon that He could be trusted.

Gideon was not from a large clan. Perhaps that was another reason God chose him for the task. Gideon was a perfect example to everyone who is smaller or less educated than his or her opponent, has fewer resources, is less known, or lacks confidence, *that the battle is never about us!* It is about God!

In fact, God often eliminates the viable reasons and resources for achieving human success so that He will be seen and known as God! He did it with Joshua at Jericho, David and Goliath, and Daniel in the lions' den. He did it with Gideon. And He'll do it with you!

The next time you hear God ask you to be His mouthpiece or warrior, lay down all your excuses. The fleece? Ask God to take away any unbelief and give you encouraging confirmation and courage to complete your assignments.

## In Paradise

*Jesus replied, "I assure you, today you will be with me in paradise."*

LUKE 23:43

E very April 27, I am reminded of the day my father died. He had suffered a heart attack a week earlier, and each of his kids flew from California to Cleveland on the first available flights. Dad was in a coma until the last sibling—me—arrived.

On Friday night, Dad was doing so well they transferred him from ICU to a step-down unit. I stayed with Dad to watch another ball game and tuck him in before heading home.

We had a few good laughs, and when the game was over I asked my dad if I could pray for him. It was such a sweet moment, but especially tender when our hands seemed to meet near his chest and fold together. I wanted him to feel comfort, so I just expressed a simple request to God that he would not be afraid, that his room would be filled with angels, and his sleep would be peaceful. As I headed down the long hospital hallway, I could hear my father say to the nurse, "Did you hear that nice prayer my daughter prayed for me?"

Those were the last words I ever heard my father say. . . .

The next morning, we received the news that Dad had suffered a final, massive heart attack and died in his sleep.

My husband called to ask if I had heard God's voice that day. Upon reading the last verse of the New Testament on April 27, I could almost hear the Lord tell me, "Your dad is with Me in paradise."

I was so encouraged by how God met my family on that day *in our daily, regular Bible reading.* You never want to miss His voice. It is priceless.

## Don't Forget

*The women were terrified and bowed with their faces to the ground.
Then the men asked, "Why are you looking among the dead for someone
who is alive? He isn't here! He is risen from the dead! Remember what
he told you back in Galilee."* LUKE 24:5-6

From the day I became a Christian, I had the distinct impression that God wanted me to share the good news about Jesus Christ with everyone in America.

For more reasons than I have space to list, I was the least likely spokesperson for God! But I didn't think about the reasons why I couldn't or shouldn't do what God asked me to do. I began telling one person at a time.

Within hours, I told my friends and coworkers about the Lord Jesus Christ. Within the next year, I enthusiastically shared with my old schoolmates, high school administrators, and family members how the Good News had powerfully changed my life. Before I had been a Christian even a year, I was asked to intern with a Christian youth organization. I became a club director in the local high school—sharing weekly with hundreds of high school students over the next decade.

Eventually I became a traveling member of a national youth-worker team, sharing with thousands of students over the next five years.

In June 1994, I shared my story in front of forty thousand people at the Greater Cleveland Billy Graham Crusade. On the last Friday of 2000, I was a guest on *The Early Show* (CBS). In five minutes, I was given the opportunity to share the Good News with over 2.5 million people. And I'm not done yet. . . .

What has He told you *from the beginning* that you must believe and accomplish?

# On Fire!

*They said to each other, "Didn't our hearts burn within us as he talked with us on the road and explained the Scriptures to us?"* LUKE 24:32

D o you know the secret to setting and keeping your heart on fire?

Theophan, known as the Recluse, said if Scripture reading and praying are practiced simultaneously, they will produce a certain feeling within the believer toward the Lord:

> *Do you wish to enter this Paradise as quickly as possible? Here, then, is what you must do. When you pray, do not end your prayer without having aroused in your heart some feeling towards God, whether it be reverence, or devotion, or thanksgiving, or glorification, or humility and contrition, or hope and trust. Also when after prayer you begin to read, do not finish reading without having felt in your heart the truth of what you read. These two feelings—the one inspired by prayer, the other by reading—mutually warm one another; and if you pay attention to yourself, they will keep you under their influence during the whole day. Take pains to practise these two methods exactly and you will see for yourself what will happen.*[6]

We underestimate the passion and intimacy available to us through prayer and the Word. We get busy and neglect our time with God, thus dousing our inner fires!

History records that *prayer combined with the Word of God* has sparked massive bonfires of revival. Prayer has the dynamite power to ignite hope and faith in individuals and in nations. Therefore, we must stay alert to outside opposition and internal complacency that keep us from maintaining a burning heart.

Like the disciples whose hearts were on fire when Jesus talked with them about the Scriptures, when you pray and read the Word, expect to be filled with an unquenchable fire to . . . move mountains, cause breakthroughs, and ignite others' fires.

# Intentional Living

*I will be careful to live a blameless life—when will you come to help me? I will lead a life of integrity in my own home. I will refuse to look at anything vile and vulgar. I hate all who deal crookedly; I will have nothing to do with them. I will reject perverse ideas and stay away from every evil.*

PSALM 101:2-4

The shows on television seem to run along these lines:

- Learn to gamble in three easy payments
- Fourth Wives Club
- Dating lessons for the loose and looser
- How to divorce your spouse without paying the prenup
- *Pornography for Dummies*
- Hollywood stars who have your horoscope

Never in history has more audiovisual information entered a home uninvited. Just surfing the channels can be dangerous these days.

But David's prayer doesn't blame culture or presume he will not face temptation. Instead, he prays to God and states his intentions—and so must you and I!

I will . . . be careful to live a blameless life in my relationships.

I will . . . lead a life of integrity in my own home.

I will . . . refuse to look at anything vile and vulgar on the Internet or television.

I will . . . reject perverse ideas and stay away from every evil counsel.

Intentional living begins with "I will . . ."

# Desperate Prayers

*He will listen to the prayers of the destitute. He will not reject their pleas.*
*Let this be recorded for future generations, so that a people not yet born*
*will praise the LORD.* PSALM 102:17-18

In June 2006, the American Film Institute named the classic 1940s film *It's a Wonderful Life* as the most inspiring film of all time. The clip they chose from the movie was the prayer of a desperate, suicidal man—George Bailey, played by Jimmy Stewart. He said, "Dear Father in Heaven, I'm not a praying man, but if you're up there and you can hear me, show me the way." A series of spiritual, serendipitous events unfold to restore the man to his family, reputation, and ultimately a wonderful life!

What is prayer and who is it for?

- Prayer is as much for the seeker, the desperate, the confused, or those estranged from God as it is for the religious.
- Prayer is not telling God what to do; it is sincerely asking Him for help, advice, or a breakthrough and expecting Him to come.
- Prayer does not hide the truth from God; most often it opens our hearts and minds to see God's escape and our rebellion.
- Prayer does not need to be formal, but respectful of the One from whom we are requesting help—He holds our lives in His grip.
- Prayer is not a monotonous, effortless pastime. It often requires agony, wrestling, or submission.
- Prayer is a two-way conversation that requires transparent honesty.

A desperate prayer, answered by the living, loving God, will change a life forever.

Never discount or deter someone from praying a desperate prayer, for God's Word says He will not reject their pleas.

## Love Language

*The LORD is compassionate and merciful, slow to get angry and filled with unfailing love. He will not constantly accuse us, nor remain angry forever. He does not punish us for all our sins; he does not deal harshly with us, as we deserve.* PSALM 103:8-10

This passage not only describes how God loves and relates to His children but also is a powerful treatise for parents on how to love and discipline their children.

The difficulty in receiving or delivering these parental concepts lies within our family of origin and view of God. It is essential to understand and accept the love of God toward you. He is . . .

merciful,

slow to anger,

unconditional in His love,

not an accuser, and

does not punish us as we deserve.

When we begin to experience and understand God's love toward us, we become not only free to love others in the same way, but compelled to do so.

How can God's love toward us practically translate from heaven to earth?

A screaming, out-of-control parent does not change a child's heart, but more likely trains him or her to be a screaming, out-of-control person. But parents who have their emotions under the control of the Holy Spirit become dependent on God's advice for each step in disciplining their children.

Parents, we must acknowledge that anger and accusation fuel a fire. We must choose to be full of compassion, use calm words, and extend unconditional love and mercy to our children—just as God chooses to relate to us with this very same language of love.

## Good News

*God loved the world so much that he gave his one and only Son,*
*so that everyone who believes in him will not perish but have eternal*
*life. God sent his Son into the world not to judge the world, but to save*
*the world through him.* JOHN 3:16-17

I have an "only son." I think I love him too much! And because he is our only child, all of our love, expectations, and dreams are showered upon him. In fact, Roger and I would agree that of all our accomplishments and treasures there is nothing or no one that has given us more joy than our only son!

When I consider the incredible relationship between God and His only Son, Jesus, the one question that most puzzles me is "How could He give up His 'one and only Son' to die so that others—who didn't even love Him—could receive the gift of eternal life?"

I can't fathom how difficult or devastating it must have been to the Father and the Son to walk through that time. The plan involved sacrifice and submission, obedience above selfishness.

John 3:16 is one of the first Scripture verses that a Christian will memorize because it has so much truth packed into one sentence. But it is more than a memory verse; it is the passion of a believer to acknowledge that God's love for us cost Him His only Son.

In *My Utmost for His Highest*, Oswald Chambers wrote, "Salvation is easy for us, because it cost God so much. But the exhibiting of salvation in my life is difficult. . . . Remain faithful to your Friend, and remember that His honor is at stake in your bodily life."[1]

Commit your ways to the lifelong privilege of sharing God's amazing love with those who are separated from Him. Remember, you have what they are looking for—the Good News!

# Take Courage

*The Israelites encouraged each other and took their positions again at the same place they had fought the previous day. For they had gone up to Bethel and wept in the presence of the LORD until evening. They had asked the LORD, "Should we fight against our relatives from Benjamin again?" And the LORD had said, "Go out and fight against them."* JUDGES 20:22-23

### Battle #1

A woman in our church is facing a second bout with breast cancer. At the suggestion of one of her dearest friends, we've gathered as a community to fast forty days—every meal—for her healing. Battle on!

### Battle #2

The younger generation in our country is being attacked by an aggressive force of sexual immorality, including pornography addiction. Do we just watch and hope that it does not affect *our* children? That would be naive. The current culture is way too invasive for us to assume our families won't be touched by this strategic onslaught of evil. We must fight.

Life is a battle. That's all there is to it. When we accept that we can't control most of what unfolds within any given day, we are in the right place—dependent upon God, looking to Him for our battle strategies.

### Judges 20:22-23 Battle Strategy

Always take your concerns first to God in prayer. (We often ask everyone's advice *except* His.) Then, encourage each other as you fight your very real battles. Stand up; stand together. Rise up, speak out, and go to the house of the Lord to weep and pray. We must physically and emotionally encourage each other as we fight our battles.

If you seek the Lord for your specific battle strategy, I firmly believe He is going to tell you how and when to "go out and fight against them."

# Keep Searching

*Search for the L*ORD* and for his strength; continually seek him.*

PSALM 105:4

Y ou have as much of God as you want . . . because what you *really* want you chase after and obsess over until you get it. Being in a passionate relationship with God is *no different* than any other relationship. God is not elusive. He speaks. He is present and real, and He waits for us.

- If you want to know God better, read the Word of God daily.
- If you want to know His thoughts, ask!
- If you want to know a specific answer, ask a specific question, then wait for His answer.
- If you want to understand more about Jesus, read the four Gospels.
- If you need more wisdom, read Proverbs.
- If you need comfort from God, read Psalms.
- If you struggle with faith or believing in miracles, read Acts and Hebrews.
- If you want to observe how a godly man endured pain and suffering, read the book of Job.
- If you want to know more about prophecy or the end times, read Daniel or Revelation.
- If you are a new believer and want to know more about Christianity, read Paul's letters in the New Testament.
- If you want to learn about God's creation or His relationship with man "in the beginning," read the book of Genesis.

These are just a few examples of how you can search for God and find Him! The psalmist knew God well and yet reminds us, "Search for the L*ORD* . . . *continually* seek him" (emphasis added). He can always be found. . . .

# Character Development

*Until the time came to fulfill his dreams, the LORD tested Joseph's character.*

PSALM 105:19

A friend of mine called after graduating from boot camp. This was our first conversation since he left home to be a marine.

I asked, "How are you—spiritually, emotionally, physically?"

He replied, "Well, I made it! If you didn't have a spiritual life before you got here, you did before you left. In fact, the training was so difficult, you quickly realized you can't make it here without God. I feel like I've matured ten years in just three months!"

He sounded different . . . like a leader.

The character of a leader will not develop unless it is tested. Joseph, among the many leadership examples in the Bible, was tested more than once. In *Spiritual Leadership*, J. Oswald Sanders writes, "Are leaders born or made? . . . Closer investigation usually reveals that the selection was not accidental but was more the result of hidden training that made the person fit for leadership. Joseph is a perfect example. . . . In fact his promotion was the outcome of thirteen years of rigorous, hidden training under the hand of God."[2]

Join the marines and you'll be tested in every way *so that* when you are under the greatest pressure, you'll respond and react as a well-trained warrior. Receive a call to lead in God's army and your training will be no different. Your character will be developed through testing.

In *Spiritual Leadership*, Sanders notes eight tests of leadership, taken from *John R. Mott* by Basil Joseph Matthews: "One should inquire of a leader whether he or she (1) does little things well; (2) has learned to focus on priorities; (3) uses leisure well; (4) has intensity; (5) knows how to exploit momentum; (6) is growing; (7) overcomes discouragement and "impossible" situations; (8) understands his or her weaknesses."[3]

# Giving Back

*"Sir, do you remember me?" Hannah asked. "I am the woman who stood here several years ago praying to the LORD. I asked the LORD to give me this boy, and he has granted my request. Now I am giving him to the LORD, and he will belong to the LORD his whole life." And they worshiped the LORD there.*

1 SAMUEL 1:26-28

H annah is the epitome of a praying woman! She asked the Lord to give her a child and God answered her! (Sounds admirable so far. . . .)

But Hannah was so grateful to God for answering her prayer that she not only dedicated her son to the Lord but gave him back to God, allowing him to leave home at a very young age and begin service in the Tabernacle.

Remarkable.

Most of us ask God to fill our needs, heal our hurts, or increase our comfort. But our normal response after we receive our answer is to ask *for more*, rather than give it back to God!

What can you or I do to give back to God?

In the most obvious way, we can begin with verbal gratitude! Like Hannah, we can acknowledge to God and others how the Lord met our specific needs.

In a more passionate, tangible way, we can give back to God the part of our lives He restored or healed in answer to our prayers.

Is it time for you to give back? Don't hesitate to give the rest of your life to working with students, helping to build homes for the homeless, volunteering at a shelter for abused women or children, teaching Sunday school, visiting the sick, or mentoring the kids of single parents.

Don't think about it—just do it.

# Rotten Jealousy

*A peaceful heart leads to a healthy body; jealousy is like cancer in the bones.*

PROVERBS 14:30

In my twenties, I was quite a bit overweight after my pregnancy. I became obsessed with my weight and often felt jealous of anyone who was skinnier or prettier than I. Unfortunately, this led to fewer friendships and lack of credibility as a leader. (Jealousy is an unhealthy sin and separates us from God and others—as any sin will do.)

At age twenty-nine, I felt my life spinning out of control—physically, emotionally, spiritually, and mentally. So I determined to pray every day for one hour. This spiritual discipline began to change *all areas of my life*. I became less concerned about food and exercise and more willing to get rid of daily sins, such as anger and jealousy. The result of daily prayer was evident to all. My relationships improved, my leadership skills had a chance to develop, my heart became more sensitive to God's Holy Spirit, and over time, I lost all of the "baby weight" and have never regained it.

That's right . . . spending time with God has been the one nonnegotiable appointment every day for over two decades that has positively impacted every area of my life. The most practical result of daily prayer has been the development of the 8 Daily To Do's (from the *Change Your Life Daily Journal*):

- Eat right
- Exercise regularly
- Forgive
- Give
- Talk to God
- Listen to God
- Detail your day
- Define your dreams

So whenever people ask me how I stay so fit or young-looking, I surprise them with my answer: "Prayer! I've prayed for one hour a day for over twenty-three years!"

# Believing Prayer

*"Tell everyone to sit down," Jesus said. So they all sat down on the grassy slopes. (The men alone numbered about 5,000.) Then Jesus took the loaves, gave thanks to God, and distributed them to the people. Afterward he did the same with the fish. And they all ate as much as they wanted.*

JOHN 6:10-11

In the 1800s, George Müller of England was called a "believing pray-er." He led a life of self-denial and was known for seeking divine guidance in prayer.

His biography, *George Müller of Bristol*, written by A. T. Pierson, records so many stories of miraculous supply that readers cannot help but be inspired by his absolute dependence upon prevailing prayer and constant obedience to God. Two miraculous accounts exhibited his ability to rest upon the unwavering "fatherly pity of God."

On the first occasion, early one morning he prayed for enough food to feed the orphanage children in his care. It didn't happen often, but by evening, there was nothing to eat for the next meal. That afternoon a poor woman came to give all she had—two pence—to the ministry. As small a gift as it was, it was "just what was at that time needed . . . to buy bread for immediate use."

Another time his faith was severely tested was on March 9, 1842. This time, the needs were so extreme that if nothing came, the ministry could not go on. Though the postal service had already delivered the day's mail, he still prayed, believing God to supply their operating expenses. Late in the afternoon, a letter was handed to him that had gone to the wrong address. In it was money enough to feed the thousands of children they had to feed daily.[4]

Over a century later, George Müller still teaches us about believing prayer—*when we ask God, we must believe that He will supply!*

## Always Full

*Jesus replied, "I am the bread of life. Whoever comes to me will never be hungry again. Whoever believes in me will never be thirsty."*

JOHN 6:35

I f you have ever partaken of a fast from eating for spiritual, medical, or physical reasons—one meal or for a whole day— you undoubtedly have experienced the bread phenomenon.

Hot, fresh bread will always catch your senses off guard! In fact, bread is often one of the first foods a person eats after undertaking a fast of any length. Why? Bread is both emotionally and physically satisfying!

I started thinking about Jesus' self-description as "the bread of life" while on an extended spiritual fast. In fact, I thought about food a lot. (You often don't realize how much you take something for granted until you can no longer have it!) And I came away with a very simple and practical explanation about the correlation between Jesus and bread.

When Jesus suggests that He is our bread, He is saying, "Only I can fill your physical, emotional, and relational needs. Your spouse can't, your kids won't. Money won't do it and your job will not. I *have* all you need. I *am* all you need."

Those who are addicted—to relationships, food, sex, or alcohol—*very often* have to return to this basic "bread of life" truth about Jesus. Until they really believe (enough to quit relapsing) that He is enough, they'll chase after anything and everything to fill their unquenchable needs.

No matter who we are, where we've been, or what we've been chasing, each of us must be willing to say, "Jesus, I get it. You're all I need to fill my hunger and quench my thirst." Has that day come for you? Do you need to return to the "bread of life"?

## Speak Out

*Give thanks to the LORD, for he is good! His faithful love endures forever. Has the LORD redeemed you? Then speak out! Tell others he has redeemed you from your enemies.*  PSALM 107:1-2

Ralph, the janitor of a church, who found me when I was about to commit suicide, was very different from me. Yet he didn't avoid me or tell me that because he was a janitor he was unqualified to talk about God. He simply asked me to pray. In one short conversation, he introduced me to Jesus, the Bible, and the Holy Spirit. And in the next twenty-four hours, I quit drinking and living with my boyfriend and became the kind of Christian that many *Christians* don't even like to be around!

So, I am compelled to be someone else's "janitor" every chance I get! And from the hundreds of conversations I've had so far, no one has stopped me abruptly or given me a negative response. In fact, most people are truly encouraged by my story.

When I have the privilege of sharing my story in front of a large group, I always ask the question, "Does anyone need a janitor? If so, I'd like to pray with you."

If God has redeemed you, speak out *today*—don't wait for tomorrow.

## Prayerlessness Is . . .

*The LORD will not abandon his people, because that would dishonor his great name. For it has pleased the LORD to make you his very own people. As for me, I will certainly not sin against the LORD by ending my prayers for you. And I will continue to teach you what is good and right.*

1 SAMUEL 12:22-23

Prayerlessness is . . . sin!

Did you know that Samuel, the great priest and God's strong and faithful leader of Israel, considered prayerlessness to be sin in his life? He believed that the prayer life of one in leadership over God's people was not just a dutiful religious practice, but a responsibility!

In 1984, I was a youth leader who was often too busy, too tired, or too lazy to pray. I sincerely believed prayer was important—but I just couldn't get myself to slow down or make the time to pray until I went to a convention where every keynote speaker (all the former presidents of Youth for Christ) talked about prayer.

The speakers begged us to become praying men and women. Quotes such as Leonard Ravenhill's "No man is greater than his prayer life"[5] landed in my heart with such conviction that I truly began to change my thinking about prayer. Instead of feeling guilty about not praying, I began to see what I was missing!

First, I understood that I was ignoring my spiritual responsibility as a leader of over two hundred students. Second, I realized that by not consulting God, I was missing His direction and intervention in their lives and mine!

At that convention, I heard 1 Samuel 12:22-23 discussed, as well as a quote by Samuel Chadwick, a nineteenth-century revival pastor: "Prayerlessness in the life of a believer is sin."[6] I felt ashamed—and proceeded to make prayer a nonnegotiable priority in my life.

What does Chadwick's quote say about your prayer life?

## Fearless Faith

*To reach the Philistine outpost, Jonathan had to go down between two*
*rocky cliffs that were called Bozez and Seneh. The cliff on the north was in*
*front of Micmash, and the one on the south was in front of Geba. "Let's go*
*across to the outpost of those pagans," Jonathan said to his armor bearer.*
*"Perhaps the LORD will help us, for nothing can hinder the LORD. He can*
*win a battle whether he has many warriors or only a few!"* 1 SAMUEL 14:4-6

Though Jonathan appeared to only have his armor bearer
by his side, he felt invincible because he believed that the
invisible, all-powerful God was with him!

A defining characteristic of fearless faith is this: Though it
sees trouble ahead—it doesn't waver. It depends on God's power,
God's Word, and God's reputation.

I grow more convinced that if we *lived like we believe* God's
Word, we'd be radical giants of faith just like the men and women
in the Bible.

What holds us back from this kind of faith? Fear.

- Fear diminishes faith.
- Fear increases doubt.
- Fear dismantles the Word of God in your heart and mind.
- Fear paralyzes you.
- Fear defeats you (if you let it).

Jonathan's faith was not overpowered by fear. He identified
his enemies and called on God to fight his battle with him. And
so must we.

You must fight against fear as the true enemy of your faith.
Identify your fears. (Are you afraid of death, rejection, poverty,
or loneliness?) Speak God's words against them. Repeat God's
words out loud over and over until you believe them.

God can win any battle whether He has many warriors or few.
Do you believe this to be true?

## Sinful Patterns

*Samuel replied, "What is more pleasing to the LORD: your burnt offerings and sacrifices or your obedience to his voice? Listen! Obedience is better than sacrifice, and submission is better than offering the fat of rams. Rebellion is as sinful as witchcraft, and stubbornness as bad as worshiping idols. So because you have rejected the command of the LORD, he has rejected you as king."* 1 SAMUEL 15:22-23

Chapters 15–16 of 1 Samuel contain the devastating record of King Saul's relationships with God and Samuel the priest. It is an absolutely gut-wrenching series of events where Saul's impulsiveness, audacity to ignore God's commands, and uncanny ability to rationalize his disobedient actions caused Samuel to never meet with Saul again and the Lord to regret He ever made Saul king of Israel (1 Samuel 15:35).

The lessons found in this account of Samuel's ministry to Saul cannot be ignored. They are both practical and profound, warning us to obey God when He speaks to us.

We've all occasionally fallen into patterns of rationalization, disobedience, procrastination, or impulsiveness. But in Samuel's estimation, such patterns can become sinful habits and are not inconsequential to God.

The most practical lesson in this account is the fact that God speaks to us—in very specific ways. And when He speaks, He gives us a choice to respond in obedience, not with excuses or impulsiveness or debate. God's willingness to use us depends on our willingness to obey His voice.

Psalm 25:14 says, "The LORD is a friend to those who fear him. He teaches them his covenant." Are you available to God? Does He call you friend? Have you heard God's voice lately? How have you responded?

# Almost Cocky

*David replied to the Philistine, "You come to me with sword, spear, and javelin, but I come to you in the name of the LORD of Heaven's Armies—the God of the armies of Israel, whom you have defied. Today the LORD will conquer you."* 1 SAMUEL 17:45-46

A t the time he faced Goliath, David was still a shepherd—not a valiant war hero yet. Remarkably, he was unmoved by his enemy's stature, or stellar battle history, and mocking threats. And he didn't cower in reply to the Philistine giant—he scalded him with rebuke and an extra measure of God's name! Ultimately, David was confident that he would gain the victory—and he did!

What was his secret? An intimate, all-encompassing relationship with the God of the Bible.

- David's God was his heavenly Father.
- David's God was his confidant and friend.
- David's God was the one true God.
- David's God was the all-powerful Commander of the army.
- David's God was able to defeat any enemy.
- David's God was trustworthy.

David had supernatural courage and indomitable strength whenever he called on God. I believe the same power, the same courage, and the same supernatural abilities that David possessed are available to *anyone* who will call on the God of the Bible. We must not hesitate to lift up His name in the face of our enemies nor fail to trust Him to rescue us.

Who is the giant that threatens your life? Put his mocking to an end. . . .

# True Freedom

*Jesus said to the people who believed in him, "You are truly my disciples if you remain faithful to my teachings. And you will know the truth, and the truth will set you free."* JOHN 8:31-32

If you've been an addict—to food, relationships, anger, alcohol, sex—you know the power of sin. It is so deceitful and shamelessly alluring that it slowly and methodically gains control over all your faculties with the intent of destroying your life. That is the truth.

But we tend to ignore the truth. For example, how many people start smoking, knowing that cigarettes cause cancer? How many junior high kids have sex and think that it could never lead to pregnancy or sexually transmitted diseases? Statistics don't lie. . . .

Jesus knows our nature. People have an uncanny ability to ignore truth and follow their own shallow impulses . . .

even though they'll become slaves to them,

even if they end in misery,

even if they are warned not to give in.

But Jesus offers freedom from slavery to sin—freedom based on *His* truth, not our idea of truth. He reminds us that we are not to be disciples of any other teaching but His.

Many years ago, Billy Graham compared the lifestyles of those who followed Christ's teachings and those who followed the sinful nature (as described in Galatians 5:16-21). He wrote, "People do many of these forbidden things in the name of freedom. What they fail to see is that such activities actually enslave those who become involved in them. True freedom consists not in the freedom *to* sin, but the freedom *not to* sin."[7]

Freedom not to sin! That is true freedom!

# Happy Mother

*He gives the childless woman a family, making her a happy mother.*
*Praise the LORD!* PSALM 113:9

I received the following letter (used with permission):

*I am writing to you to share about how the Lord spoke to me the day after I attended your prayer conference on May 16. . . .*

*My husband and I have been struggling with infertility for the past two years. We have had three miscarriages, and after many tests, it is inconclusive why those miscarriages are happening. We have been praying and asking the Lord for direction, and He has spoken to us many times through Scripture.*

*After our last miscarriage, He gave us Psalm 20. We decided we would put our trust in Him for our fertility. . . .*

*So this brings me up to the night of your conference. I went, even though I need a lot of sleep. . . . When I came home I was unable to sleep. . . . Finally somewhere around three, I fell asleep. I really felt tired, but I decided I would still wake up at 5 a.m. to pray. So my alarm goes off at 5 and I stumble down my stairs and get out my* Change Your Life Daily Bible *and prayer notebook.*

*I read May 17. And my amazing Father met me. As I read Psalm 113 (the passage for the day) it read, He settles the barren woman in her home as a happy mother of her children. Praise the Lord. Can you imagine my joy and praise?*

*To be honest, Becky, I would have missed this because May 17 would have been a day that I would have skipped my quiet time due to lack of sleep and busyness.*

Don't miss God's voice today in your life!

# Kinney's Ginny

*May the LORD richly bless both you and your children. May you be blessed by the LORD, who made heaven and earth.* PSALM 115:14-15

Kinney, my prayer partner and friend, was unable to have a baby. After many attempts and much disappointment, she and her husband began adoption proceedings. To add to their broken hearts, an adoption fell through at the last minute.

Just about that time, Kinney and I were scheduled to attend a women's conference. Because Kinney could not seem to regain hope after this series of discouraging events, we decided to visit the prayer room at the conference.

In that quiet room, we knelt by two chairs and cried our hearts out, asking God for a baby.

That night, we attended a concert with hundreds of other women. Before it began, a woman behind us tapped Kinney on the shoulder and said, "I understand you are looking for a baby." We were awestruck.

This woman lived hundreds of miles away from us. She had been to lunch with a woman from Kinney's church and heard her story. At this same time, a young girl in her church was giving her unborn child up for adoption through a private agency. The woman at the concert offered to connect Kinney to the right people.

The first step was to write a letter to the young mother—which Kinney did. Baby Ginny was born on December 8 and went home to Kinney six weeks after the women's conference. One month after that, much to the surprise of everyone, Kinney became pregnant! The two sisters are less than a year apart in age!

The Lord richly blessed Kinney and her children. They are a testimony to the faithfulness of God, who hears our prayers and answers them in wonderful ways!

# Lifestyle Praying

*I love the LORD because he hears my voice and my prayer for mercy. Because he bends down to listen, I will pray as long as I have breath!* PSALM 116:1-2

People who have heard me speak or read one of my books often ask, "Do you still pray one hour a day?" I sometimes think they secretly wish I'd admit failure. But instead I reply, "Yes, for over twenty-three years—almost eight thousand, five hundred hours—and counting. I haven't missed a day!"

The truth is, I haven't missed my appointment with the King, not because *I'm* innately disciplined, but for the following reasons:

1. God waits for me. He gives me wise counsel, great comfort, encouragement, and the perfect blend of love and discipline. I'd be crazy to miss a personal appointment with the One who always listens to me, loves me, and knows me better than anyone else!

2. I plan my hour with God *one day in advance*. (When I was the mother of a toddler, that meant I had to set my alarm before dawn! When I travel, I have to take into account flight times, time zones, and where I can find a quiet place.) My hour with God happens at a different time every day— but it happens!

A lifestyle of prayer takes planning. In *The Way of the Heart*, Henri Nouwen wrote,

> *The very first thing we need to do is set apart a time and a place to be with God and him alone. The concrete shape of this discipline of solitude will be different for each person depending on individual character, ministerial task, and milieu. But a real discipline never remains vague or general. It is as concrete and specific as daily life itself.*[8]

# Romans Road

*Jesus told her, "I am the resurrection and the life. Anyone who believes in me will live, even after dying. Everyone who lives in me and believes in me will never ever die. Do you believe this, Martha?"* JOHN 11:25-26

When I read Jesus' intimate conversations with His friends, I am struck with His level of confrontation. He didn't just strongly suggest that He would be resurrected, He asked Martha if she *believed* that He was indeed the resurrection and the life.

I truly think Jesus was looking for an answer. He wanted to know if she believed in Him. Her eternal destiny was at stake.

Our goal as believers is not to persuade people to think or act like us. We are to present Jesus to them.

*You will encounter skeptics.* And though you might have to work hard to debate apologetics with them, don't end the conversation until you've asked, "Do you believe?"

*You will encounter family members, old friends, or coworkers* who consider you the least plausible expert on spirituality with whom they want to engage in conversation about God. Don't take it personally. Overcome your feelings with the thought of where they will spend eternity.

*You'll be divinely placed into the lives of strangers.* You'll know it; you'll feel it. Your story of how you met Christ or your nonjudgmental, nonchurchy persona will allow you to share your heart with them.

As a youth worker, I learned the "Romans Road" as a simple but complete way to share Christ using four verses in Romans: 3:23; 5:8; 6:23; and 10:9-10.

*Do you believe?*

# Trust God

*It is better to take refuge in the LORD than to trust in people. It is better to take refuge in the LORD than to trust in princes.* PSALM 118:8-9

I often look back on how I raised my son. And I remember the day I realized that I no longer had as much influence over him as I'd once had. . . . When Jake came home for a break during his first semester of college, he stayed out all night and didn't come home until the next day. I was surprised, though I didn't immediately think of all the bad things he might have done. But by the time I rounded him up at a friend's house late into the next afternoon, I was angry. I worried about him drinking and driving.

He walked in the door and sat on the couch across from his father and me.

I said, "Jake, what were you doing staying out all night?"

He said, "Mom, I don't live here anymore, and I have to make decisions for my life by myself."

I was stunned. He was right! He lived at school. He was never going to live in our house 24-7 again. Most of the hands-on training had been completed. Now it was up to him.

I knelt by the couch and said, "Honey, I'm going to pray for you and fast for you regularly as you make these decisions. But don't make them without God's voice in your life, please. Read the Word daily. Let Him speak to you. Listen to His counsel."

It was all I had to give. But it was enough.

If you teach your kids to recognize God's voice, to obey Him instantly, and not to run from Him . . . it will be the best counsel you can give.

## Quick Temper

*The heart of the godly thinks carefully before speaking; the mouth of the*
*wicked overflows with evil words.* PROVERBS 15:28

Many of us grew up around cursing and angry outbursts. Many of us work around foul-mouthed coworkers and find ourselves repeating their language. Many of us struggle with a quick temper. We not only hurt others, we have a bad reputation. None of these are excuses . . . they are sinful habits which must be addressed by those who want to live godly lives.

To rid yourself of a quick temper, you must clean your heart!

- First, set aside time to think about (or journal about) your childhood. Were you raised in a home with a lot of yelling or name-calling? Were you criticized frequently? Do you find yourself repeating this behavior? (My counselor husband reminds me often that the things we don't like in other people are most likely faults in our own lives!) Be honest.
- Second, ask yourself, "Have I hurt anyone with my words in the past week or month?" Of course, we are most vulnerable at home, but conversations with coworkers and service workers might come to mind as well. List the occasions— and be specific.
- Third, confess your sin to God. (Yes, angry outbursts and judgmental accusations are sins.) Identify when you do it, then stop doing it—one person, one conversation, one emotional moment at a time.
- Fourth, forgive and ask for forgiveness. Ask God to forgive you. Forgive others face-to-face or in your heart (through meditation, prayer, or journaling). Tell others that you are going to change. Ask them to keep you accountable.

You can't change your past, but you can change the way you speak to others *from this moment forward*.

# Scripture Memory

*I have hidden your word in my heart, that I might not sin against you.*

PSALM 119:11

Whom my son, Jake, was in elementary school, he was required to memorize Scriptures every week. It was a great idea, but difficult for those of us who have a hard time concentrating!

Every week I had to make Jake review his Scriptures. He usually found a way to either procrastinate or forget them within minutes of repeating them. We soon fell into the pattern of waiting until the last day to start.

One day in particular, everything fell apart. Jake was assigned to memorize a series of verses in 1 Corinthians 13—the love chapter! Each week we agonized over the exact words in every verse. By the time we got to verse 4, both of us were exasperated!

I can still see him standing by the foot of his bed in his little school uniform. I had my hands on his shoulders, looking sternly in his eyes. With a very controlled but frustrated voice, I began to slowly repeat, "Love is patient and kind. . . ." He could not seem to get the order of the words. He grew sweaty and whiny. I got angry. . . . As my voice escalated, I caught myself rudely repeating, "First Corinthians 13:4—'Love is patient and kind. . . .'"

I was being anything but patient and kind with my little son.

I realized that God's great plan in having Jake memorize Bible verses was to get his mother to do so as well. And not just memorize them, but live them out in my daily life *so that I might not sin* against God or others! What a novel idea!

143

# Discipleship Training

*Don't let your hearts be troubled. Trust in God, and trust also in me.*
*. . . I am the way, the truth, and the life. No one can come to the Father*
*except through me. . . . I tell you the truth, anyone who believes in me will*
*do the same works I have done, and even greater works, because I am going*
*to be with the Father. You can ask for anything in my name, and I will do*
*it, so that the Son can bring glory to the Father. Yes, ask me for anything*
*in my name, and I will do it!* JOHN 14:1, 6, 12-14

The fourteenth chapter of the book of John is mesmerizing. First, Jesus tells His disciples that He is leaving them, but He promises to prepare rooms for them in His Father's heavenly house. Then He pledges to come back for them. . . .

Next, He eases their concerns about His relationship to the Father. He assures them that He is the only way to God the Father. They must be convinced of this fact, and convince others of it as well. Though He must leave them, He reminds them that there is much work for them to do.

This passage is equally powerful for you and me, His twenty-first-century disciples.

First, we must not worry about our earthly lives. Instead, we must be eternity minded. Those of us whose hearts and minds are with Christ in eternity have great peace on earth and do not fear death. We do not feel separated from God. We know He will come for us when it is time, because He said so. Second, we must not vacillate in our belief about the way to the Father—Jesus is the only way. In our personal and professional lives, we will meet opposition on this issue. We must be strong enough to uphold this truth in our words and actions. Third, we must step out in supernatural faith and do greater works than He did while on earth.

Jesus' discipleship training takes incredible conviction to follow! No wonder He began His teaching with "Don't let your hearts be troubled. Trust in God, and trust also in me."

## Holy Spirit

*When the Father sends the Advocate as my representative—that is, the Holy Spirit—he will teach you everything and will remind you of everything I have told you.* JOHN 14:26

In the last two years, I've heard hundreds of confessions of sexual immorality by far too many people who call themselves Christian. I've been an eyewitness to more than a dozen Christian leaders who have fallen morally in the past twenty years. And based on the statistic that 43 percent of first-time marriages end in divorce (including those of Christians),[9] I feel strongly that the average Christian could use a refresher on the indwelling power of the *Holy Spirit*! (Christians may often be considered religious or spiritual, but we're sure not often known by observers as *holy*.)

In *Spiritual Leadership*, J. Oswald Sanders writes, "Each of us is as full of the Spirit as we really want to be."[10] There it is! If we neglect, reject, or ignore the Holy Spirit in our lives, we are going to live less Holy Spirit–filled lives, as a great many of us do.

Much of Sanders's book focuses on the impact that the Holy Spirit is meant to have in a believer, especially a leader. He writes, "To be filled with the Spirit is to be controlled by the Spirit. . . . Through the work of the now ungrieved and unhindered Spirit, all the fruits of the Spirit start to grow in the leader's life. His witness is more winsome, service more steady, and testimony more powerful."[11]

When you and I daily listen to and obey God's promptings, we'll be filled to overflowing with His Holy Spirit. The result will be holy lives!

## First Lessons

*Remain in me, and I will remain in you. For a branch cannot produce fruit if it is severed from the vine, and you cannot be fruitful unless you remain in me. Yes, I am the vine; you are the branches. Those who remain in me, and I in them, will produce much fruit. For apart from me you can do nothing.*

JOHN 15:4-5

Most of my early Bible training came from the janitor who led me to Christ. He purchased a cassette player and the New Testament on tape for me to listen and learn as the Word of God was so foreign to my way of living and thinking. Listening to God's Word on tape daily cleansed my mind.

My next Bible training came as a volunteer in youth ministry. I stayed only one step ahead of the students I mentored as each week the volunteers were given basic biblical principles from the Bible to apply to our lives as well as to teach our youth group.

Then I became a mom. Attending the weekly women's Bible study at our Christian Missionary Alliance Church was the "thing to do" for all young women. A mature, beautiful, articulate woman taught our class. Her series was taken from the text in John about the vine and the branches.

I will never forget the spiritual surgery those verses performed on me. My young heart and mind were so hungry to learn. This teacher made us *want* to stay near to God. She made the consequences of detachment clear: We would no longer be useful to God—an unbearable thought!

# Big Collapse

*David confessed to Nathan, "I have sinned against the LORD." Nathan replied, "Yes, but the LORD has forgiven you, and you won't die for this sin."*

2 SAMUEL 12:13

David had sinned grievously. People around him must have hidden—and even enabled—his sin until Nathan came to him.

If David, who was so in love with God, could be so vulnerable, are we any less of a target? You see, sin chases us—especially God's leaders. And this story proves that even one who consistently seeks after and serves God must be surrounded with accountability. We must come under the protection of accountability partners to whom we give authority to confront us anytime.

In his book *Heart After God*, Luis Palau wrote, "Immorality begins with tiny things. Little things. Yet, if you don't crucify them, if you don't bring them to judgment, if you don't face up to them for what they are—sin—they can destroy you. They can blur your moral judgment at a critical, irreversible juncture in your life. No one sees the little flaws. But everyone sees the big collapse."[12]

My pastoral counselor husband has been involved in a weekly accountability group of Christian leaders for many years. He often jokes, "This is not a grace group. If you want a grace group, you'll have to go somewhere else." In fact, the moral failures of Christian leaders in our area have been numerous. But the reality is that very few people in leadership are surrounded by men and women who can and will be honest with them, who will call them on improprieties, and ask them the tough questions on a regular basis.

## Encouraging Word

*I am worn out waiting for your rescue, but I have put my hope in your word.* PSALM 119:81

We all experience bouts of hopelessness upon the receipt of bad news or repeated delays. Psalm 119 is the prayer of one who knew how to overcome hopelessness and receive hope—through the Word of God.

- He prays, "Revive me by your word" (verse 25).
- He prays, "Encourage me by your word" (verse 28).
- He prays, "Give me life through your word" (verse 37).
- He prays, "Reassure me of your promise" (verse 38).
- He prays, "I do not turn away from your instructions" (verse 51).
- He prays, "Your decrees have been the theme of my songs" (verse 54).
- He prays, "I promise to obey your words!" (verse 57).
- He prays, "Teach me your decrees" (verse 64).
- He prays, "I have put my hope in your word" (verse 81).

I have taken this advice literally! Daily I wait for and expect God to open a door, answer a prayer, and speak to me.

The Word of God is where I hear God's voice. It is where He comforts, corrects, and advises me. Near the beginning of every hour in prayer, I open the Word of God. For over two decades I have used a one-year Bible—and for almost a decade, a special edition of *The One Year Bible* called the *Change Your Life Daily Bible*.

Each day, I simply open the Bible to today's date and read from the selected New Testament, Old Testament, Proverbs, and Psalms passages. And every day *without fail*, I underline or highlight one or more verses that give me hope to wait a bit longer or fight a bit harder! And, I don't leave my time with God until I receive hope.

He promises to give us hope through His Word. Receive it!

# Every Time!

*We can make our plans, but the LORD determines our steps.* PROVERBS 16:9

Over a span of twenty-nine years of marriage, my husband and I have purchased six homes. Always, we laid out our plans. Each time we could see how the Lord rearranged circumstances and determined our steps.

First home: We were engaged to be married and had no money for a down payment on a home. One month before we were to be married, my fiancé's van was stolen and burned. We used the insurance settlement as the deposit on a two-bedroom condo.

Second home: While riding bikes in our neighborhood, we stopped to chat with an elderly couple who told us they would be selling their home in the spring. We gave them fifty dollars down, which held their home for over six months.

Third home: We moved just two blocks from my childhood home. That house sold in a day.

Fourth home: We moved to California from Ohio and couldn't afford *anything*. Suddenly a bank offered us a 10 percent down, forty-year loan!

Fifth home: We found a sales listing on a scrap of newspaper in the trash can while sweeping the garage floor!

Sixth (and current) home: We had been looking to move for over a year. Our home finally sold, and our agent heard of a retiring couple whose home was not yet listed. We went to visit them and made an offer that they accepted. The home never went on the market.

What's next? We know one thing: We can make the plans, but every time, the Lord has always determined our steps.

# Heavenly Kingdom

*Jesus answered, "My Kingdom is not an earthly kingdom. If it were, my followers would fight to keep me from being handed over to the Jewish leaders. But my Kingdom is not of this world." JOHN 18:36*

When I first met my husband, Roger, he was the director of the Youth for Christ / Campus Life Club in the high school I once attended. He had recently come to Christ after a painful personal experience and was sold out for God!

He was so different from any other single man I had met. First, he maintained a level of personal purity and integrity through his words and actions. He wouldn't flirt, swear, or drink. He read the Bible every day and loved going to church . . . qualities the men I had been around since college did not possess. His integrity was very attractive. But the real uniqueness Roger possessed was a Kingdom attitude about living and dying! He wasn't afraid to die. In fact, he looked forward to heaven! Roger looked forward to being with Jesus—and he wasn't even thirty years old!

He often quoted Scriptures about living as if true life began when you died. He particularly repeated Paul's comments in Philippians 1:20-24.

Honestly, those of us who volunteered in the ministry thought he was strange at first. But his faith gave him fearlessness, strength to overcome weakness, and an incredible ability to do the right thing when it was not easy or convenient. He always reminded us that our reward was in heaven! His eternal perspective had a powerful appeal to all of us.

Do you live with eternal perspective?

# Wake Up!

*I rise early, before the sun is up; I cry out for help and put my hope in your words.* PSALM 119:147

I usually make time for the things I love to do. But for many years, although I claimed to love God, I made excuses for not spending time with Him.

- I don't have time! I'm so busy!
- I need my sleep. I'm working too many hours. God understands.
- I'll do it later today. I will. . . .
- I'll get back into a habit of daily prayer after my vacation.
- I don't really feel like praying now. I'll wait until I feel like it. . . .

As the adage goes, "If you fail to plan, you plan to fail."[13]

And I did—miserably. I had no consistency in prayer, no passion, and no power in my life. I had never taken the tour through the classic authors who wrote zinging one-liners on prayer, such as "No man is greater than his prayer life" (Leonard Ravenhill)[14] or "Neglect prayer, neglect God" (O. Hallesby).[15]

I seemed to be able to fit everything *but prayer* into my day in one-hour increments: the gym, luncheons, meetings, television shows. One February weekend in 1984 I admitted my laziness to God and made a decision to never again miss my time with Him. Every day since then I've met with God for one hour . . . to pour my heart out to Him and listen to Him.

For over twenty-three years, there has been one nonnegotiable appointment in my day—one hour with the King. It was that simple. And if I can do this, you can do this.

Make an appointment with God one day in advance—and keep it.

## Miraculous Signs

*The disciples saw Jesus do many other miraculous signs in addition to the
ones recorded in this book. But these are written so that you may continue
to believe that Jesus is the Messiah, the Son of God, and that by believing
in him you will have life by the power of his name.* JOHN 20:30-31

I am the child of an alcoholic. My dad was the child of an
alcoholic.

Statistics show that if you are the child of an alcoholic,
you have a greater chance of becoming an alcoholic. So it should
have been no surprise that by age sixteen, I had already progressed
through the stages of alcoholism—blacking out and passing out
every time I drank.

Unfortunately, this went on for five more years. I added
drugs to my drinking and partied to oblivion nightly until I was
twenty-one.

I never called myself an addict or alcoholic . . . until I hit
bottom, slamming so hard that I considered suicide the only way
out of my shame and pain.

On that day, in desperation, I prayed and asked God to help
me, change me, and forgive me. I immediately hated what I used
to love. I stopped drinking that day. It was a miracle to every
person who knew me—my parents, who had lived through five
years of my alcoholism, car accidents, and carousing, and my
coworkers, who saw me hungover every morning. When God
healed me, many of my family and friends became believers.

I believe in miracles. I truly expect God to do miracles for
people who were just like me—hopeless, desperate, or unworthy.
I tell of His power so that others may believe in His name.

# Hudson's Secret

*I took my troubles to the LORD; I cried out to him, and he answered my prayer.* PSALM 120:1

Hudson Taylor, physician, evangelist, and pioneer missionary to China, experienced intense troubles in his life—yet he served God more profoundly, passionately, and sacrificially than most. His life continues to inspire contemporary Christians to know God as he did.

Hudson took his troubles to the Lord every minute of every day. And when life got tough—family members died of diseases, coworkers were murdered—he did not quit or grow bitter toward God.

His secret?

There was a turning point between 1869 and 1870, when he found new release in casting his cares on God rather than striving. In *Hudson Taylor's Spiritual Secret*, by Dr. and Mrs. Howard Taylor, Taylor's letter to a fellow missionary records his journey: "How then to have our faith increased? Only by thinking of all that Jesus is and all He is for us; His life, His death, His work, He Himself as revealed in the Word, to be the subject of our constant thoughts. Not a striving to have faith . . . but a looking off to the Faithful One seems all we need; a resting in the Loved One entirely, for time and for eternity."[1]

When I journal in my prayer notebook every morning, in essence, I am handing my troubles to the Lord. I cry out to Him for help and He answers me. He reminds me that my troubles are not bigger than He is.

Be encouraged to take your troubles daily to God. He has the answers you need to overcome.

## Soulwinner

*You will receive power when the Holy Spirit comes upon you. And you will be my witnesses, telling people about me everywhere—in Jerusalem, throughout Judea, in Samaria, and to the ends of the earth.* ACTS 1:8

Charles Spurgeon was a powerful preacher at the Metropolitan Tabernacle in England, an inspirational teacher at a pastor's college, and a student of revivals and revivalists during the late 1800s.

In *The Soulwinner*, excerpted lessons from the pastor's college, he gives details of his relationships with some of the great evangelists of his generation. In each of his examples, he gives the distinct impression that these men were not special, but were simply fully obedient to witness with power from on high.

He wrote about attending a George Müller lecture: "He was there only in his personality as a witness to the truth, but he bore that witness in such a manner that you could not help saying, 'That man not only preaches what he believes, but also what he lives.' . . . Holiness was the preacher's force."[2]

Of D. L. Moody he wrote, "[He] would have never spoken with the force he did if he had not lived a life of fellowship with the Father, and with His Son, Jesus. The great force of any message lies in what has gone before it."[3]

Spurgeon inspired greatness for God. He taught others how to become godly soulwinners. Consider Spurgeon's seven qualities of a soulwinner:

1. You must believe you are called by God.
2. You must believe God has given you a message.
3. You must have great faith in God's Word.
4. You must be earnest and passionate.
5. You must be humble.
6. You must have pure motives—to work for the glory of God.
7. You must be able to stand firm and alone.

# Victory Song

*David sang this song to the LORD on the day the LORD rescued him from all his enemies and from Saul.* 2 SAMUEL 22:1

JUNE 4

Have you ever written a victory song? David wrote fifty verses detailing the story of how God rescued him! (See 2 Samuel 22.) He gives a vivid picture of his warrior God who saved and protected him.

Make this paraphrased version of 2 Samuel 22 your prayer.

*O Lord, You are my Rock, my fortress, and my Savior.*
*You are my shield, the power that saves me, and my place of safety.*
*You are my refuge. . . .*
*The waves of death overwhelmed me. . . .*
*You heard me from Your sanctuary; my cry reached Your ears.*
*You shot arrows and scattered my enemies.*
*Your lightning flashed, and they were confused.*
*You reached down from heaven and rescued me.*
*You led me to a place of safety.*
*O Lord, You are my lamp.*
*You make me as surefooted as a deer,*
*enabling me to stand on mountain heights.*
*You train my hands for battle. . . .*
*You show your unfailing love to Your anointed.*
*You live! Praise be to You, my Rock of salvation! Be exalted!*

# Wise Guy

*From a wise mind comes wise speech; the words of the wise are persuasive.*

PROVERBS 16:23

I often joke that God saved me a lot of money by allowing me to marry a counselor! It's really not such a joke. I am married to someone who is wiser than most. And because I came to Christ with so many personality struggles and addictions, and a lack of discipline, I've saved more than money—I've experienced great healing and growth because of his wise counsel.

I must add, though, that his counsel is rarely comforting. That may sound odd, but it has been a common theme of our conversations for almost three decades. I still suggest that he "lighten up" on me when giving me counsel. And he still replies, "Do you want help or comfort?" Good question.

Wisdom is not meant to be comforting, but helpful.

Recently while chatting with two dozen moms who regularly gather to pray for their own and others' kids, we talked about the pressure to be popular. And we weren't talking about the students. We were bemoaning *our* lack of neighborhood popularity for not allowing our kids to attend certain events.

It takes incredible discernment, understanding, and persuasiveness to be a wise and godly parent, spouse, or friend in the twenty-first century.

A deeper study in the book of Proverbs reveals that wisdom is truth. And though we might not like it, truth doesn't change. Godly men and women must speak truth to each other and their kids.

Can we persuasively present the wisdom of God and still be popular or comforting? Probably not. . . .

But if God's wisdom resides in you, then speak His truth in love . . . even if it is unpopular and uncomfortable. You never know when God will use you to save a life.

# Powerful Name

*Peter, filled with the Holy Spirit, said to them, "Rulers and elders of our people, are we being questioned today because we've done a good deed for a crippled man? Do you want to know how he was healed? Let me clearly state to all of you and to all the people of Israel that he was healed by the powerful name of Jesus Christ the Nazarene, the man you crucified but whom God raised from the dead. . . . There is salvation in no one else! God has given no other name under heaven by which we must be saved."* ACTS 4:8-10, 12

J esus' name is powerful.

There is no other name that creates more synergy or more distance in an instant. You do not have to know a person for more than a minute if you both know Jesus, and you can strike up a conversation as if you were old friends! His presence is real in your midst. But if you know Jesus, and another person does *not* know Him or is hostile toward Him, you feel tension.

His name is powerful—enough to save, heal, and divide.

*To save:* I was taught to pray using Jesus' name whenever I was afraid or tempted. It was that simple. I wasn't given a phone number to call, but a name. I was told, "Say Jesus' name out loud. Ask Him to help you in that moment."

*To heal:* Just as the disciples prayed for the healing of others using the powerful name of Jesus, so can you. If someone is sick, pray for him or her and speak Jesus' powerful name.

*To divide:* Can you articulate who Jesus is to one who does not know Him? Though His name may divide, He is the God who loves. Tell His story.

## Wild Things!

*We are witnesses of these things and so is the Holy Spirit, who is given by God to those who obey him.* ACTS 5:32

The fifth chapter of Acts is *wild*!

It begins with the story of Ananias and Sapphira, who sold some property and then lied about the amount of the sale. And because they lied, they died within three hours of their deception.

The chapter continues with the apostles having such a public crusade and healing ministry that crowds of men and women were being saved. (See verses 14-16.)

Now, you'd think these miraculous healings would have created great enthusiasm from the high priest and his officials. Instead, the apostles were arrested because of the religious leaders' jealousy. But they didn't stay in jail long—an angel freed them. (See verses 19-20.)

After being freed, Peter stood in front of the high council and said, "We must obey God rather than any human authority" (verse 29). He then explained that the Jews killed the Messiah, and the Holy Spirit was their witness. (Way to get the high priest's blood boiling again!)

A strange intervention occurred when a Pharisee, Gamaliel, advised the council, "Let them go. If they are planning and doing these things merely on their own, it will soon be overthrown. But if it is from God, you will not be able to overthrow them" (verses 38-39). They accepted his advice and ordered the disciples to never speak the name of Jesus again. (Really?)

The book of Acts reads like a wild adventure—it makes me wonder if we're missing something in the twenty-first century? Shouldn't it be a little more wild and exciting to be a Christian?

## Angel Face

*At this point everyone in the high council stared at Stephen, because his face became as bright as an angel's.* ACTS 6:15

Stephen was described as "a man full of God's grace and power, [who] performed amazing miracles and signs among the people" (Acts 6:8) . His "acts" once again fueled the fire of another sect—the Synagogue of Freed Slaves.

Infuriated, they convinced some men to lie about Stephen and strike a public debate with him. They ultimately created such dissension among the teachers and elders of the religious law that he was brought before the high council.

Though he was surely under severe scrutiny, Stephen was asked if the accusations against him were true. Instead of defending himself, he delivered a lengthy, all-encompassing discourse, beginning with Abraham and ending with the betrayal and murder of Jesus Christ by the Jews.

By the time he finished speaking, he was finished with living . . . for the people rushed at him, dragged him out of the city, and stoned him.

As they stoned him, Stephen prayed, "Lord Jesus, receive my spirit" (Acts 7:59).

And with that Stephen was the first martyr of the church. Jesus promised that all believers will face persecution. He said, "Here on earth you will have many trials and sorrows" (John 16:33). Many of us, if we're honest, will admit to being afraid to face those "trials and sorrows" on behalf of His name. Yet He promises to be with us as He was with Stephen. If you're facing persecution, consider Jesus' concluding words in John 16:33: "But take heart, because I have overcome the world."

## Our Reward

*Children are a gift from the Lord; they are a reward from him.* PSALM 127:3

$\infty$

In our premarital counseling session, Roger and I discussed and agreed (in front of our pastor) that we were never going to have children. Both of us mentored dozens of students and programmed events and meetings for hundreds of other students on a weekly basis. And most of them had "all access" passes to us. They knew where we lived and they had our phone numbers! We couldn't fathom being responsible for any more children.

Three months after we married, Roger sheepishly approached me. "I think the Lord wants us to have a baby."

I said, "Well, I don't."

He replied, "Well, just read your Bible and see what He says." I panicked.

My Bible was old and cracked at the spine. If I set it down too abruptly, it would fall open to Psalm 127. For the next few days, I couldn't get near my Bible without it opening to the verse above.

I got pregnant that week. Ten days after our first anniversary, I delivered a little baby boy, Jacob, named after my father and grandfather.

When Jacob was born, I had more love for him in an instant than I could imagine was possible! By the time Jake left for college, I realized that our precious gift, our special reward from the Lord, was going off to make a difference in the world!

Now in his late twenties, Jake is a missionary and soccer player. He loves to travel the world and dreams big dreams of impacting young children's lives for the Lord through the gifts God has given him.

The greatest challenge a parent will face is the desire to make your child a little *you*! But God asks us to present our children back to Him—as Christ-followers: those who know and love *Him* more than anyone or anything else.

# Choleric Control

*Better to be patient than powerful; better to have self-control than to conquer a city.* PROVERBS 16:32

My friends Florence and Marita Littauer developed a series on the four personality types. (One book is *Personality Plus*.[4]) Most of us have both a primary and a secondary personality type.

- The **sanguine** personality is the fun-loving life of the party. He or she is easily distracted and often disorganized, but fun!
- The **choleric** personality is the one who likes to be in charge. He or she is often bossy and impatient, but gets things done.
- The **melancholy** personality is detailed and meticulous. He or she can sometimes be moody, but is incredibly organized.
- The **phlegmatic** personality is very easygoing. He or she is often late and a bit slow, but gets along famously with everyone.

In my life-coaching practice and Roger's premarital counseling, this personality test helps us better understand the people with whom we are working. The personality profile also comes in handy for parenting and relating to coworkers.

Each of the personality types has strengths and weaknesses. No type is better or less problematic than another.

My primary personality type is choleric. Yes, I like to be in charge. Some who've worked with me mispronounce my last name: "Tirabossy." I have struggled most of my life to exhibit patience. I have to pray and take deep breaths to calm myself. Sometimes, I have to close my mouth and not say anything, or I'll surely have to apologize for some strong or insensitive comment I let slip out.

If you struggle with impatience and lack of self-control, join me in asking God—daily—to control your emotions with His Holy Spirit!

## Wholehearted Devotion

*Solomon stood before the altar of the LORD in front of the entire community of Israel. He lifted his hands toward heaven, and he prayed, "O LORD, God of Israel, there is no God like you in all of heaven above or on the earth below. You keep your covenant and show unfailing love to all who walk before you in wholehearted devotion."* 1 KINGS 8:22-23

I n this biblical record of Solomon's prayer, I am reminded one more time that written prayer is not a new idea!

For over twenty-three years I have written my prayers in *My Partner Prayer Notebook*, using a four-part pattern (PART) for talking to God. In the first section, "Praise," I open my heart to God in prayer by reminding Him (and myself) that He is the all-powerful, all-knowing God who loves me. If you are overwhelmed and fearful when you come to God in prayer, the habit of telling Him how strong and awesome He is immediately discounts doubt and fear.

In the next section, "Admit," I confess my sins to God in writing. The healthy habits of a fully devoted follower of God must include regular confession. First John 1:9 says, "But if we confess our sins to him, he is faithful and just to forgive us our sins and to cleanse us from all wickedness."

The third section is "Requests." Like Solomon, I ask God, "May your eyes be open to my requests and to the requests of your people . . ." (1 Kings 8:52). It is both a responsibility and a privilege to intercede on behalf of others.

The fourth section in my prayer notebook is "Thanks." Solomon, David, and the other psalmists were among many whose words of gratitude to God for specific blessings serve as historic proof that God listens to our prayers.

Try praying, using the PART method, this week.

## God Answers

*The LORD appeared to Solomon a second time, as he had done before at Gibeon. The LORD said to him, "I have heard your prayer and your petition. I have set this Temple apart to be holy—this place you have built where my name will be honored forever. I will always watch over it, for it is dear to my heart."* 1 KINGS 9:2-3

Recorded for generations to read is the Lord's response to the prayer Solomon prayed for the Israelites at the Temple dedication. (See 1 Kings 9.) Interestingly, the Lord's answer to Solomon includes an *if/but* scenario.

God's *if* statement is very broad: "As for you, if you will follow me with integrity and godliness . . . then I will establish the throne of your dynasty over Israel forever" (verses 4-5).

God's *but* statement was much more detailed: "But if you or your descendants abandon me and disobey the commands and decrees I have given you, and if you serve and worship other gods, then I will uproot Israel from this land" (verses 6-7).

Prayer is a two-way conversation! We often tell God what we want, but then we don't wait for His response or we expect Him to answer us in a specific way. When we pray, we must not only listen for His response . . . but be willing to follow it.

In *The Pursuit of Holiness*, author Jerry Bridges explains that God's voice can be heard by the average believer in four ways:

1. Memorize key passages for immediate recall.
2. Listen for Scripture used in sermons that impact your life.
3. Study Scripture intently for special counsel.
4. Read the Bible regularly to know God's viewpoint in all aspects of life.[5]

Prayer is not just talking to God—it is also listening to Him by reading and meditating upon His Word.

JUNE 12

# Chosen Instrument

*Instantly something like scales fell from Saul's eyes, and he regained his sight. Then he got up and was baptized. Afterward he ate some food and regained his strength. Saul stayed with the believers in Damascus for a few days. And immediately he began preaching about Jesus in the synagogues, saying, "He is indeed the Son of God!"* ACTS 9:18-20

Saul watched as Stephen was stoned, then set out for Damascus in an attempt to arrest believers and return them to Jerusalem in chains. On the way, he was struck with blindness and met by Jesus in a "white light" moment. After three days of waiting in Damascus, God sent a believer, Ananias, to find Saul and give him a word from God. At first, Ananias resisted. But in obedience, he told Saul that God had sent him with a message so that he might regain his sight and be filled with the Holy Spirit. Instantly Saul could see. Then he got baptized and immediately began to preach! As the record continues, all who heard him were amazed. And his preaching became more and more powerful.

God often chooses unlikely instruments. God can take any man or woman, with or without training, and make him or her His instant spokesperson! The list of unlikely but chosen instruments of God begins early in the Old Testament and continues through the New Testament. And history has not finished writing about the many surprising men and women whom God chose to preach His Word through music, books, and meetings:

- *John Newton*, a reformed slave trader and author of the hymn "Amazing Grace"
- *John Bunyan*, an uneducated prisoner and author of *Pilgrim's Progress*
- *D. L. Moody*, a shoe salesman, evangelist, and founder of Moody Bible Institute

What impact will your life make for Christ?

## "I Cannot . . ."

*"No, I cannot," he replied. "I am not allowed to eat or drink anything here
in this place. For the LORD gave me this command: 'You must not eat or
drink anything while you are there, and do not return to Judah by the
same way you came.'" But the old prophet answered, "I am a prophet, too,
just as you are. And an angel gave me this command from the LORD: 'Bring
him home with you so he can have something to eat and drink.'" But the
old man was lying to him.* 1 KINGS 13:16-18

W hile reading this story, I couldn't help but wonder,
*What would I do in a similar situation?*
Then I remembered one of the first times
God told me to do something and almost immediately someone
pressured me to ignore Him. I had been a sober, sexually pure
Christian for a few weeks when my old boyfriend returned from
his vacation and asked why I moved out of our apartment.

I said, "Oh, I've become a Christian and I can't live with you
until we're married."

He looked at me and almost sneered. "Becky, people who love
each other live together. The Bible is old-fashioned."

I said, "I cannot live with you anymore. I am a Christian."

Then he suggested that we talk over a drink.

"Oh, I can't do that. I'm an alcoholic and I can't drink."

He was livid. "You are not an alcoholic. Just slow down."

"I can't slow down. I don't know how to slow down."

"I cannot . . ." saved my witness, my sobriety . . . my life.

When the Holy Spirit prompts you, do not hesitate to say,
"I cannot" to others.

# Brotherly Harmony

*How wonderful and pleasant it is when brothers live together in harmony!*

PSALM 133:1

I've said this before, but being married to a counselor comes in handy more often than you'd imagine, especially for someone like me!

Roger has the greatest tools for better relationships, such as "8 Steps to Conflict Resolution," "A 6-Step Anger Management System," "The 5 *A*s," and "15 Skills for Effective Listening." In fact, I'm not the only beneficiary. He requires all his premarital classes and marriage counselees to use these tools at the first sign of trouble.

Roger has spent over thirty years counseling pastors, couples, and students. And with all that research, he concluded that poor communication will blow up any relationship! In fact, he sides with C. S. Lewis's theory in *The Screwtape Letters*—our enemy has a detailed plan to destroy our relationships and uses us against each other much of the time!

Be proactive. Put powerful strategies in place to protect your relationships and live in harmony with your family, friends, and coworkers. Here are a few of Roger's 15 Skills for Effective Listening to get you started. . . .

- Don't name call, blame, or shame others.
- Listen without interrupting.
- Speak the truth in love.
- Use *I* statements, not *you* statements.
- Use specifics, not generalizations.
- Don't withdraw or isolate.
- Don't demand, ask!
- Don't use the words *never* or *always*.
- Identify the enemy!

## Henrietta's Commandment

*Love prospers when a fault is forgiven, but dwelling on it separates close friends.* PROVERBS 17:9

Henrietta Mears, one of the original members of the 1947 Fellowship of the Burning Hearts, was a powerful influence in the lives of hundreds of students. Her legacy includes encouraging four hundred men and women to enter full-time Christian work, including Bill Bright, founder of Campus Crusade for Christ, and Richard Halverson, former chaplain of the U.S. Senate. She also founded a Christian campground and a Christian publishing company. Both organizations continue to impact lives today.

She lived by a personal set of Ten Commandments that guided her relationships, especially with students. Of the ten, the commandment that stuck out to me more than all the others was:

*I will never let anyone think I am disappointed in him.*[6]

When I first read this mandate of hers in July 2000, I was immediately ashamed of myself. When offended, I usually made certain the other person knew he or she disappointed me! I admired Henrietta's life and legacy so much that I determined to make her commandment my own. The first thing I did was take the word *disappointed* completely out of my vocabulary!

Interestingly, the other nine commandments are directly related to Christian training, evangelism, and discipleship. Not letting someone think he or she disappointed you certainly seems out of place until you consider it more deeply. The sign of a true disciple is love!

Quickly forgiving a fault shows Christ's love more than any other action. It is not only Henrietta's commandment but our Lord's! I encourage you to eliminate *disappointed* from your vocabulary and extend love instead!

## Keep Looking

*Elijah said to Ahab, "Go get something to eat and drink, for I hear*
*a mighty rainstorm coming!"... Finally the seventh time, his servant*
*told him, "I saw a little cloud about the size of a man's hand rising*
*from the sea."* 1 KINGS 18:41, 44

E lijah had visionary faith . . . he would not stop looking for God's answers, even when he—and others—could not see evidence of them. And therein is the difference between Elijah and most of us—he didn't care what others saw or said! He kept looking for God's answer. (For the record, rarely will a crowd of cheerleaders surround you after the third or fourth time you've looked and seen nothing. I know. I've been in that lonely spot more than once!)

Elijah's prophetic faith didn't look at circumstances or delays or even possibilities—he only listened for God's leading and followed His voice. Hebrews 11:1, 6 says, "Faith is the confidence that what we hope for will actually happen; it gives us assurance about things we cannot see. . . . And it is impossible to please God without faith. Anyone who wants to come to him must believe that God exists and that he rewards those who sincerely seek him."

Elijah kept looking . . . until he received.

The record continues, "And soon the sky was black with clouds. A heavy wind brought a terrific rainstorm, and Ahab left quickly for Jezreel" (1 Kings 18:45).

I am incredibly inspired by people of this importunate ilk. They have a faith that will not quit. They hear God telling them, "Keep looking," and they keep looking!

Bible translator J. B. Phillips in speaking of Bible legends said, "Perhaps if we believed what they believed, we would achieve what they achieved."[7]

# Stop Quarreling

*Starting a quarrel is like opening a floodgate, so stop before a dispute breaks out.* PROVERBS 17:14

There are certain personality types that seem to attract arguments! Yet the wise advice in this proverb does not take into account a person's rights or reasons for quarreling. It simply says stop before you start!

This is universal counsel for parents with children, spouses, siblings, coworkers, roommates, and even strangers who find themselves about to tangle. Because you cannot determine how another person will react, this proverb asks *you* to take the responsibility of stopping a quarrel before it starts. (Let's be honest! Do you really expect a heated quarrel to end *without* some level of emotional or physical damage? So why not take the advice and avoid the inevitable?)

The key to any biblical principle is turning it into a lifestyle. So if you want to stop a quarrel before it breaks out . . .

*Don't attack.* Before saying anything, take a few seconds to consider the seriousness of the situation. Usually, it is not that serious.

*Be slow to speak and quick to listen.* (See James 1:19.) We are all flawed. Keep your voice low. It will keep your temper down.

*Be empathetic.* In most instances, people are not trying to hurt you. They may be selfish, insensitive, or impulsive, but rarely does a dispute come from a malicious heart. Think of a time when you hurt someone in a similar way, *then respond the way you would want to be treated.*

One final thought . . . the choice to start or stop a quarrel usually happens within a few seconds. Making amends for impulsive accusations or hurtful actions often takes *much more* time, energy, and humility than stopping a quarrel before it starts!

Make a habit of making the wise choice. . . .

# Hands On

*After more fasting and prayer, the men laid their hands on them and sent them on their way.* ACTS 13:3

In November of 2005, I felt that God prompted me to call students to forty days of nonstop prayer. As the itinerary unfolded, twenty-three college campuses signed up to pray, starting on January 20, 2006. My initial purpose for going was to fan the flame of revival prayer erupting on many campuses. After identifying the willing campuses, I determined to be the baton passer, linking each campus's twenty-four- or seventy-two-hour prayer room with the next.

From the beginning, I focused on the end of the forty days, thinking the tour would culminate in a furnace of prayer for revival that would explode into a nationwide bonfire! The reality proved much different. From the first campus to the final one, I was surprised at how much my focus changed. It seemed I was not only sent to fan the flame of revival prayer but I was also sent to meet certain people, most of whom I'd never met before, and lay hands on them and pray. Each person was so precious and had a very specific, often very serious, prayer request.

Over the forty days, I received much confession of sin. I also prayed for many students who had requests for physical healing for themselves or family members. Many times I prayed for emotional healing, especially for young women who had been sexually abused. I prayed repeatedly for God to remove apathy, addiction, and anger and to restore hope.

Something happens when you lay hands on someone and pray for him or her. Prayer connects you to that person and God. It opens your heart to listen and join in his or her plea.

The one who lays hands on another feels an enormous responsibility. . . .

# Workout Praying

*Though I am surrounded by troubles, you will protect me from the anger of my enemies. You reach out your hand, and the power of your right hand saves me. The LORD will work out his plans for my life—for your faithful love, O LORD, endures forever. Don't abandon me, for you made me.*

PSALM 138:7-8

When I finally accepted that God's plan for my life would be worked out one day at a time, prayer became the time, place, and method where God accomplished His work in me. Very quickly, the psalms became one of my greatest daily sources of comfort, courage, and strength.

The psalmists became my prayer teachers. I learned through their written prayers that it is valid to simultaneously cry for God's help *and* confirm His promises to rescue. As I began to express myself to God in writing, I often paraphrased the psalms, making them my personal praise prayers. The psalmists taught me to pray boldly, because they prayed boldly.

Therefore, just as the psalmist prayed, I have also prayed for years, "I have confidence that Your love for me, God, will endure forever. You will work out Your plans for my life even when I can't feel or see the results right away."

Confessing in writing that God is faithful to finish the plans in your life will alleviate your anxieties, diminish any lurking lies you might be entertaining, and help lift your eyes to Him and off your situation.

Written prayer, formed from God's Word, is a stress reliever, a confidence builder, and a doubt defeater. I encourage you to pray Scriptures, especially the Psalms, for yourself and others.

Open your prayer notebook alongside the book of Psalms today, and create your own praise prayers.

# Daily Revival

*Search me, O God, and know my heart; test me and know my anxious thoughts. Point out anything in me that offends you, and lead me along the path of everlasting life.* PSALM 139:23-24

D r. Joe Church was a medical missionary to Rwanda in the 1940s. Because he had been part of a twenty-year revival in East Africa, his perception of revival was much different from that of others. He felt that Western Christians had the strange idea that revival occurred at meetings where "the roof blew off." He believed that true revival is when "the bottom falls out." This was true for me.

In 1984, after almost a decade of striving to be a good Christian and failing regularly, I realized—like so many others—that sin was never going to stop chasing me. I was never going to stand up against it *without an intentional, daily action plan.* So I made a commitment to let God examine my heart daily.

Verses 23 and 24 in Psalm 139 became the ideal words to pray. These verses immediately ushered God's searchlight into my heart, allowing daily revival to begin!

At the beginning of this daily habit, the bottom fell out! Though I was a Christian in ministry, God's searchlight exposed unconfessed sins such as uncontrolled anger, jealousy, selfishness, laziness, and greed. Those days are over. . . .

For the record, in over twenty-three years, I have never forgotten or neglected to pray this psalm. Not a day has gone by when I didn't have sin to confess.

Are you willing to let God search your heart every day—as often as necessary?

# Unhappy Christian?

*A cheerful heart is good medicine, but a broken spirit saps a person's strength.*

PROVERBS 17:22

A man was asked, "Are you a Christian?"

He answered, "Yes."

The inquirer then responded, "Then tell your face."

An unhappy Christian is an oxymoron!

Do you possess joy, a fruit of the Holy Spirit and one of the defining attributes of a Christian? Do you consider it a choice to be a joyful, cheerful Christian?

*The Pulpit Commentary* describes *cheerfulness* as (1) "commended in Scripture," (2) "exert[ing] a healing influence over the individual soul," (3) "a source of healthy influence for others," and (4) "best attained in the Christian life."[8]

How can we develop cheerful hearts and rise above those things that want to break our spirit and steal our joy?

Jesus set the standard for joy, as Hebrews 12:1-2 explains: "Therefore, since we are surrounded by such a huge crowd of witnesses to the life of faith, let us strip off every weight that slows us down, especially the sin that so easily trips us up. And let us run with endurance the race God has set before us. We do this by keeping our eyes on Jesus, the champion who initiates and perfects our faith."

In Philippians 4:8, Paul taught the secret to living a joyous life. "Fix your thoughts on what is true, and honorable, and right, and pure, and lovely, and admirable. Think about things that are excellent and worthy of praise."

Being positive is not a psychological cliché, it is a biblical principle! Exert the joy of the Lord over yourself and others by your words, countenance, and actions. Don't be an oxymoron!

## Sexual Sin

*Don't let me drift toward evil or take part in acts of wickedness. Don't let me share in the delicacies of those who do wrong.* PSALM 141:4

There is a book by Jack Hayford that I would suggest as a manual for every home in America: *Fatal Attractions: Why Sex Sins Are Worse Than Others*. It is both honest and heart-breaking and includes letters from parents, students, single adults, and leaders who were entrapped (often very young in life) and who *continue* to struggle against the addiction and guilt.

Perhaps the reason I so strongly resonate with Hayford's treatment of the subject is because I, too, have spoken to far too many Christian men and women who are addicted to pornography or struggle with other issues such as same-sex attraction. Rarely is there peace—or purity—in their lives. They are in a constant battle.

Hayford cites that one of the reasons why sexual sin is so destructive to every aspect of a person's life is the fact that "sex sins . . . beget further immoral behavior."[9] In almost every case, the extremely addicted person thought he or she dabbled in something harmless at first. In speaking of a young man's progression, he writes, "What gave such compelling power to the images that Pete watched on the video, the *idol* he 'worshiped' by looking at the magazines, was the *demon spirit* behind them. That's the definition of idolatry—*worshiping an image behind which a demon spirit resides*."[10]

Drifting into the sexual immorality of culture is the start of a spiritually deadening cycle of demonic activity designed to steal a believer's intimacy with God and others. Don't believe me . . . believe God's Word.

## Restoration Prayer

*I cry out to the L*ORD*; I plead for the L*ORD*'s mercy. I pour out my complaints before him and tell him all my troubles.* PSALM 142:1-2

A confused child knows this prayer.
A recovering addict knows this prayer.
A wounded friend knows this prayer.
A person in pain knows this prayer.
A wanderer knows this prayer.
A betrayed spouse knows this prayer.
An overwhelmed single parent knows this prayer.
A discouraged pastor knows this prayer.
An overlooked team member knows this prayer.
A discounted sibling knows this prayer.
A barren woman knows this prayer.
An embattled warrior knows this prayer.
A desperate parent knows this prayer.
A humbled sinner knows this prayer.

True prayer is not the expression of one's personal perfection to a holy God, but a sincere cry by any of His children for His intervention.

The living, loving God hears your prayer. He knows your heart. He will respond. He can be trusted.

## Jesus' Name

*One day as we were going down to the place of prayer, we met a demon-possessed slave girl. . . . Paul got so exasperated that he turned and said to the demon within her, "I command you in the name of Jesus Christ to come out of her." And instantly it left her.* ACTS 16:16, 18

I recently met a young woman who attended a church youth group through junior high and high school. She went to a Christian college for one semester before transferring to a local private college. On her new campus, she quickly made friends with other young women. They confided in each other and began a search into alternative religions. It just so happened that there was a "witch's coven" on their campus that dabbled in Wicca. They got involved.

Frankly, I was shocked that I had known her for a few weeks and was just uncovering this information about her. I asked her some questions about her involvement. She considered it harmless initially. After a few more questions, she mentioned that the other girls were much more involved than she. Finally she divulged that she *was* more involved than she should have been. She left the school after a terrifying experience and continued to have a lingering fear about the impact Wicca had on her life.

Based on her current spiritual confusion, past relationship struggles, and repeated sexual promiscuity, I asked, "Have you ever renounced with a pastor or Christian counselor all of this demonic activity in Jesus' name?"

She replied, "Not really."

We immediately set up an appointment to meet at church and pray with a pastor.

Commanding demons to leave people was a common practice for the early church. I am convinced it needs to become a much more common practice for the twenty-first-century church!

## Berean Believers

*That very night the believers sent Paul and Silas to Berea. When they arrived there, they went to the Jewish synagogue. And the people of Berea were more open-minded than those in Thessalonica, and they listened eagerly to Paul's message. They searched the Scriptures day after day to see if Paul and Silas were teaching the truth. As a result, many Jews believed, as did many of the prominent Greek women and men.* ACTS 17:10-12

I'm from Berea—Berea, Ohio.

As a teenager, I attended a church that followed the denominational tradition of providing confirmation classes for junior high students. I don't remember very much of what I learned during that lengthy series, but I do remember that I received a gift from the church—a white leather Bible with gold-edged pages with my name engraved on its cover.

On the first page of my Bible, there was a beautiful inscription with my name and a reference to Acts 17:10-12. In curiosity, I opened the Bible to the verses. I smiled and thought it was nice that Berea was mentioned in the Bible. I packed it away with my other keepsakes, and it moved from apartment to apartment for many years.

I've had numerous Bibles since then. And in a very wonderful way, the teacher's inscription about the Berean believers has become a reality in my life.

Almost four decades later, I still smile at the reference to the Bereans who eagerly listened to Paul's message and daily searched the Scriptures. I am such a Berean! In fact, there are at least eight of us from Berea, Ohio, who live near one another in California and who have made it a lifelong habit to read from the Bible daily!

## Lifelong Mentor

*Joash began to rule over Judah in the seventh year of King Jehu's reign in Israel. He reigned in Jerusalem forty years. His mother was Zibiah from Beersheba. All his life Joash did what was pleasing in the LORD's sight because Jehoiada the priest instructed him.* 2 KINGS 12:1-2

I t is surely not a coincidence that Joash became king at the young age of seven or that he remained a king who pleased the Lord for forty years (when many kings reigned for much shorter seasons). I am convinced that the secret of his resolve can be traced to Jehoiada the priest.

In 2 Chronicles, there is more information about Jehoiada. "In the seventh year of Athaliah's reign, Jehoiada the priest decided to act. He summoned his courage and made a pact with five army commanders" (23:1).

Jehoiada urged everyone to move into immediate action to make Joash king by overthrowing Athaliah. The Levites were instructed to form a massive bodyguard around the young boy and kill anyone who entered the Temple.

When Athaliah, the mother of Ahaziah (Judah's former king), realized what was happening, she hurried to the Temple and witnessed the crowning of young Joash. He was surrounded by commanders, singers, trumpeters, and Levites leading the people in a joyous celebration. As ordered, they seized her, led her out of the Temple, and killed her. Joash's priest, Jehoiada, then made a covenant between himself, the king, and the people that they would be the Lord's people.

And that was *just the beginning* of the relationship between Joash and his lifelong mentor. . . .

Please, open your heart and mind—and home—to those God brings into your life who need a spiritual parent, mentor, or family!

## God's Mercy

*Joyful are those who have the God of Israel as their helper, whose hope is in the LORD their God. He made heaven and earth, the sea, and everything in them. He keeps every promise forever. He gives justice to the oppressed and food to the hungry. The LORD frees the prisoners. The LORD opens the eyes of the blind. The LORD lifts up those who are weighed down. The LORD loves the godly. The LORD protects the foreigners among us. He cares for the orphans and widows, but he frustrates the plans of the wicked.*

PSALM 146:5-9

The comfort in this psalm is immeasurable. The Lord wants you to know and believe that . . .

- He is your helper.
- He is the Creator, *your* Creator.
- He keeps every promise He makes.
- He gives justice to those who are oppressed.
- He feeds the hungry.
- He frees the prisoners.
- He opens the eyes of the blind.
- He lifts up those who are bowed down.
- He loves the godly.
- He protects the foreigner.
- He cares for orphans and widows.
- He frustrates the plans of the wicked.

I encourage you to read this psalm and *own* it. Meditate on these words until you can grasp the depth, height, and width of God's available love and power. Let these words eradicate your doubts and dismantle your fears. In the midst of every trial, call on the powerful name of the Lord your God.

## Impossible Situations

*He takes no pleasure in the strength of a horse or in human might. No, the LORD's delight is in those who fear him, those who put their hope in his unfailing love.* PSALM 147:10-11

In *Spiritual Leadership*, J. Oswald Sanders captures the experience of a leader who feared God more than man.

> *Moses faced an impossible situation when Israel reached the Red Sea. On one side was the desert and Pharaoh's army; on the other side was water, and Israel had no boats. Moses was in a cul-de-sac, and the people were getting edgy. Complaints started flying as morale dropped: "Is it because there were no graves in Egypt that you have taken us away to die in the wilderness?"*
>
> *Moses, great man of faith, stayed himself on God. His order must have sounded like sheer fantasy but in point of fact it was a defining moment of his leadership.*
>
> *"Do not fear!" he cried, against every good reason to fear.*
>
> *"Stand by!" he cried, as Pharaoh sped toward them.*
>
> *"See the salvation of the Lord!"*
>
> *So on that strange and wonderful day the people of Israel saw their God in action, their hopes affirmed, their enemies crushed. The bracing lesson is that God delights to lead people, and then, in response to their trust, to show them power that matches every impossible situation.*[11]

If you're currently facing an impossible situation, don't count on physical strength to sustain you. The matchless power of the living, loving God is available to you now and in the future. Resist fear. Put your hope and confidence in the invisible, almighty, all-knowing God. Let His unfailing love draw you out of your impossible situation and into a deeper faith.

## Father's Heart

*Hezekiah trusted in the LORD, the God of Israel. There was no one like him among all the kings of Judah, either before or after his time. He remained faithful to the LORD in everything, and he carefully obeyed all the commands the LORD had given Moses. So the LORD was with him, and Hezekiah was successful in everything he did.* 2 KINGS 18:5-7

The "good" king / "evil" king report is a pattern often repeated in the Old Testament. Matter-of-factly each king's reign is defined by how he followed the Lord and to what degree he shadowed his father's ways.

You would think that the evil kings would consider their idolatrous ways in light of their predecessors' fates. But few did. Most gave in to culture by worshipping idols.

If a king's heart was bent toward evil, he inevitably and miserably failed himself, his family, and the nation. But if a king's heart was open to the Lord (like Hezekiah's), he found God's favor. The choice was always his.

What are the traits of one who follows after the Lord's heart?

First, he or she trusts the Lord and has the courage to wait on Him. Every faculty of his or her being is under His control. This person shows trust in His timing and instruction . . . not only with words but also actions.

Second, he or she is faithful in everything—not just in the big things and not just when others aren't looking. A faithful person makes the right decisions in public or in private. He or she has integrity and keeps his or her word even when it is inconvenient or costly.

Finally, this person willingly learns God's Word and obeys it.

The choice to follow after the heart of the Father is always up to you. . . .

# Rumor Mill

*Rumors are dainty morsels that sink deep into one's heart.* PROVERBS 18:8

The dictionary defines *rumors* as . . .

- unverified reports,
- idle speculation, or
- opinions of uncertain reliability.

The Bible suggests that rumors also have a powerful emotional effect on you—and others.

Have you been caught in the rumor mill?

Have you flippantly, angrily, or persuasively given your opinion about someone to another which nudges that person toward or away from the other?

Have you secretly envied someone, presuming to know his or her motives? This can impact how others relate to the one with whom *you* struggle.

Have you heard something "juicy" about someone? You can't verify the information, yet you pass it along to a few others, suggesting that you are not sure it is true . . . but you've planted the seeds.

Or have you shared a personal struggle with your small group and two weeks later, an acquaintance mentions that he or she heard about your struggle and is concerned about you? The rule of thumb for every small group or support group is confidentiality . . . so what happened?

Do you think people are talking about you when you *are not* in the room? When you *are* in the room, you notice looks between people that seem to insinuate something. . . . You feel left out of the loop.

Do you feel a distance between yourself and another for some unknown reason? Something has changed, but what? Perhaps a rumor was started.

Avoid the rumor mill.

# Worship Wave

*Praise him with a blast of the ram's horn; praise him with the lyre and harp! Praise him with the tambourine and dancing; praise him with strings and flutes! Praise him with a clash of cymbals; praise him with loud clanging cymbals. Let everything that breathes sing praises to the Lord! Praise the Lord!* PSALM 150:3-6

One Sunday night, I sat in church with almost one thousand young adults. We enjoyed hearing our copastor teach a series on Proverbs. As usual, a worship band followed the message with thirty minutes of worship songs blended together as if they were one song.

It was one of those nights when I seemed to know and really like every song in the worship set. As I stood and took Communion, I felt like I was being swept up by a wave. My spirit soared. The lead singer's acoustic guitar seemed to strum to the beat of my heart. I didn't want to lose the feeling, so I remained standing. I was not alone on the wave! Young men and women popped up out of their seats to sing praises to the Lord.

At this juncture, the drummer found his way to the stage, and the energy in the room increased even more. Though the pace of the songs never seemed to speed up, our voices raised higher, as did our hands and faces. We lifted our eyes and opened our palms in surrender.

The final worship song released a round of spontaneous clapping. The leader closed us in prayer, then said, "It was amazing to stand up here and hear your voices showering over me. I know it was pleasing to the Lord!"

If you've never been swept up by a worship wave, just let yourself go next time!

## His Story

*[Ananias] told me, "The God of our ancestors has chosen you to know his will and to see the Righteous One and hear him speak. For you are to be his witness, telling everyone what you have seen and heard. What are you waiting for? Get up and be baptized. Have your sins washed away by calling on the name of the Lord." ACTS 22:14-16*

The first time we read Paul's testimony early in Acts, it is happening *to* him. Every time after that, he is telling others of his experience of meeting Jesus and how that changed his life! Each time he highlights different details in his testimony to relate something more about God to whomever he is speaking.

I've probably told my testimony over one thousand times to more people than can be counted. In fact, I've probably shared some detail of my conversion experience at least once a week for thirty years! Though I have been invited to give my testimony at hundreds of meetings and have written my story at the request of publishers, most often I find myself sharing it with a stranger or a new acquaintance.

Each of us has a unique story of how we met God. But it's not just *our* story—it is God's story! Those of us who have met God during or after great failure or heartache have a story of redemption and restoration. Yet many others have a story of consistent, unshakable faith since childhood. Their walk with God equally spurs others to desire a similar relationship.

What is your story or the testimony of how God met you and changed you—and continues to change you every day? Through God's hand upon your life, you show others how much God loves them and how He desires to be in a personal relationship with them. Don't hesitate to tell your part in His story.

## Relationship Fireworks

*Spouting off before listening to the facts is both shameful and foolish.*

PROVERBS 18:13

- Quick temper.
- Quick to interrupt.
- Quick, piercing comeback.
- Quick reply; last to speak.

Though there are plenty of hurtful qualities people possess, "spouting off" happens to be one of mine.

The trouble with any personality flaw is that it will wreak havoc on your relationships. Fireworks fly, people get hurt, you feel ashamed, and someone acts or looks foolish. Distance results. The cycle repeats itself until . . . you change.

Consider where your personality flaws derive, but not as a continued excuse for repeating the behavior. Did you learn this behavior from someone close to you? Were you a "smart mouth" as a child? Can you see the negative result it is having on any or perhaps all of your relationships? Are you willing to change or even call it sin in your life?

The Bible has a great deal to say that is very sobering to those of us who have not taken seriously the challenge to tame our tongues. James 1:26 says, "If you claim to be religious but don't control your tongue, you are fooling yourself, and your religion is worthless." The tongue is a powerful tool that can be used for good or for evil. It can ruin your witness and wound those you love. If you're like me, you must always put your tongue on the table for review in your daily conversations with God. You must beg God to change you.

Consider your relationship fireworks—and disarm them.

## Sweet Sleep

*I lay down and slept, yet I woke up in safety, for the LORD
was watching over me.* PSALM 3:5

From the time I was born, we went to church every Sunday.
And as soon as I could speak, I was taught a prayer:

*Now I lay me down to sleep.
I pray the Lord my soul to keep.
If I should die before I wake,
I pray the Lord my soul to take.*

This prayer created a growing sense of terror within me by
the time I was four or five years old. As my mother tucked me in
each night, I wondered, *Why are they teaching me an I'm-going-to-die
prayer? Is it because I'm going to die?*

That deep fear about death started my search for the meaning
of life. I repeatedly asked my parents for answers. The impression I
received from them was, "If you are good, you will go to heaven."
But even a young child has bad days. My fears only grew stronger.

Then over a brief period, a string of deaths came in rapid
succession: Grandma, then Grandpa, a family friend, another
grandpa, and a U.S. president. I literally thought a casket was in
my closet!

I couldn't sleep at night. Not only was I fearful over what
would happen when I died, I was concerned about the where-
abouts of people who had already died.

But on the day that I asked Christ into my life at age twenty-
one, the sweetest words I heard were, "When you die, you will be
with Jesus in heaven, not because you deserve it or earned it, but
because He paid the price for your sins."

I felt the assurance of my salvation rush into my heart. I've
never feared death since. I hit the pillow and I'm sound asleep.

# Time Out

*Don't sin by letting anger control you.*
*Think about it overnight and remain silent.* PSALM 4:4

I've heard it said that you shouldn't "stuff" your anger or it will cause internal problems. That is correct, but neither should you shove it on others!

My husband is in the business of teaching anger management to couples. That's right. Anger is one of the most common passion stealers within a marriage! The Bible (the original marriage guidebook) gives practical advice for managing anger, rather than letting anger control you.

Based on Scripture, Roger has developed a three-step anger management system.

First, protect your relationship. How? Take a "time-out" before saying or doing anything. (Time-outs are not taken to watch television, isolate, or avoid talking.) Take a few deep breaths, count to ten . . . or one hundred . . . and pray. Get connected with God so you can get your anger under His control. As an added benefit, this action step will build character! (See Romans 5:3-4.)

Second, identify the enemy. Remember, it is *not* the person with whom you are angry! Ephesians 6:12 says, "For we are not fighting against flesh-and-blood enemies, but against evil rulers and authorities of the unseen world, against mighty powers in this dark world, and against evil spirits in the heavenly places." Next, identify how the enemy is causing you to judge or accuse the other person. Combat these emotions by providing evidence of the good qualities that your spouse or friend possesses. Reverse the role of accuser and become the other person's advocate.

Third, speak the truth in love. (See Ephesians 4:15.)

If "now" is not a convenient or plausible time to discuss the situation, set an agreed-upon time to come back together.

Managing your anger is not an option—it is God's mandate!

## Happy Hour

*O LORD, hear me as I pray; pay attention to my groaning. Listen to my cry
for help, my King and my God, for I pray to no one but you.
Listen to my voice in the morning, LORD. Each morning I bring
my requests to you and wait expectantly.* PSALM 5:1-3

There is only one reason that has motivated me to pray for
one hour a day for over twenty-three years: to spend time
with God!

All the other reasons to pray have a downside:

- It takes time.
- It requires planning.
- It will likely reveal possible internal or external problems.
- It produces change whether I'm ready to change or not.
- It can be costly. I'll be asked to send, do, give . . .

One day I had a meltdown and realized that the Christian
life was never going to be perfect or easy. Every day I would face
financial or relationship challenges. I was always going to wake up
and have to resist sin and temptation. I continually needed God's
intervention.

Too tired, too lazy, too busy doing ministry . . . were no
longer acceptable reasons to keep me from God's presence or
power. I no longer wanted to go even one day without consulting God! Because I knew how to do "life without prayer" (and
it wasn't working), I determined to *never* miss one day of talking
to God and listening to Him.

One Saturday afternoon in February of 1984, I made a commitment to pour my heart out to God and listen for His answers by
reading His Word for one hour a day for the rest of my life.

It's my happy hour—the most fulfilling, filling hour I've ever
known.

# Answered Prayer

*The LORD has heard my plea; the LORD will answer my prayer.* PSALM 6:9

Do you *expect* God to answer your prayers? My level of expectation to receive answers to prayer was heightened with every book I read by Andrew Murray, an outstanding nineteenth-century religious leader whose ministry greatly impacted the church in South Africa from the mid-1800s until his death in 1917.

His classic prayer handbook, *With Christ in the School of Prayer*, teaches a follower of Christ to develop a prayer life that reaches deeper into God with every two-way conversation.

When I first discovered Murray, I was hungry to enter into the powerful prayer life he spoke of—I was at least willing to pray for one hour a day. I wanted to learn the secret of asking and receiving. I was most surprised to find the limitlessness and willingness of God to answer prayer!

Even though I have seen great and exciting answers to prayer over the past two decades, I still open Murray's book to refresh my spirit and to refocus my thinking. I regularly need a stronger heart, a larger heart to enter into daily prayer as my most powerful spiritual exercise. I read Murray to remind me that "the power to believe *a promise* depends entirely on faith in *the promiser*."[1]

You do not have to question whether God answers prayer. You can be confident, knowing that when you talk to God and listen to Him, you will receive answers from Him. But when you ask, make certain your request is in agreement with God's Word. Carefully consider your motives and never give up praying for something until you receive God's answer.

Your part is to ask and expect, not to tell or demand. His part is to answer you. Amen?

# Treasure Hunt

*The man who finds a wife finds a treasure, and he receives favor from the LORD.* PROVERBS 18:22

Upon returning home to Ohio at the age of twenty-one, I had a compulsion to tell the assistant principal and former teachers at my high school about my new life in Christ. Though they didn't know what to do with my exuberant faith, they were happy to hear that I'd quit doing drugs, drinking alcohol, and smoking cigarettes.

Everyone assumed I would continue working in an office. But I wanted to *do something for the Lord* with my life. I wanted to make a difference, to tell my story to students who were like me—lost! The principal and my teachers suggested that I meet our school's Campus Life director, Roger Tirabassi, a former guidance counselor at the high school.

I made an appointment to meet with him and another Campus Life staff member on the following day.

As I recall, it was close to Thanksgiving. Immediately following our initial interview I was asked to become a volunteer. I attended weekly training dinners, weeknight club meetings, and staff retreats—with Roger.

He became my mentor and identified my spiritual gifts. After nine months, he encouraged me to intern with Campus Life / Youth for Christ during the summer, raise support, and join the staff full-time.

On the following Thanksgiving, he asked me to marry him. I said, "Yes!" We were married two months later. And we've been married—and in ministry—for over twenty-nine years.

My husband found me—without even trying! Sometimes your treasure is right in front of you!

# Disgraceful Ending

*Saul died because he was unfaithful to the LORD. He failed to obey the LORD's command, and he even consulted a medium instead of asking the LORD for guidance. So the LORD killed him and turned the kingdom over to David son of Jesse.* 1 CHRONICLES 10:13-14

I t is disheartening to read the epitaph of Saul in two painfully sad verses.

Saul was handsome, skilled—and chosen by God. He had Samuel as a mentor and Jonathan as a son. Both men would be considered outstanding assets to any leader. Yet Saul consistently ignored them and disgraced God, his nation, and his family.

Saul was not deceived. At critical junctures he made specific choices to turn away from God and even consult a medium rather than seek the Lord. "So the LORD killed him."

If there is a lesson behind the disgraceful ending in Saul's life, it is this: It was avoidable!

Saul had one of the most renowned spiritual advisers in history available to him. That he repeatedly ignored Samuel's advice put a nail in Saul's coffin, so to speak. His defiance and disobedience to the Lord's specific instructions is also a matter of record. And even when he could have repented, he refused to do so. Instead, he rationalized his behavior.

I believe these two verses serve as a warning to every Christian.

Look around you. Do you regularly open God's Word and follow His advice? Do you recognize the godly spiritual advisers He has placed in your life? Do you make time for them? Do you listen to their teaching, especially their warnings?

Saul proved ignoring God's chosen instruments might cost more than your reputation, your family, or your ministry. It could cost your life.

# Revival Preacher

*For the next two years, Paul lived in Rome at his own expense. He welcomed all who visited him, boldly proclaiming the Kingdom of God and teaching about the Lord Jesus Christ. And no one tried to stop him.* ACTS 28:30-31

The autobiography of Charles G. Finney, originally published in 1876, reads like a modern-day book of Acts. As Paul was a central figure in Acts, Charles G. Finney was a revival preacher during the nineteenth century through whom over a half million people converted to Christ.

It was said of his preaching that sinners were converted at once under his influence. He was uniquely driven by God. His life story reveals that he considered his greatest teachers to be the Lord and the Bible.

Having no formal training, Finney began to preach where he was invited, filling pews with people from all walks of life—often the unchurched and uneducated. He wrote, "I borrowed my illustrations from their various occupations. I tried also to use language they would understand. . . . I sought to express all my ideas in a few words, and in words that were in common use."[2]

Wherever he held a revival, the citizens of an entire town would attend and their lives would be turned upside down! His experiences were so widely reported that eventually he taught and wrote extensively on revival. His treatise *Lectures on Revival* has remained in publication for well over a century.

Finney seemed purely motivated and powerfully equipped to preach the gospel message of Christ. He wrote, "Without the direct teaching of the Holy Spirit a man will never make much progress in preaching the gospel."[3]

# Good News

*I am not ashamed of this Good News about Christ. It is the power of God at work, saving everyone who believes—the Jew first and also the Gentile.*

ROMANS 1:16

Charles Spurgeon said, "The gospel will be found equal to every emergency—it is an arrow that can pierce the hardest heart, a balm that will heal the deadliest wound. Preach it, and preach nothing else. Rely implicitly on the old, old Gospel. You need no other nets when you fish for men; those your Master has given you are strong enough for the great fish and have meshes fine enough to hold the little ones."[4]

Peter Marshall, former chaplain of the U.S. Senate and a pastor in Washington DC during the late 1940s, was a modern-day fisher of men. He reeled in many of the nation's political leaders, packing them into pews—sometimes with standing room only—by the creative way in which he chose to share the gospel.

In a sermon recorded in his life story, *A Man Called Peter,* he spoke of Jesus:

> *He Himself said:"I came not to invite the pious, but the irreligious."*
> *Perhaps that applies to some of you?*
> *He is calling you.*
> *Christ is here—a thousand times more alive than when He walked in the flesh up and down the sun-baked trails of that little land. . .*
> *Have you ever said to the Galilean,"I believe in You.*
> *I am with You, come what may"?*
> *Have you ever told Him that?*
> *If you have not, why not do it—now?*[5]

You and I have what people want to hear—the Good News! Frame it, shape it, cast it like a fishing net. Don't ever be ashamed of it . . . it is God's power to save.

## Exact Words

*God abandoned them to do whatever shameful things their hearts desired.*
*As a result, they did vile and degrading things with each other's bodies.*

ROMANS 1:24

At the end of one very late evening meeting, a young man approached me. He didn't have a prayer request; he disagreed with my comments regarding same-sex attraction. Quite upset, he said, "I don't believe that gay sex is sin."

Those were his exact words. I was very tired, so I said, "Well, it's obvious that I'm not going to change your mind in a short conversation. So I have a question. Would you be willing to pray with me tonight and ask the Holy Spirit to fully come into your life?"

I was surprised at his quick reply: "Okay." I added a disclaimer: "I don't know what will happen when we pray this prayer."

His response made me smile. "You're the third person who has said that to me recently."

I wondered, *What will happen?* All I knew was that the power of God was available to us. I took his hands and bowed my head, then stopped. I looked right in his eyes and asked, "Would you ever be involved in pedophilia?"

He promptly replied, "No."

When I started to bow my head again, I couldn't. I looked into his eyes, but had nothing to say.

But he did. He said, "Yes, I do fear that I could be involved in pedophilia."

My mouth dropped open. What just happened? I had never asked a person that question before!

When we bowed our heads to pray, the first words out of his mouth were, "Lord, I believe gay sex is sin." Those were his exact words.

# Spiritual Direction

*That same night God said to Nathan, "Go and tell my servant David,*
*'This is what the LORD has declared: You are not the one to build a*
*house for me to live in.'" . . . So Nathan went back to David and told him*
*everything the LORD had said in this vision. Then King David went in*
*and sat before the LORD and prayed.* 1 CHRONICLES 17:3-4, 15-16

I n the Old Testament, God assigned spiritual directors to
every leader. And each leader was free to decide if he would
confer with the spiritual director or even maintain the special
relationship. Repeatedly, God's leaders came to important crossroads and chose either to ignore or embrace God's counsel given
through their spiritual directors. Their futures, very often, were
decided in those moments.

David had numerous interchanges with Nathan, but at this
juncture of their relationship, the climate was neither demand-
ing nor impulsive. Their conversation seems very much like two
friends brainstorming.

In the few recorded conversations between Nathan and David,
there is both an order and a mutual respect between them. But
I see one more characteristic they possessed that makes their
relationship work: Both men were leaders in their own right.
Therefore, they expected God to speak to them individually, to
confirm or convict them.

Oh, to be so fortunate to have wise, godly people in our lives
who confirm, advise, and pray with us regarding our decisions! My
husband is my spiritual director. He loves my visionary faith, often
agrees with me, always prays for me, but also is quick to warn me
when he sees something I can't—or am unwilling to—see.

I've learned that listening to his wise counsel usually saves us
time, money, . . . or heartache.

# Heart Change

*A true Jew is one whose heart is right with God. And true circumcision is not merely obeying the letter of the law; rather, it is a change of heart produced by God's Spirit. And a person with a changed heart seeks praise from God, not from people.* ROMANS 2:29

Blaming others . . . often keeps us from change.

I meet many college students who are bitter. At their parents . . . or God . . . or both. They resent something about their upbringing which keeps them from moving on.

I listen, empathize, then lovingly remind students, "As long as you blame your parents or others in authority for their shortcomings instead of examining your own heart, you'll never find peace. In fact, you'll be so wrapped up in others' stuff that you'll miss the change of heart that God wants to produce in you."

Many students respond immediately. They humbly understand that God's mandate for each believer is that he or she become a fully devoted follower of Christ, regardless of age or upbringing. This includes forgiving flawed people, especially parents. When students quit wallowing in self-pity and begin to forgive others, they can let God into their hearts and amazing changes occur, including family reconciliation and deep emotional healing.

But sadly, people of all ages struggle for years with unforgiveness, entitlement, and bitterness. They refuse to let God heal them and change their hearts.

A change of heart can happen at any age, to anyone.

Where God leads you, how He speaks to you, what He requires of you will be unique to you—your daily cross to bear.

Do you find yourself blaming others or unwilling to forgive? Perhaps it is time to ask God for a "Holy Spirit change of heart" in your life.

# All Fall

*We are made right with God by placing our faith in Jesus Christ. And this is true for everyone who believes, no matter who we are. For everyone has sinned; we all fall short of God's glorious standard.* ROMANS 3:22-23

Upon coming to Christ, my visible sins—drunkenness, cursing, and sexual immorality—were purged in such rapid succession that my new, unexplainable moral behavior became outward evidence to many of my supernaturally changed life. For a short while, I lived with a false sense of security—thinking I was invulnerable to sin simply because I was a Christian.

But hidden sins lurked within me—jealousy, uncontrolled anger, and greed. Eventually, they caught up with me and became visible to others. I was awakened to the daily cycle of indwelling sin. I realized if I didn't regularly come clean with God, or daily "die to myself," my "self" was going to humiliate God.

Recently, I discovered an author who not only described my experience, but made practical sense of indwelling sin. John Owen, a seventeenth-century theologian, wrote extensively on sin and temptation. He was a thinker who impacted other great theologians, such as Jonathan Edwards. He wrote, "But when Christ Himself comes as Conqueror to visit the soul, He finds no resting place. He must fight for every inch of territory—within the mind, within the affections, within the will. . . . Even when God's grace enters the soul of man, sin is still there, and pervasively so. . . . Sin never wavers, yields, or gives up in spite of all the powerful opposition it encounters from the law of the gospel."[6]

Open your eyes! Be on guard. Kick out any known sin in your life. Fight back. Fight hard. *Fight always.*

Let *no* sin find a comfortable resting place in your heart or mind.

# Intense Companionship

*O LORD, how long will you forget me? Forever? How long will you look the*
*other way? How long must I struggle with anguish in my soul, with sorrow*
*in my heart every day? How long will my enemy have the upper hand?*
*Turn and answer me, O LORD my God! Restore the sparkle to my eyes,*
*or I will die.* PSALM 13:1-3

David's honest conversations with God throughout the book of Psalms reveal much about the intensely intimate companionship they shared. David petitioned the Lord and trusted Him not to turn away. Repeatedly and without hesitation, David asked God for an answer. He shared every beat of his heart—his needs and expectations—with his Lord.

Many of the psalms expose David's tenacity in prayer. They give me great encouragement to come to God also with my every concern. They encourage me to trust God, to know with certainty that He will respond to my heart's cry. And though I don't always receive an answer in the way or at a time I would have chosen, I *always* sense His presence for every situation.

Nikos Kazantzakis wrote of his similar ongoing conversations with God in *The Saviors of God: Spiritual Exercises*:

> *My prayer is the report of a soldier to his general: This is what I did*
> *today, this is how I fought to save the entire battle in my own sector,*
> *these are the obstacles I found, this is how I plan to fight tomorrow.*
>
> *My God and I are horsemen galloping in the burning sun or*
> *under drizzling rain. Pale, starving, but unsubdued, we ride and*
> *converse.*[7]

Ask God to make Himself known to you. Do not hesitate to call on Him. Call on Him, even now, to send you help.

# Radical Faith

*Abraham never wavered in believing God's promise. In fact, his faith grew stronger, and in this he brought glory to God. He was fully convinced that God is able to do whatever he promises.* ROMANS 4:20-21

You and I must come face-to-face with impossible faith and ask ourselves, *Do I possess this kind of radical faith?* Perhaps it is at those "no hope" junctures, just as Abraham encountered, when we reach out and take hold of radical faith— to believe what we can't see, to believe in that which makes no sense, to believe in Him who is invisible!

In every century there are faith healers, faith lovers, faith preachers, and faith leaders. They are not usually the most wealthy or educated. Most often, they are the humble orphanage founders, the first missionaries in an isolated country, or brilliant doctors and impressive preachers who give up certain societal advantages to answer a mysterious, less prominent call from God.

Radical, biblical faith has the same expression in any century:

- It will leave comfort for suffering, if God asks . . .
- It will move away from family to settle in an unfamiliar territory, if God asks . . .
- It will articulate God's plans to outspoken skeptics and critics, if God asks . . .
- It will follow God's directions (for example, building an ark on dry land), even when everyone around ridicules the unusual behavior, if God asks . . .
- It will fearlessly declare the Good News, even at the risk of personal safety, if God asks . . .

Faith like Abraham's keeps hoping, never wavers, and is convinced that God is able to do what He promised.

In this century . . . God asks you and me, "Will you possess radical faith?"

## Public Proclamation

*So now, with God as our witness, and in the sight of all Israel—the LORD's*
*assembly—I give you this charge. Be careful to obey all the commands of*
*the LORD your God, so that you may continue to possess this good land and*
*leave it to your children as a permanent inheritance.* 1 CHRONICLES 28:8

Marriage is a perfect example of a modern-day public vow. At a wedding ceremony, in front of family and friends, a couple makes a proclamation to God and each other—to remain faithful all their lives. A marriage is intended to reflect God's love toward us.

Yet marriage has lost its significance in our culture, either as a lifelong commitment or as a sacred union that brings glory to God. At the turn of the twenty-first century, statistics sadly reveal that 43 percent of American couples will divorce regardless of their religious beliefs.[8]

Restoring the marriage vow to its high calling has been an incredibly intense effort for Christian premarital counselors and pastors like my husband. They feel a great responsibility to equip engaged couples to honor God through their marriage. These counselors spend weeks and months reeducating couples on the biblical, sacred meaning of their union, equipping them for the nuances of relationship management, and challenging them to grasp the higher calling within their vows.

A public vow signifies intent, commitment, integrity, and longevity. When a vow includes God, it most often includes a promise.

In today's Scripture—as in the marriage vow—God rewards those who keep His commands. Most importantly, He promises to be with us. . . .

Before you make a vow to someone, carefully consider the principles and promises in God's Word so that you may honor God with your words and leave a lasting legacy with your life.

# Ruinous Dominance

*Do not let sin control the way you live; do not give in to sinful desires.*

ROMANS 6:12

John Owen, a seventeenth-century English statesman and theologian, wrote three treatises that were later compiled into a single edition: *Sin and Temptation*. Though he died in 1683, his words are powerfully relevant to the twenty-first-century Christian who battles the very same sins that have chased, deceived, and opposed believers in every century.

Owen's constant contention is that God has given believers two practical methods in which to overcome sin—prayer and meditation!

Owen suggests four values of prayer and meditation:

1. *Meditation will reveal all the "secret workings and actions of sin."* Owen believed that "prayer does not exist" if we are unwilling to express our very real needs to God—our fears, weaknesses, and temptations.

2. *Prayer is the method of communication that God has designed to give our hearts "a deep, full sense of the vileness of sin."* Prayer is the place where sin will be exposed. Avoiding prayer gives sin time to hide or to become even exciting to you.

3. *Prayer is the place, the way, to obtain power against sin.* You must fight against any apathy or discouragement in prayer. Don't neglect to pray—it is where you access God's supernatural and available power to overcome sin.

4. *Prayer and meditation "counteract all the deceitful workings of sin."* Not only do prayer and meditation reveal our weaknesses and God's hatred toward sin, but they are where the battle is fought.[9]

Owen encourages Christians with these words: "Prayer weakens a prevalent sin. . . . As long as the soul engages itself with God, it is certain sin cannot rise up in ruinous dominance."[10]

## Glorious Presence

*The trumpeters and singers performed together in unison to praise and
give thanks to the LORD. Accompanied by trumpets, cymbals, and other
instruments, they raised their voices and praised the LORD with these words:
"He is good! His faithful love endures forever!" At that moment a thick
cloud filled the Temple of the LORD.* 2 CHRONICLES 5:13

On a few occasions in my life, I have been in a church
service or revival meeting when everything stopped—
the music, the preaching, the singing, and the praying.
The silence became the loudest "noise" in the room. No one dared
to move. Actually, I didn't get a scary feeling—more of a holy
feeling.

Recently, this phenomenon happened at two meetings a week
apart.

I invited students to join me for a time of worship and prayer
in the main auditorium on campus. In both meetings, student
musicians were willing to play and sing all night! The program
wasn't planned in advance—we would simply open with worship,
have a time of sharing, invite a few people to share testimonies,
and then pray. There would be no stated closing time, and anyone
who wanted to pray with someone was invited to come to the
altar for prayer.

Interestingly, both student meetings lasted almost four hours
and the worship bands played almost the entire time. In both
meetings, there was silence near the end as the musicians, one by
one, simply stopped playing without being asked to do so. There
was stillness, as if someone or something else had filled the room.
And both times I asked the same question to the remaining fifty-
plus students, "Why are you still here?"

And both times I received the same answer . . . "Because He's
here."

## Mind Control

*Those who are dominated by the sinful nature think about sinful things,
but those who are controlled by the Holy Spirit think about things that
please the Spirit. So letting your sinful nature control your mind leads to
death. But letting the Spirit control your mind leads to life and peace.
For the sinful nature is always hostile to God. It never did obey God's
laws, and it never will.* ROMANS 8:5-7

Paul cuts right to the core of sin—he tells you how it works so that you can be alert and informed. He challenges you to win the battle against sin by making moment-by-moment choices to please God, rather than yourself. Just as sin rallies for your affection, so does God. Whom will you please?

Do you know which sin vies for control in your life? Your willingness to identify the specific sin that tempts you is critical. You must name it; it can never remain vague if it is going to be eradicated from your life!

In *My Utmost for His Highest*, Oswald Chambers suggests, "There are certain things in life we need not pray about—moods, for instance. We will never get rid of moodiness by praying, but we will by kicking it out of our lives. . . . It is a continual struggle not to listen to the moods which arise as a result of our physical condition, but we must never submit to them a second."[11]

Chambers challenges his readers further: "The problem that most of us are cursed with is simply that we *won't*. The Christian life is one of spiritual courage and determination lived out in our flesh."[12]

Today, name those sins that are hostile to God, but reside in you. Anger, hatred, jealousy, addiction . . . don't submit to them for a second. Win the battle in your mind.

# He Rescues

*He reached down from heaven and rescued me; he drew me out of deep waters. He rescued me from my powerful enemies, from those who hated me and were too strong for me.* PSALM 18:16-17

I met a cute young gal (we'll call her Sally) at a large state university during my forty-day campus tour in the winter of 2006. She was a strong campus leader by title and personality, but on the inside she was crumbling.

She was the second person to approach me when I offered to pray for anyone who wanted to confess any sexual impurity. She had been raped by a youth minister at a camp the previous summer, but had never told anyone.

I tried to imagine how I'd feel if I were her, but I was too overcome with a different distress—like a mother whose daughter had been violated. I tried to comfort her, but I didn't feel as if I had done enough to alleviate her significant pain.

Then God gave me an idea. I frantically began to look for Sally. When I finally found her, I asked her permission to write a letter to the founder of the camp and tell him what happened.

That week, I wrote the letter and received a very swift, humble response. A few months later, I heard from Sally: "I may never be able to thank you enough. I am indebted to you for taking action in a place where I was still weak. Since you left I have been trying to get my feet on the ground, trying to find some way to trust people again, desperately wandering back into God's arms. Now, as I am writing this, I am learning to fly."

When God prompts you to bring relief or rescue or help to a weaker brother or sister, respond immediately.

## God's Love

*I am convinced that nothing can ever separate us from God's love. Neither death nor life, neither angels nor demons, neither our fears for today nor our worries about tomorrow—not even the powers of hell can separate us from God's love. No power in the sky above or in the earth below—indeed, nothing in all creation will ever be able to separate us from the love of God that is revealed in Christ Jesus our Lord.* ROMANS 8:38-39

Young believers are often given a few classic Bible verses by older believers who know the Word of God has the power to sustain them when the inevitable difficulties of life confront their newly found faith. Romans 8:38-39 are two verses that were etched in my mind during my early Bible-training days. They were instrumental in helping me view my new relationship with God—and my faith in Him—as different from any other relationship.

In these verses, Paul lists every imaginable threat to our relationship with God and reminds believers that *nothing* can separate us from the love of God, not even . . .

death or life
demons or angels
fear or worry
created beings, *or*
creation itself.

At the time I met Christ, not only was it difficult for me to believe that someone could faithfully love me, but I also feared that I could not be trusted to love others!

Love is so hard to do well or even understand.

So Paul reminds every believer—especially new ones—that God's love is not like any love we've ever experienced. We can't earn His love and we can't lose it. Nothing will ever separate us from the living, loving God!

There is no one who loves you like God loves you.

## Holy Tension

*How can I know all the sins lurking in my heart? Cleanse me from these
hidden faults. Keep your servant from deliberate sins! Don't let them
control me. Then I will be free of guilt and innocent of great sin. May the
words of my mouth and the meditation of my heart be pleasing to you,
O LORD, my rock and my redeemer.* PSALM 19:12-14

David's pattern of confession to God was the process in
which he daily consecrated his life to God, becoming a
clean vessel for His use at His pleasure!

Though David's prayer expressed his deep desire to be kept
from sin, he knew his choices would be the final test. He articulated what we all know—there is a constant tension between
pleasing ourselves and living our lives with such a pure passion
that we truly please a holy God.

In *A Gift for God*, Mother Teresa spoke of this holy tension:
"Our progress in holiness depends on God and ourselves—on
God's grace and on our will to be holy. We must have a real living
determination to reach holiness."[13]

The admission of deliberate or hidden sin in our lives cannot
be an occasional or random exercise. It must be intentional. "If you
keep yourself pure, you will be a special utensil for honorable use.
Your life will be clean, and you will be ready for the Master to use
you for every good work" (2 Timothy 2:21).

Do you want the Master to use you? Make David's prayer
yours: "Lord, search me and show me where I hide from You.
Purge me of anything that would shame me—or Your name! I give
You control over my life today. I will live my life to please You, my
Lord and my Redeemer."

# Heart's Desires

*May he grant your heart's desires and make all your plans succeed.*

PSALM 20:4

I love Psalm 20 because it provides an exciting component to my prayer life. For the many minutes I spend in confession each day, because of David's example, I have a freedom to also spend time asking the Lord to grant the desires of my heart and make my plans succeed!

Though most Bible teachers, preachers, or authors hold a certain opinion about praying for your desires and success, David's psalm gives us permission to request God's favor, to ask Him to give us the desires of our hearts and make our plans succeed.

I like that perspective. I have that passion! Therefore, I am continually encouraged by David's absolute transparency with God as I read and reread his psalms. He ushers me into passionate prayer, giving me the courage to say, "Lord, You know my desires. You know what is in my heart. You've put those desires there. Please make my plans succeed."

What David *isn't* doing is telling the Lord, "This is my plan, please bless it." Nor is David praying about plans that have been completed, offering a quick, "This is what I decided to do. I hope it was okay."

David doesn't tell God what to do, but asks God to . . .

- Hear his cry
- Keep him safe from all harm
- Strengthen him
- Rescue him by His great power
- Send help

Does it sound like David is talking to a God who is reluctant or unwilling? No.

If you are hesitant to pray about your heart's desires, I encourage you to allow God's Word to be your teacher, to guide you into transparent, two-way conversations with the living, loving God.

## God's Battle

*After this, the armies of the Moabites, Ammonites, and some of the Meunites declared war on Jehoshaphat. . . . Jehoshaphat was terrified by this news and begged the LORD for guidance. He also ordered everyone in Judah to begin fasting. So people from all the towns of Judah came to Jerusalem to seek the LORD's help.* 2 CHRONICLES 20:1, 3-4

I regularly read this Old Testament account because . . .

- I often find myself in a place of great need for God's intervention, and
- I want my reaction toward fear to resemble Jehoshaphat's response!

Though Jehoshaphat admitted that he was powerless over the vast approaching army, he acknowledged that God was *not* powerless. Significantly, Jehoshaphat called on God in front of the entire community. He proclaimed the limitless power of God and acknowledged that prayer was the way in which God invited His people to come to Him. Then Jehoshaphat gave God the details of Judah's situation, saying, "O our God, won't you stop them? We are powerless against this mighty army that is about to attack us. We do not know what to do, but we are looking to you for help" (20:12).

Men, women, and children stood before the Lord, and the Lord spoke to them through the prophet Jahaziel. He gave them a word from the Lord that detailed their victory, including specific directions and great encouragement: "But you will not even need to fight. Take your positions; then stand still and watch the LORD's victory. He is with you, O people of Judah and Jerusalem. Do not be afraid or discouraged. Go out against them tomorrow, for the LORD is with you!" (verse 17).

Can this be any more encouraging? Now you know why I read this so often! (For the final outcome, read 2 Chronicles 20.)

# Godly Children

*The godly walk with integrity; blessed are their children who follow them.*

PROVERBS 20:7

Most couples can't begin to anticipate the challenges they will face when they become parents! They blissfully see the stages of birth, toddlerhood, and elementary school . . . not anticipating the traumas of their children's teens and twenties!

Yet the wisdom in this proverb is not offered to the children, but to the parents. It challenges a parent to model integrity *so that* his or her children will have a pattern to follow.

When I look back at over twenty-eight years of parenting, I don't remember the times my *son's* character was required to change. I wince at how many times *my* character was challenged to change. I agonize over the times that I had to apologize to my son for my lack of integrity or uncontrolled anger. There were also many difficult moments when my husband and I made choices for our young son that would set him—and us—apart from other families because of our convictions. Those were not fun times. But we lived through them.

By the time my son was in high school, I felt the Lord nudge me. "Your son will never have a more devoted person in his life that will pray and fast for him as much as you. Commit yourself to weekly fasting. Pray for him specifically and daily. Pray for his friends. Pray for his future wife. This is your greatest work as his mother." So I did, and still do.

If I added anything to the proverb above, I would say, "Worry less about how your children will turn out and instead spend that time in prayer. Pray for yourself, first, to be a godly parent. Ask God for wisdom and discernment to love your children unconditionally and to discipline them fairly."

# Different Lives

*Dear brothers and sisters, I plead with you to give your bodies to God because of all he has done for you. Let them be a living and holy sacrifice—the kind he will find acceptable. This is truly the way to worship him.* ROMANS 12:1

Of the many men and women throughout history who have literally given their lives for the cause of Christ, Dietrich Bonhoeffer is one of the most unforgettable people in the early twentieth century.

He was a Lutheran theologian and professor who spoke out vehemently and publicly against Hitler, knowing it could cost him his life. And it did. His repudiation led to his imprisonment and death.

For this reason, Bonhoeffer's life and teaching detailed in *The Cost of Discipleship* has had a profound impact on the modern-day Christian who seems so unfamiliar or at least uncomfortable with sacrifice.

Like Paul in speaking to the Romans, Bonhoeffer pleaded with believers to willingly give their lives back to the One who died for them. Both men challenge us not to live easier lives, but *different* lives—perhaps more dangerous, less self-serving, more outspoken, and from a different motivation than the world around us. In *The Cost of Discipleship*, Bonhoeffer wrote, "Yet it is imperative for the Christian to achieve renunciation, to practise self-effacement, to distinguish his life from the life of the world."[14]

We may never be faced with torture or imprisonment for the cause of Christ, but we are faced with daily choices that, if made in light of Christ's sacrifice for us, would set us apart.

Give yourself to Christ—as much as you can each day—not out of duty, but because of what He has done for you, give yourself to Him . . . just as you are, right where you are . . . as a living and holy sacrifice.

## Tough Times

*The LORD is my shepherd; I have all that I need. He lets me rest in green meadows; he leads me beside peaceful streams. He renews my strength. He guides me along right paths, bringing honor to his name. Even when I walk through the darkest valley, I will not be afraid, for you are close beside me. Your rod and your staff protect and comfort me.* PSALM 23:1-4

During those tough times, whether they last an hour, a week, or even a month, the Lord wants to be your greatest comfort and mine.

I had one of those months recently. My thirteen-year-old black Labrador became very ill. I've never had to put a dog to sleep before, nor have I nursed a dying dog. It was an emotionally painful and draining experience.

During the same time period, I hurt someone close to me by something I said. It took two lengthy appointments to reconcile. Within the same week, I discovered (by way of e-mail) that someone I hadn't seen in over five years held something against me. I couldn't recall anything specific that happened between us, so I began the process to reconcile—but it was a slow process.

Then exciting news I had been waiting for . . . fizzled.

The words of Psalm 23 often came to me. They consoled me even though I created my own distress in many ways.

Because this psalm is embedded in my heart and mind, the words came out of my mouth when my heartache grew unbearable.

Though trouble and pain will assail you, you are not alone. Your shepherd, the One who comforts and protects you, will never leave your side. He will lead you to the place of quiet reflection and renewed strength. He will forgive and restore you.

He will always be with you.

## Unnecessary Stumbling

*Yes, each of us will give a personal account to God. So let's stop condemning each other. Decide instead to live in such a way that you will not cause another believer to stumble and fall.* ROMANS 14:12-13

An alcoholic can never justify having a drink. Oh, we'll try. We think a toast here and there is harmless. But an alcoholic can't drink—ever—without risking a relapse. Relapsing after months or years of sobriety is a devastating experience.

When I finally determined that I could never drink again, I avoided all parties or places where alcohol was served. I couldn't even be around drinkers. Thankfully, I never returned to the party scene. Most important, I married a man who, on our honeymoon, graciously offered never to drink again for my sake. And significantly, for the first eight years of my sobriety, I worked for a youth ministry that required its staff to abstain from alcohol.

But for the past twenty years, I have observed how alcohol is abused in the church.

As a youth worker, it simply made sense not to drink, because we worked with underage students. But for most of my years in ministry, it has been difficult to watch Christians drink like non-Christians. Though abstinence can appear noble—even legalistic—in some cases, in my case, it is essential. A recovering alcoholic can't drink—ever. And because there are millions of us in the church who are alcoholics—some newly sober, others sober many years like myself, others still struggling to overcome an addiction to alcohol—I see no place for alcohol in church functions.

I've never been able to persuade drinking Christians, especially those in ministry, not to drink, but I still try, because there is a lot of unnecessary stumbling going on. *Just a thought.*

# Wholehearted Pursuit

*In all that he did in the service of the Temple of God and in his efforts to follow God's laws and commands, Hezekiah sought his God wholeheartedly. As a result, he was very successful.* 2 CHRONICLES 31:21

In one word, we are given a glimpse into Hezekiah's pursuit of God—*wholehearted*. This implies that his relationship with God was sustained by enthusiastic, godly obedience deeply motivated by love.

In *Religious Affections*, Jonathan Edwards, a central figure in New England's first Great Awakening, wrote about the balance between expressed emotion and dutiful obedience toward God. He listed "twelve signs of gracious affections," concluding that "true religion" must result in a wholehearted, holy affection toward God. He strongly believed that an authentic Christian should, over time, *increasingly* (not decreasingly) desire to grow closer to God and continuously seek to be more like Him. He wrote:

> *Multitudes often hear the Word of God and have knowledge about it. But it will be totally ineffective and will make no change in their behavior or character if they are not affected by what they hear. . . . They also hear the clear commands of God and of His gracious warnings and sweet invitations of the gospel. They hear all this and yet there is no change of behavior. This is simply because they have not been affected by what they heard. I am bold to assert that no change of religious nature will ever take place unless the affections are moved. . . . In summary, nothing significant ever changed the life of anyone when the heart was not deeply affected.*[1]

How can you become more wholehearted in your devotion and pursuit of God?

I believe your whole heart will be daily and deeply affected to love God more fully when you willingly give to Him that which is precious to you—*your time.*

# Great Power

*Be strong and courageous! Don't be afraid or discouraged because
of the king of Assyria or his mighty army, for there is a power
far greater on our side!* 2 CHRONICLES 32:7

I recently heard of a young woman, a missionary in Africa, who was almost gored by a bull. She was on the side of the road with nothing to protect herself from the charging bull. For no apparent reason, it stopped three feet from her and never harmed her.

I listened to an Indian preacher give report of an orphan who fell into a coma. The doctors said that her illness was irreversible. Her classmates, little Christian orphans, prayed believing . . . and she awoke days later, completely recovered.

A friend sent with a team on a short-term mission to Bosnia experienced a flat tire in a location that would prove deadly if the team was stopped by the opposition army. Unbeknownst to them, friends in the States were awakened in the middle of the night to pray for them. How they drove on a flat tire for over six hours, just reaching the safe border before dark, never seen by those who could harm them, was evidence of God's great protection over them.

During a tragic tsunami that devastated entire villages, a Christian orphanage director loaded every child under his care into a small boat, then headed the overweight vessel directly into the approaching wave. They all survived.

Our God is an awesome God—His love is deeper, His presence more real, and His power greater than any other. Though we recognize we have an enemy, most importantly, we must put our confidence in God to save us. We cannot freeze in the face of attack. We must look to and trust our great God to rescue us.

# Bold Prayer

*Declare me innocent, O LORD, for I have acted with integrity; I have trusted in the LORD without wavering. Put me on trial, LORD, and cross-examine me. Test my motives and my heart. For I am always aware of your unfailing love, and I have lived according to your truth.* PSALM 26:1-3

David makes truly bold statements in this psalm—asking God to declare him innocent *and* cross-examine his motives! David was not professing his innocence and integrity *to others*; he was speaking truthfully and transparently to the Lord, knowing that He already knew the circumstances.

I can't say I've ever had the guts to articulate my innocence to God as David did, but twenty-three years ago, I became aware that I am strongest when I operate out of a right relationship with God. To develop a more intimate relationship with God, I knew I had to be completely and regularly honest with Him about my motives and what is in my heart—even on an hourly basis.

Prior to that, though a Christian, I did not regularly ask God to examine me—and the result was a great lack of integrity; I was not the same person in public that I was in private. In order to change the pattern of rationalizing my flaws, I determined to ask God to search my heart daily. In the "Admit" section of *My Partner Prayer Notebook* (the prayer system I use), I confess my sins in writing to God. (The habit of daily coming under God's searchlight, asking Him to examine you, actually circumvents much sin and temptation that might otherwise catch you unaware.)

Obviously, written confession isn't a new idea—it is a centuries-old method God has given us to maintain honest communication with Him. If you find yourself resistant to this idea . . . make it a matter of prayer!

# Liftoff

*The LORD is my light and my salvation——so why should I be afraid? The LORD is my fortress, protecting me from danger, so why should I tremble? When evil people come to devour me, when my enemies and foes attack me, they will stumble and fall. Though a mighty army surrounds me, my heart will not be afraid. Even if I am attacked, I will remain confident.*

PSALM 27:1-3

An unexpected message . . . negatively impacted me one morning. It began with a little "hit" to my heart—an emotional arrow shot at me. Each time I gave thought to it, I grew less motivated, more restless and critical, and eventually it just seemed to hover over me.

The emotional and spiritual attacks lasted most of the day.

By evening, I was temporarily distracted when my husband and I went out for dinner and a movie. But as I was sitting in the dark theater, waiting for the show to start . . . I began to think about the situation again. Instead of nursing feelings of hopelessness, I decided to observe the feelings that had taken hold of me. I thought, *What if I hadn't received this news today? Would I have had a significantly different, happier day? Yes. Would I have had a more productive day? Yes. Should this news have impacted me so intensely? No. By dwelling on the negative aspects of this situation, might I have given the enemy of my soul a foothold in my life? Yes.*

I whispered, "Lord, I need Your help against my enemy who has taken my thoughts captive. Break these thoughts off of me, expose any lies of Satan, and remove my fear. Fill me with Your presence. Return me to a place of nearness toward You."

I felt something leave. It was gone.

# God Calling

*Hear me as I pray, O LORD. Be merciful and answer me! My heart has heard you say, "Come and talk with me." And my heart responds, "LORD, I am coming."* PSALM 27:7-8

I just love the picture that David paints in this psalm: God calling to us—asking us to visit with Him! Yet many Christians tell me they find it very difficult to regularly spend time with God. What's missing? I think we forget how *real and present* He is. . . .

Early in my Christian life, I was lulled into thinking that prayer was a spiritual discipline that I might master someday. Because I wasn't the "disciplined" type, I considered prayer an optional, only-when-desperate exercise.

But at age twenty-nine, I realized what I was doing and, more importantly, what I was missing! When I rushed out the door, too busy to meet with God, I was not only missing His counsel, but I was hurting His feelings.

At that juncture, I made a nonnegotiable decision to spend time with God every day. I changed my perspective and priorities about prayer and planned for our appointments one day in advance. I *finally understood* that prayer was the avenue through which I would learn to know God better.

Often, when speaking to any size audience, I ask, "What would you do if Jesus entered through the back door right now? Would you bow down on the floor in awe or sheepishly slide down into your seats? I bet you'd rush toward Him, try to get close, even touch Him. Surely you'd listen to what He had to say."

That's prayer. He waits for you to open your eyes in the morning! He has so much to tell you— I know He just loves when you say, "Lord, I'm coming!"

Why not make an appointment with the King—one day in advance—and keep it? It will change your life.

## World Changers

*Dear brothers and sisters, when I was with you I couldn't talk to you as*
*I would to spiritual people. I had to talk as though you belonged to this*
*world or as though you were infants in the Christian life. . . . And you still*
*aren't ready, for you are still controlled by your sinful nature.*
*You are jealous of one another and quarrel with each other.*
*Doesn't that prove you are controlled by your sinful nature?*
*Aren't you living like people of the world?* 1 CORINTHIANS 3:1-3

L ast night we had a little get-together at our house with
friends from church. When it came time for my husband to
share his prayer request, he shared something completely
surprising to all of us. He was deeply burdened. He began by
saying, "I don't know if people are naive, blind, or just plain rebellious, but so many of today's Christians—and I'm not talking
about new or baby Christians, I'm talking about those who have
been Christians for a while and are in leadership positions—act
like they don't even know God."

Dietrich Bonhoeffer apparently felt the same exasperation.
In *The Cost of Discipleship*, he wrote, "We are no longer sure that
we are members of a Church which follows its Lord. We must
therefore attempt to recover a true understanding of the mutual
relation between grace and discipleship. The issue can no longer
be evaded. It is becoming clearer every day that the most urgent
problem besetting our Church is this: How can we live the
Christian life in the modern world?"[2]

Over seven decades later, the same question, the same
urgency is on the lips of those who minister.

If we would focus on how to reflect our holy God in our daily
lives—we would absolutely change our world.

## Defining Delays

*The work on the Temple of God in Jerusalem had stopped, and it remained
at a standstill until the second year of the reign of King Darius of Persia.*

EZRA 4:24

The book of Ezra describes a delay in building the Temple of God. The story ends in Ezra 6:22 with a completed Temple and a huge celebration. What happened in between those verses can only serve as great encouragement to anyone who has ever heard God instruct him or her to build or rebuild an organization, facility, or ministry. Ezra's record of the Israelites' experience provides great insight into the tenacity it takes to follow the call of God.

Pastor Rick Warren's book *The Purpose-Driven Life* awakened an estimated 25 million people to the truth that each person has been created by God with a unique purpose he or she must fulfill in order to experience a meaningful life.

Yet common to all of us are the delays which hinder us from either discovering or fulfilling our life's purpose! In fact, when we experience even a *little* inconvenience and discomfort, or a lot of rejection, many of us find it easier to withdraw from—even give up—rather than *fight for* God's plan for our lives.

We must not focus on the difficulties or the delays—but keep looking with expectation—to the completion! As recorded in the book of Ezra, the building of the Temple would not have been completed if those who heard God's voice did not speak up and encourage others to rally, fight, build, and finish the work God assigned to them.

I encourage you (and myself) not to give up. Do whatever you can do today to move toward the finish line, to complete the project God has given you to do.

AUGUST 7

## In Position

*Ezra arrived in Jerusalem in August of that year. He had arranged to leave Babylon on April 8, the first day of the new year, and he arrived at Jerusalem on August 4, for the gracious hand of his God was on him. This was because Ezra had determined to study and obey the Law of the LORD and to teach those decrees and regulations to the people of Israel.*

EZRA 7:8-10

Y ou can almost become jealous of Ezra, who details four times (in chapters 7 and 8) how the "gracious hand of his God" was upon him!

If you have ever felt the gracious hand of your God upon you, you never forget it. It is just as Ezra describes . . . an unexpected door opens, someone with a necessary skill shows up out of the blue, or you are the recipient of something special you didn't earn or deserve.

In Ezra's account there are two agents involved in experiencing the gracious hand of your God.

The first agent is God Himself. He chose when, where, how, and with whom He would orchestrate the beautification of the Temple. Though Ezra sought God's instruction, obeyed His marching orders, and continually offered praise to God for the way He chose to help them, Ezra never took credit for the way the details fell together. He always pointed his fellow sojourners toward the power and person of God.

The second agent is a commitment to studying the ways and Word of God, as shown by Ezra. God favored Ezra because he "determined to study and obey the Law of the LORD" and teach it to God's followers.

Based on Ezra's example, those who diligently study God's Word recognize His voice. If they obey His Word, they will be in a position to receive His favor.

## Powerful Disciplines

*There by the Ahava Canal, I gave orders for all of us to fast and humble ourselves before our God. We prayed that he would give us a safe journey and protect us, our children, and our goods as we traveled.*

EZRA 8:21

I love this picture of Ezra, who is extremely motivated to accomplish a God-size task, but equally convinced that it won't happen without a total dependence upon God and utter fearlessness in front of unbelievers.

In this verse we are given the secret of where godly fearlessness is formed—in the powerful disciplines of fasting and prayer.

In the mid 1990s, Bill Bright, founder of Campus Crusade for Christ, delivered a similar impassioned call to the believers of his generation.

He called for two million believers to pray and fast for revival in America for forty days before the end of the year 2000. Through his challenge, people like me—not coworkers in his organization, but believers from every walk of life who shared his passion—responded to his call.

Some amazing men and women fasted forty days in a row. Others (like me) set aside forty nonconsecutive days to fast and pray over the designated period of time. In expectation, each of us waited and wondered how our prayers would impact the great commission.

On the last weekday of the year 2000, I was given the opportunity to share my testimony on a national network morning show. On December 29, 2000, in front of 2.5 million people, in only four minutes, I shared the story of how a janitor of a church led me, a suicidal alcoholic, to Jesus Christ in a simple prayer. I've never reached *more* people with the gospel message before or since that day.

# Hot Shower

*Don't you realize that those who do wrong will not inherit the Kingdom of God? Don't fool yourselves. Those who indulge in sexual sin, or who worship idols, or commit adultery, or are male prostitutes, or practice homosexuality, or are thieves, or greedy people, or drunkards, or are abusive, or cheat people—none of these will inherit the Kingdom of God. Some of you were once like that. But you were cleansed; you were made holy; you were made right with God by calling on the name of the Lord Jesus Christ and by the Spirit of our God.* 1 CORINTHIANS 6:9-11

Initially, I rationalized living with my boyfriend because "we loved each other and planned—someday—to marry." At times I felt ashamed of my lifestyle because I had been raised to believe that sexual promiscuity was wrong—but I always ignored the low level of guilt that hung over me . . . especially after a few drinks.

One night, everything changed when I had a sexual escapade with a stranger following a drinking binge. Not even knowing the name of the man by whom I could be pregnant, I fell into deep despair and such self-disgust that I quickly became suicidal.

I could no longer defend the life I was living. I hated myself.

When you find yourself that low, there is only One who still loves you. The Lord Jesus Christ found me, broken and ashamed.

In a simple prayer in front of a janitor of a little California hillside church, I confessed to Jesus every sin I could think of and asked for His forgiveness. The forgiveness came in a whoosh. I felt like I was standing in a hot shower while caked-on mud was dissolved from every part of my body. I stood under the shower for a long time . . . and I cried and cried and came out clean.

# Common Denominator

*They said to me, "Things are not going well for those who returned to the province of Judah. They are in great trouble and disgrace. The wall of Jerusalem has been torn down, and the gates have been destroyed by fire." When I heard this, I sat down and wept. In fact, for days I mourned, fasted, and prayed to the God of heaven.* NEHEMIAH 1:3-4

In every century, there are men and women who plead with God to revive the faith of His followers. And in every century, the word *revival* elicits as many negative as positive connotations when mentioned among believers!

Very often a revival is equated with an emotional meeting or a weeklong event. But a revival is a time when God greatly pours His Spirit out upon His people, calling them to a new level of holiness, resulting in a massive outreach to nonbelievers.

Revival accounts in every century, especially in America, reveal a common thread—they were birthed in prayer. Most often, revival beginnings can be traced back to a handful of humble, praying and fasting men and women who would not stop petitioning God until His Holy Spirit poured down on them.

Nehemiah was cupbearer to the king—and a praying man. When he heard of the captivity of God's people, he was burdened to fast and pray for an outpouring from God to change the situation. And God mightily used him—and his prayers—to bring about a national, spiritual change.

Charles Finney, D. L. Moody, and Bill Bright were also called out of their business positions by God to become ministers of the gospel and dynamically impact their generations. They were praying men first and foremost.

Prayer is the common denominator of every revival—does it have a significant and powerful place in your life?

## Fully Devoted

*I want you to be free from the concerns of this life. An unmarried man
can spend his time doing the Lord's work and thinking how to please him.
But a married man has to think about his earthly responsibilities and
how to please his wife.* 1 CORINTHIANS 7:32-33

I've observed that most single women want to get married as
soon as possible and most single men want to remain single
for as long as possible (secretly wondering if someone better
might come along). And just as often, those who are married
(especially with kids) daydream about their previous, carefree
single days!

In essence, most of us want what others have . . . or at least,
what we don't have.

Though Paul suggests serving the Lord is less complicated
as a single person, I believe it is possible, though not easy, to be
married and fully devoted to the Lord.

As a single adult and a new Christian, I immediately got
involved with a youth ministry organization that utilized as many
volunteers as they could recruit. There were so many single adults
who weekly met for training that the possibility of meeting someone with the same passion for serving the Lord was really great!

When my mentor and boss asked me to marry him, I had
a great assurance that he would help me fulfill my call in life
as much as I would encourage him to fulfill God's call. And at
every juncture, in almost thirty years of marriage, we have made
prayerful, mutual decisions about our family priorities, ministry
workloads, speaking/travel schedules, even sharing chores and
parenting roles that were not always traditional.

I contend that it is possible to stay focused on Christ whether
single or married—if each person keeps God first in his or her
life.

## Unseen Enemies

*Sanballat, Tobiah, Geshem the Arab, and the rest of our enemies found out that I had finished rebuilding the wall and that no gaps remained—though we had not yet set up the doors in the gates. . . . They were just trying to intimidate us, imagining that they could discourage us and stop the work. So I continued the work with even greater determination.*

NEHEMIAH 6:1, 9

Each year as I read through the book of Nehemiah, I am encouraged by Nehemiah's dogged determination and refusal to be intimidated by his enemies! I, perhaps like you, am continuously intimidated and distracted by negative thoughts and feelings—that keep me from doing God's work and following His plan for my life.

Our best defense in those situations is to acknowledge the truth: We have an enemy—the devil! Even so, many believers seem oblivious or uninformed about the spiritual forces that not only exist, but strategize to defeat them. First Peter 5:8-9 powerfully exposes the tactics of our enemy: "Stay alert! Watch out for your great enemy, the devil. He prowls around like a roaring lion, looking for someone to devour. Stand firm against him, and be strong in your faith."

In *The Screwtape Letters*, C. S. Lewis used a creative literary approach to expose the truth and tactics of a believer's unseen enemy. In the preface he writes, "There are two equal and opposite errors into which our race can fall about the devils. One is to disbelieve in their existence. The other is to believe, and to feel an excessive and unhealthy interest in them."[3]

Whether you share Nehemiah's tenacity or memorize 1 Peter 5:8, you must have a strategy against the devil—because he is not going to go away . . . ever.

# Solemn Assembly

*Ezra read from the Book of the Law of God on each of the seven days of the festival. Then on the eighth day they held a solemn assembly, as was required by law.* NEHEMIAH 8:18

A t a recent pastors' meeting, I was asked to share my strongest impressions while visiting the prayer rooms on twenty-three college campuses over a forty-day period beginning in January 2006. I began my talk with, "I stumbled over confession. . . ."

Though every campus had a uniquely designed prayer room, each had similar forms of prayer available—a wailing wall, a map of the nations, a healing wall to name those with special needs, and journals for recording prayers. But the surprising pattern that emerged on every campus was the sincere, tear-filled time of confession that most students experienced.

One campus in particular reflected the solemn assembly described in Nehemiah 9.

I spoke to the students at a chapel service that morning, asking them to simply consider coming to the prayer room some-time the following day. I was certain not all students considered prayer a priority—or even of interest—but I truly believed that if they just set aside time to be with God, He would be there to meet them.

By 11 p.m. over four hundred students had come through the prayer room doors. It was amazing to sit by the door and watch so many students enter with smiling, curious faces, but leave with tear-stained, humbled faces. Almost every student spoke of how God met them very personally, how His thoughts were deeply convicting, and how surprised they were with their compulsion to confess every known sin to Him.

Campus after campus, student after student, I stumbled over confession. . . .

## Sobriety Check

*The temptations in your life are no different from what others experience.
And God is faithful. He will not allow the temptation to be more than
you can stand. When you are tempted, he will show you a way out
so that you can endure.* 1 CORINTHIANS 10:13

I have a few friends whom I randomly e-mail to check on their sobriety from a variety of addictions.

I always hold my breath until I hear back from them. They are dear to me, but they seem unable to kick their specific addictions out of their lives—for good.

Here's the pattern: They can articulate exactly how God provided one of many, many escapes . . . which they ignored. Because they were either too lazy to implement these escapes or unwilling to say that their hideous sin had no real or damaging hold over them, they relapsed. Rarely will they admit that their addiction and continuous fall in the same area . . . is hurting and humiliating God as much as anyone.

It is not enough to understand that your temptation is common to others. It is not enough to feel remorse or shame. Those reasons won't help you overcome temptation. Victory comes when you admit to God and others that you need help and are willing to do whatever it takes to get sober or be set free from your temptation.

If you struggle with addiction, you cannot ignore God's methods of escape for you. You must look for and respond to His escape methods—which often, if not always include submitting to real accountability. Commit, today, to turn from that which tempts you . . . or you'll be its slave.

## So Broken

*The LORD hears his people when they call to him for help. He rescues them*
*from all their troubles. The LORD is close to the brokenhearted; he rescues*
*those whose spirits are crushed.* PSALM 34:17-18

I was on my way out of the building when I caught her eye. She was seated in the back of the large auditorium by herself. Her sad, somber eyes made me ask, "Would you like to pray?"

She nodded, not willing or able to say anything more. I sat in the row of seats in front of her so I could look into her eyes and hear her better . . . but I could barely hear her. Realizing that what she wanted to share was going to be painful, I asked if she preferred to move to another part of the auditorium so we could speak more privately.

She agreed. Her prayer request came in the form of questions: "How do you get over . . . ?" "How can you forgive . . . ?" "How can God love a person who . . . ?"

I couldn't ever remember hearing a story of worse abuse. I realized that she rarely spoke of her past to others. Yet the devastating effects were all over her. She was emotionally paralyzed and had become physically self-destructive. Life seemed almost impossible.

Though I could not pretend to understand her pain, I knew how to usher her into the Lord's presence. I knew He was able and willing to meet her and rescue her broken, battered heart. I just had to connect them to each other in prayer in that very moment. And from that moment, I have remained her friend . . . answering her many questions, exposing the lies that Satan continually feeds her, telling her just how much God loves her.

# Personal Holiness

*I purged out everything foreign and assigned tasks to the priests and Levites, making certain that each knew his work. I also made sure that the supply of wood for the altar and the first portions of the harvest were brought at the proper times. Remember this in my favor, O my God.*

NEHEMIAH 13:30-31

Over the past few years, I've been on a reading frenzy of the spiritual classics. Many are out of print; others are freshly covered and reprinted. One of the common threads I am finding is how anticultural these authors and their titles seem. For example, John Owen's *Sin and Temptation* or Dietrich Bonhoeffer's *The Cost of Discipleship* are just two examples of works that call readers to become revolutionaries for Christ—to be sold out to Him above all else. Other authors . . . William Wilberforce, Jonathan Edwards, Charles G. Finney, Hudson Taylor, and A. W. Tozer echo each other, causing readers like me to hunger for more of their noncontemporary, unfamiliar words. . . .

In fact, I have been drawn into the resurgence of the classic authors—and their biblical message—not by my peers, but by those either much, much younger or much older than I! It is as if many in my generation have rejected or perhaps never seen modeled the radical call to resolutely live holy lives.

For these authors holiness is not a onetime experience. It is a call to a continual purging. Perhaps holy living is more basic, more immediate than we allow?

Is the fire on the altar of your heart burning brightly? Have the daily sacrifices been burnt, the confessions made, and all things foreign purged?

"When Christ calls a man," says Bonhoeffer in *The Cost of Discipleship*, "he bids him come and die."[4]

# No Yelling

*It's better to live alone in the desert than with a quarrelsome, complaining wife.* PROVERBS 21:19

My husband has been known to throw out this verse to me every once in a while . . . as if it is biblical ammunition to make me feel ashamed of myself or at least back off. Well . . . it works! Fortunately, he usually rifles it at me in such a humorous manner that I can take it at face value, rather than as a personal attack. (Granted, that understanding comes after almost thirty years of marriage!)

Actually, within our first month of marriage, we came to an agreement that we were not going to have a "yelling home." There were many reasons for this. . . .

- Yelling is demeaning to the recipient.
- Screaming is unsettling to observers, especially children.
- Accusations are usually embellished and create new arguments.
- Defensiveness often escalates into harmful, irretrievable words.

You don't have to be married very long to admit that the best way to avoid a quarrel is never to get it started! But it takes two people to speak the truth in love, deal with conflict unemotionally (using a proven conflict-resolution system), and control anger. And though you might not always achieve success—it will be wise to make "no yelling" a standard in your marriage.

Developing healthy communication habits requires great effort and sincere intention. And of course, it isn't *always* or *only* the wife who starts a quarrel. But I'm convinced that when women diligently control their anger and emotions with their spouses and children, they create happier, emotionally safe homes for everyone.

# Lord Jesus

*I want you to know that no one speaking by the Spirit of God will curse Jesus, and no one can say Jesus is Lord, except by the Holy Spirit.*

1 CORINTHIANS 12:3

Before I came to Christ, I was asked if I could say the phrase "Jesus is Lord." I remember being unable to do so. I wasn't rebellious or resistant; I simply could not make those words come out of my mouth!

After becoming a Christian, the memory of that conversation came flooding back to me when I read this verse for the first time. It made sense. . . . When the Spirit of God is not in you, you cannot call Jesus your Lord!

Recently, I met a young man who was uncertain about the validity of the Bible. His uncertainty created an intense inner conflict, especially while attending an event for Christian leaders as his church's assigned leader! He confessed to me that he was unable to call himself a believer for intellectual reasons. He felt too ashamed to tell anyone of his uncertainty.

I asked, "Can you say, 'Jesus is Lord'?"

He could not.

I said, "Can you say that you believe Jesus died on the cross for your sins?"

He tried to whisper those words, but I could barely hear him. It was evident that he struggled to believe. I talked with him about the step of faith every Christian must take to accept Jesus' death on the cross as the payment for his sins.

I asked a second and a third time if he believed Jesus died on the cross for his sins. The third time, he spoke firmly as tears burst from his eyes. Then I asked him to tell God what he believed. . . . He didn't stop crying or praying for quite a while. . . .

## Fasting Prayer

*Esther said, "If it please the king, and if I have found favor with him, and if he thinks it is right, and if I am pleasing to him, let there be a decree that reverses the orders of Haman son of Hammedatha the Agagite, who ordered that Jews throughout all the king's provinces should be destroyed. For how can I endure to see my people and my family slaughtered and destroyed?"*

ESTHER 8:5-6

I f you haven't read the book of Esther, you owe it to yourself to read an account of two cousins whose bravery, obedience, honor, and fasting prayer—changed a nation! At least it will force you to examine your faith!

The story of Esther begins with the disposal of her predecessor, Queen Vashti, who refused to come to King Xerxes at his request. The search for a new queen was extensive, and Esther, a young Jewish orphan whose cousin Mordecai raised her when her parents died, was taken to the palace to be considered as a future queen. Xerxes was so delighted with her that he crowned her queen.

From then on the story becomes a nightmare! Haman, an enemy of the Jews, convinced the king to allow all the Jews in the land to be killed. Upon hearing this news, Mordecai went to Esther and begged her to go to the king to expose the plot, knowing that Esther could be killed for approaching the king without an invitation. Even so, she considered his request and called for a corporate, three-day time of fasting and prayer before visiting King Xerxes.

Honestly, it would take a movie to capture the astonishing twists that evolved as Haman's plot was overthrown and Mordecai promoted to a high position of leadership in the land!

If prayer and fasting can reverse the irreversible, you don't want to neglect them.

# Final Word

*Satan replied to the Lord, "Skin for skin! A man will give up everything
he has to save his life. But reach out and take away his health, and he will
surely curse you to your face!" "All right, do with him as you please," the
Lord said to Satan. "But spare his life."* JOB 2:4-6

I have a friend who is suffering with inoperable cancer. She is a
powerful prayer warrior, a mother of five boys, and a faithful
wife. It just doesn't seem fair.

It really doesn't make sense . . . until you read the biblical
record of Job's life. And even then, it is difficult to understand.

My friend never blames God for her illness. She consid-
ers herself in a battle waged against her by the most sinister of
enemies . . . she would tell you that she doesn't doubt that the
disease racking her body is in part retaliation for her years of
prayer for revival.

Our church has gone to battle with her.

Her friends have set up a forty-day schedule of nonstop prayer
and fasting for her healing before she makes further decisions
about the treatment that God would have her take against this
aggressive cancer.

We're all aware that we do not know how or when God is
going to move on her behalf. We know that He loves her, that
there is power in prayer and fasting, and that He invites us to ask
Him to answer impossible prayers.

We can neither judge nor speculate the reason a person goes
through something negative. But we can certainly come alongside
of them. In the end, we'll all see that God has the final word.

## Prayer Life

*Put your hope in the LORD. Travel steadily along his path. He will honor you by giving you the land. You will see the wicked destroyed.* PSALM 37:34

Hudson Taylor was a nineteenth-century British physician and missionary who took the gospel to China at a dangerous time in history.

What God asked of him and the God-size success that he achieved required such incredible sacrifice, humility, perseverance, and prayer . . . that it seemed Taylor possessed supernatural powers!

It is almost impossible to conceive how he sustained his faith during repeated bouts of poverty, loss, and personal tragedy. Both the continued legacy of his ministry and his undying love for God seem beyond the reach of the average Christian. Yet the only explanation for Hudson Taylor's exceptional life is his exceptional *prayer life*. The record of Taylor's mission work is not just sprinkled with prayer; his achievements were documented by prayer. His prayer life was. . .

- the source of his endless passion for the lost,
- the power behind incredible miracles,
- the strength to sustain his waiting upon God,
- the balm to comfort the loss of a child and spouse to illness, and
- the secret to his clear vision.

If there is any lesson that the average Christian might learn from Hudson Taylor, it is that the prayer life of a man or woman holds the key to success or failure for God.

Without hearing God's voice or being sustained by His Holy Spirit you simply cannot travel steadily down a long road that will deliver risk or pain. Without prayer, you will lose hope. But if you remain in constant communication with God, you will break through impossible barriers.

# Public Confession

*I am on the verge of collapse, facing constant pain. But I confess my sins;
I am deeply sorry for what I have done.* PSALM 38:17-18

A young friend almost drowned in her bathtub after a drunken binge. Shortly after returning from a treatment center, she joined a local group for addicts. As part of sustaining her sobriety, she helps other young women—especially those sober for only a few weeks. Her favorite phrase is "I keep my bottom close to me."

At meetings, she shares her story with broken, addicted people who are struggling. Of course, her friends and family have not always understood why she is so public about her shortcomings. For her, it is one of the most powerful ways to avoid a relapse.

Those who make public confessions find their power to be far greater than the power of secrecy. Public confession exposes the truth about our sin to others—which usually has a consequence. But except in cases when it would cause undue harm, confessing the truth to others forces us to humbly work toward reconciliation, ultimately finding healing and lifelong sobriety. (See James 5:16.)

Are there downsides to public confession? It is usually more humiliating, most often requires restitution, and its sting doesn't go away quickly—vivid reasons to keep you from going back to your sin. Isn't that the goal, anyway?

# The Janitor

*So, my dear brothers and sisters, be strong and immovable. Always work enthusiastically for the Lord, for you know that nothing you do for the Lord is ever useless.* 1 CORINTHIANS 15:58

I am forever grateful that a janitor named Ralph took time to talk to, pray with, and disciple me. He invited me to church and Bible studies, introduced me to other Christians, and helped me find a house to rent from a Christian woman when I needed to move. He even bought me a cassette player to play the Bible on tape!

Ralph has been my role model. I regularly find strangers along the way whom I know God has given to me; they are "mine."

Most recently I reached out to a young man at the corner store who shared his struggles with me.

Though he wasn't a follower of Christ, I enthusiastically talked with him about God—as if he really was interested. Then the day came when he became interested! I invited him to come to a Burning Hearts meeting on a local college campus. I knew he wasn't going to fit in—he knew it too. But he seemed more excited about coming to a prayer room than some of the Christians I know! He even had to arrange a ride to meet me there.

God seemed to be waiting for him. Upon entering the room, he opened up to me even more in a time of confession and asked Christ to come into his life. I gave him a book and a Bible . . . and kept inviting him to church and Bible studies.

It is the call and commission of every Christian to enthusiastically share Jesus with others! If you need encouragement to answer the call, take a class, read a book, and pray for courage!

# Stand Alone

*Be on guard. Stand firm in the faith. Be courageous. Be strong.*
*And do everything with love.* 1 CORINTHIANS 16:13-14

The current American collegiate culture is so steeped in sexual immorality and inebriation that it is no longer possible to ignore the impact it is having on our students. Thirty years ago, when I was a binge-drinking college student—it wasn't popular; I was considered "loose." Now "girls gone wild" is the rage! Those who seductively exhibit themselves stand out as datable, sexy, and popular. What used to be "loose" and vulgar is the standard to which many collegians aspire.

First Corinthians 16 is more pertinent to today's Christian than ever before. You cannot afford to be naive or unaware. If you are a young adult who is so hungry for love that you'll do anything to get it, you are a vulnerable target to those looking to consume the precious innocence of others.

I don't believe I'm overestimating the onslaught of sexual promiscuity, pornography, or drunkenness prevalent on American college campuses. You only have to spend a few days on a campus to see it for yourself.

In fact, Vigen Guroian, a professor at Loyola College, confirmed my assessment. Guroian warned about the promiscuity among college students[5]—yet his warning didn't seem to make the kind of impact I thought it would.

So who or what *will* make a difference? One student, one family, one administrator at a time must stand firm against the trends of culture.

In the end, you must guard your heart, refusing to partake in those things that compromise your faith. Indeed, you might well have to stand alone to be a courageous *Christian* man or woman in your culture.

It won't kill you to stand alone, but it could save your life.

## Comfort Others

*He comforts us in all our troubles so that we can comfort others.
When they are troubled, we will be able to give them the same
comfort God has given us.* 2 CORINTHIANS 1:4

A ugust 26 is the day every year that I celebrate—with more enthusiasm than the day I was born—my spiritual birthday—the day a janitor led me to Christ.

On that day, I told everyone what God had done for me. Most of my friends and coworkers were not terribly excited that I had "become religious," but they couldn't deny that my foul mouth and drunken, immoral craziness had come to a dramatic halt.

After a few months, my enthusiasm . . . didn't wear off! And it seemed best that I leave California and return home to start my life over.

Upon returning to Cleveland, I went to my local high school. I was compelled to talk to teenagers—to tell them what I'd found: true love. I knew what students were looking for!

God had a plan for my life at that high school. Within a year, I became a youth worker there. And it was the beginning of a thirty-year (so far) ministry to students.

I am still passionate about telling people of all ages, especially students, that God loves them. I have never forgotten the day God intervened to change the course of my life. I love to tell others how He forgave me and gave me a second chance . . . to comfort others in the way that I have been comforted.

Yes, I absolutely love to celebrate my spiritual birthday.

## A Person

*It is God who enables us, along with you, to stand firm for Christ.*
*He has commissioned us, and he has identified us as his own by placing*
*the Holy Spirit in our hearts as the first installment that guarantees*
*everything he has promised us.* 2 CORINTHIANS 1:21-22

Twentieth-century pastor and author A. W. Tozer gave a
powerful perspective on the Person of the Holy Spirit in
his books *The Pursuit of God*, *The Knowledge of the Holy*, and
*Keys to the Deeper Life*.

> *The Holy Spirit is a Person. He is not enthusiasm. He is not cour-*
> *age. He is not energy. . . . The Holy Spirit can communicate with you*
> *and can love you. He can be grieved when you resist and ignore Him.*
> *He can be quenched as any friend can be shut up if you turn on him*
> *when he is in your home as a guest. Of course, he will be hushed into*
> *hurt silence if you wound him, and we can wound the Holy Spirit.*
> *That is the reason most people don't want to be filled with the Holy*
> *Spirit—they want to live the way they want to live and merely have*
> *the Holy Spirit as a bit of something extra. I can tell you the Holy*
> *Spirit will not be an addition. The Holy Spirit must be Lord, or He*
> *will not come at all.*[6]

Consider your life. God has commissioned you and identi-
fied you as His own *by placing the Holy Spirit in your heart as the first*
*installment. . . .*

Have you invited the Holy Spirit into every area of your life?
Is there any part of your current lifestyle that has wounded Him?
Is there any way you push the Holy Spirit away from you? Are you
filled with the Holy Spirit?

# Depression Antidote

*Why am I discouraged? Why is my heart so sad? I will put my hope in God!*
*I will praise him again—my Savior and my God! . . . But each day the*
*LORD pours his unfailing love upon me, and through each night*
*I sing his songs, praying to God who gives me life.* PSALM 42:5-6, 8

I n this psalm, David describes a season of life that every believer
encounters: discouragement.

In fact, perhaps the most comforting aspect of the psalms
is that they candidly reveal the emotional battles that God's
anointed leaders so often faced. Not ignoring their feelings, they
expressed them to God in the expectation that He would touch
their lives and resolve their situations. We should have no less
expectation that God is present and willing to reach into our lives.

One of the most encouraging, faith-empowering authors who
taught the way through despair was Charles Spurgeon. An English
preacher, Spurgeon pastored the world's largest independent
congregation during the nineteenth century. If you read excerpts
of his sermons, you'll know why he was so popular. He inspired
indomitable faith, making it attainable for the average believer.

Spurgeon wrote, "Under no conceivable circumstances ever
give place for an instant to the dark thought that God is not true
and faithful to His promises. You may not know why He deals
with you so strangely, but never think that He is unfaithful for an
instant. Never cease your prayers. No time is wrong for prayer.
The glare of daylight should not tempt you to cease, and the
gloom of midnight should not make you stop your cries."[7]

Wishing, worrying, complaining will not change things.
Prayer changes people and circumstances.

When you have nothing to hold on to, not even hope, you
have prayer.

# Covenant Eyes

*I made a covenant with my eyes not to look with lust at a young woman.*

JOB 31:1

I was a very new Christian when I became a youth ministry volunteer. At the time, I had not read through the entire Bible. In fact, I had probably only read portions of the New Testament and none of the Old Testament. The book of Job was not on the top of my reading list.

Our volunteer staff was made up primarily of single Christians in their twenties. It was really fun to attend staff meetings, weekend camps, and weekly club meetings!

Our leader, Roger—an older Christian than most of us— was also single. He had been through a very devastating experience in a previous relationship, so his perspective on dating—or even flirting—was much more reserved than those of us who were younger in the faith.

In many aspects, we were immature. To look in from the outside, you might have observed that we weren't much different from the culture around us—except for Roger. He seemed more cautious, more responsible. When our conversations inevitably turned to dating, love, sex, or marriage, he would always refer us to Scripture. He reminded us to base every aspect of our lives on what the Bible taught, not on how our peers lived.

We were all taken by surprise when Roger gave us his standard for relating to women, referring to the verse above from Job. I remembered thinking, *Who even reads the book of Job?*

We all admired the standard Roger set for us—even though it was quite the opposite of our culture. We understood that the integrity with which he treated the women on his staff was the way God wanted us to relate to each other, and especially the young students we mentored.

## Tough Skin

*We are pressed on every side by troubles, but we are not crushed. We are*
*perplexed, but not driven to despair. We are hunted down, but never*
*abandoned by God. We get knocked down, but we are not destroyed.*

2 CORINTHIANS 4:8-9

The early Christians lived under intense persecution. Certainly they didn't enjoy beatings, imprisonment, or trials, but they did expect them. And when they came, the believers faced them courageously.

The early church was tough.

The modern Western church? Many of us are more likely to encounter difficult situations and consider them unfair or not worth the fight. We quickly ask, "Why me?" We struggle with entitlement. Our observers don't usually perceive us as strong.

I remember the words a friend snarled at me when he discovered I had recently become a Christian. It felt like he wanted to shame me into running back to the pigpen. As if to inform me of what everyone else knew, he said, "Becky, Christians are weak people. They need a crutch."

I refused to turn my back on the God who loved me, so I turned my back on my friend. Though it scared me to let go of someone I could see in order to hold on to Someone invisible— I did it anyway. Looking back, I exhibited more courage in that moment than I ever did as a nonbeliever. It was just the beginning of getting knocked down and having to get up. . . .

Truth be told, the Christian life is a pretty tough life. It requires tough skin. It takes dogged persistence not to give up or give in. It means fighting for what is worthwhile, even if you fight alone.

Today, if you find yourself overwhelmed or troubled, grab on to Paul's encouragement for living the Christian life. (For further reading see 2 Corinthians 4:6-7.)

# Go Outside

*The lazy person claims, "There's a lion out there! If I go outside,*
*I might be killed!"* PROVERBS 22:13

I n the midst of a series on Proverbs, my pastor recently used this verse. He made quite a funny observation. He reminded us that in the middle of Israel there are very few lions roaming the streets. So for a person to make a lion his excuse for not going outside was rather irrational! The point he made? Most excuses *are* irrational!

Whether we are lazy or procrastinating or afraid, if we pay attention to the excuses we make, they can serve as helpful indicators of what is really going on inside of us!

Zig Ziglar, a motivational speaker and businessman who inspired many leaders through his presentations and resources, said, "Fear, to a degree, makes procrastinators and cowards of us all."[8]

Fear paralyzes. And it doesn't even have to be real or rational to keep us from "going outside"!

Fear immobilizes. It can lead to panic, worry, laziness, or procrastination.

Fear is a powerful barrier to hinder us from achieving even the smallest tasks.

Fear *can* be overcome. Like any other barrier, it must be removed!

The next time you hear an irrational excuse come from your mouth, say a prayer. Whisper (or shout) the name of Jesus and tell the lie, fear, or temptation to leave. And if your fear is rooted in jealousy, envy, or even hate, ask God to immediately fill you with His love and give you courage to "go outside."

## First Job!

*This means that anyone who belongs to Christ has become a new person.*
*The old life is gone; a new life has begun! And all of this is a gift from*
*God, who brought us back to himself through Christ. And God has given us*
*this task of reconciling people to him. . . . So we are Christ's ambassadors;*
*God is making his appeal through us. We speak for Christ when we plead,*
*"Come back to God!"* 2 CORINTHIANS 5:17-18, 20

I often wonder what my life would be like if the janitor who led me to Christ had not taken his discipling role so seriously. Immediately after praying together, he quoted 2 Corinthians 5:17 to me and boldly told me that I was new—my old life was gone! Can you imagine how liberating that thought would be to such a sinner? My past was so ugly and the consequences of my behavior loomed so large that to be told that somehow God was going to make my life new gave me incredible hope.

But that was not all. He shared even more of 2 Corinthians 5 with me. He said, "Now, you've been given a job to reconcile others to God, to be Christ's ambassador!" Again, I was amazed that someone as lowly as I would be so undeservedly and immediately entrusted with the Good News.

I went back to work that afternoon and asked the girl at the switchboard to come to church with me on Sunday. It took some begging, but she came. After the service, I asked her to meet with the janitor. She prayed the same prayer I'd prayed days earlier, asking Jesus into her heart.

We went to work on Monday wondering, *Who can we tell now?*

## True Ministers

*We live in such a way that no one will stumble because of us, and no one will find fault with our ministry.* 2 CORINTHIANS 6:3

I t is easy to look at these verses and judge how your minister is ministering. But the New Testament makes it clear that all believers in the Lord Jesus Christ are ministers of the gospel! We *each* have spiritual gifts in order to be an active part of His church.

In your home, workplace, and neighborhood, you are God's messenger! Because the Holy Spirit of the living God resides in you, you have an assignment to reach out to others with His love.

What might it look like to be a minister in your home, if you live with roommates or family members? Begin by carefully choosing the entertainment you view or hear in your home. Talk often about the Bible. Pray at meals and bedtimes. Pray regularly for those in your home, for friends and other family members. Prayer is a very powerful ministry.

When you see yourself as a minister in your workplace, it will impact how you talk, act, and present the gospel. Start a prayer group with other Christians before work. Pray for each person you work with by name.

Finally, being a minister in your neighborhood includes caring for the people on your block and at your corner shopping center. Discuss your faith while waiting in line. Invite people to church. Pray for them regularly. Speak kindly toward them (even when it is difficult). And be aware of the impromptu times they might need your practical help.

When you see yourself as God's minister—it gives your life purpose from the moment you wake up until your head hits the pillow each night.

## Come Out

*Therefore, come out from among unbelievers, and separate yourselves from them, says the Lord. Don't touch their filthy things, and I will welcome you. And I will be your Father, and you will be my sons and daughters, says the Lord Almighty.* 2 CORINTHIANS 6:17-18

Shortly after becoming a Christian, I looked for the person with whom I had spent the night during my last drunken binge. He was a popular athlete in my hometown. I wanted to tell him that I was an alcoholic and could never drink again. More importantly, I wanted to share how I became a Christian. Finally, I wanted him to know that as a Christian, sex outside of marriage was wrong in God's eyes. Because I had slept with him, I was humiliated and sorry.

The only place I knew to find him was the local college bar. When I asked if I could speak with him, he was friendly and suggested we sit in a booth.

I was so nervous. He graciously listened, and I never walked into the bar again after that night.

At the time, I had no idea what significance either my public confession or profession of faith would have upon my reputation.

A few years later, I became the cheerleading coach and Campus Life Director at the public high school. The games were played at the college football field where many of the town's former and current college athletes sat in box seats along with the high school coaches. Every home game, I would have to step down his row, in front of him and his wife. My credibility in ministry hinged upon our conversation years earlier and my willingness to honor God.

## Final Celebration

*A good reputation is more valuable than costly perfume. And the day you die is better than the day you are born.* ECCLESIASTES 7:1

The thought that "the day you die is better than the day you are born" never seemed to make sense to me until I heard a pastor preach about it. He was sharing about the life of one of the young elders in his church who had recently and unexpectedly died. The young father was a great contributor to the community and an exemplary follower of Christ.

In fact, the impact he made on the entire community—not just the church—was beyond what anyone could have imagined. The pastor revealed that the many trips and fun events the young man attended were not the memories that were discussed by those at the funeral. It was his character, the way he boldly shared Christ with others, his generosity, and the incredible leadership skills and passion for God that he exhibited that people talked about.

Those most touched by his life had been challenged to know God better because of him.

In reflecting upon the young man's life during the week leading up to the funeral, it was apparent that it was not his life but his death that caused everyone to consider more seriously their own mortality and their walk with God, and to honestly assess the impact their lives were making on others.

Yes, a funeral has a refining influence on us—it can be a celebration of a life well lived for Christ and a catalyst for reflection and renewal in the lives that were touched by the one who died!

# Don't Forget

*Don't let the excitement of youth cause you to forget your Creator.*
*Honor him in your youth before you grow old and say,*
*"Life is not pleasant anymore."* ECCLESIASTES 12:1

A 2003 Barna report revealed a 58 percent drop in church attendance of those eighteen to twenty-nine years old.[1] Of course, this information had a lot of older adults in an uproar! Teams of men and women from every denomination and student ministry frantically assessed the cause, to determine what could be done to change this downward direction.

I have a few suggestions that might bring some "bored" students and empty nesters together in your ministry:

*Increase your youth budget.* If you are on a church or youth ministry board, raise more money for activities, speakers, and bands. Because students love excitement, they'll go where the action is! Arrange adventure trips and invite older adults to come along. Let their wisdom and love for the Lord rub off on the young ones.

*Improve your youth facilities.* Build (or rent) a basketball gym, a workout center, or a coffee lounge. Add a foosball table and a Ping-Pong table, and secure an outside field for softball or soccer. Since most students love sports, regularly bring in Christian athletes to speak to every age-group. You'll have so many kids and so much excitement that the old coaches and cooks in your organization will have to come out of retirement!

*Increase your volunteer staff.* Ask members with boats, vacation homes, or mountain cabins to donate their prized possessions for a weekend.

When young adults are genuinely cared for, called, visited, regularly e-mailed, and prayed for . . . over an extended period of time, they won't want to disappoint you or God.

Don't forget what it is like to be young!

# Dual Purpose

*We are careful to be honorable before the Lord, but we also want everyone
else to see that we are honorable.* 2 CORINTHIANS 8:21

There are few men and women who have mastered the "dual
purpose" life—living honorable lives in front of God *and*
others.

I am very fortunate that my greatest living example of a God-
honoring man has lived with me for over twenty-nine years!

When I first met Roger, he was a relatively young Christian.
And because he had not been raised in an evangelical Christian
home, he had few role models by which to frame his walk with
God.

The first week he was a Christian, his public school secretary
invited him to a week of special services at her church. His walk
with God began with regular church attendance and daily Bible
reading—and it has remained the same for over thirty-five years.

Within a few short years, he was asked to lead a citywide
evangelical youth ministry. He took his responsibility very seriously—when the first payroll could not be met, he withdrew the
balance from his savings account.

With the permission of culture to be sexually promiscuous,
he chose not to kiss or date the woman he asked to marry him
(me), even though his fiancée would have been less strict! Though
engaged, he remained sexually pure until the honeymoon.

While on their honeymoon, when he realized his new wife
could never drink, this new husband (of one day) decided he
would join her in abstaining from alcohol all the days of their
marriage.

My husband's walk with God has modeled to me and others
that a God-honoring life *is achievable* for the average man or woman.

## Exclusive Lover

*I am my lover's, and he claims me as his own.* SONG OF SONGS 7:10

I recently heard a college professor teach on the inability of today's single adults to *get* married, much less *stay* married. He felt that the greatest hindrance to marriage is the fear of unhappiness. People are simply afraid that if they get married, someone better will come along. He suggested that men especially have a strong resistance to commitment and blamed the surge of images of beautiful women in magazines, in movies, on the Internet, or on television. He contended that these images skew reality, causing single men and women to expect the majority of the dating pool to be made up of perfect bodies, sparkling white teeth, and endless infatuation.

Because those images are simply *not* (nor ever have been) what determines true love, expectations of the opposite sex are completely unrealistic, and relationships quickly fizzle. . . .

By the twenty-first century, the average age of newlyweds has crept higher, as has the divorce rate.

History suggests that there is only one rule to having one lover for life: Divorce is not an option. My parents and in-laws were married over fifty years. Though all fifty years were not "happy," they stuck to the no-divorce rule.

For any generation, fidelity requires a firm, nonnegotiable commitment to honor your spouse by keeping your eyes and heart focused on him or her all the days of your life!

Though it takes effort to keep your mind and eyes on one person all the days of your life, the Song of Songs is surely the book in the Bible in which to find ways to explore the more physical aspects of becoming a great lover.

Don't miss reading the entire book with your spouse.

## Settle This

*"Come now, let's settle this," says the LORD. "Though your sins are like scarlet, I will make them as white as snow. Though they are red like crimson, I will make them as white as wool."* ISAIAH 1:18

Every individual of every generation must not take for granted the cost of salvation and forgiveness. Neither can it be bought or earned. Only God can take a stained, broken, rebellious sinner and make him or her spotless and holy.

Andrew Murray, a nineteenth-century South African pastor and evangelist, deeply wanted believers to understand God's dynamic invitation to be holy. In *Holy in Christ*, he wrote, "Happy is the soul who is willing to learn the lesson that, all along, it is going to be the simultaneous experience of weakness and power, of emptiness and filling, of deep humiliation and the wonderful indwelling of the Holy One."[2]

Murray suggests that you will only understand how to live a holy life with God when you settle the matter of sin in your life.

Sin stains you. Therefore, you must actively be cleansed from it. You must regularly acknowledge any known sin, repent of it, and receive forgiveness for it. The repentance process, as Murray suggests, is lifelong. You must be willing to identify your weaknesses and the enemy's continual attempts to divide you from God.

You simply cannot be a happy Christian unless you are clean before God! Let the joy that comes with true repentance and forgiveness be your lifelong pursuit. Invite the indwelling power of the Holy Spirit to enter your life on a daily basis.

# Be Discerning

*Even Satan disguises himself as an angel of light.* 2 CORINTHIANS 11:14

∽

Have you ever asked yourself, How does Satan disguise himself as an angel of light in my life?

*First*, you must admit that Satan exists—that he is real and destructive. If you have yet to be convinced, just open the Bible. Satan is everywhere. . . . He came to Eve as a talking snake (Genesis 3), tempting her to question her God. Satan also appeared before God in the book of Job, suggesting that Job only loved God because God blessed him so abundantly. And of course, Satan tempted Jesus while He was in the desert (Matthew 4).

*Second*, you must be alert. The devil hates you and God. In the Word of God, believers are given ample ammunition to expose the many ways Satan comes to God's chosen people to torment, tempt, ridicule, blind, and even curse them.

*Third*, you must recognize that Satan often works through other people. You must carefully discern when others claim to speak to you on God's behalf.

1. Does the message agree with God's written Word? It is *always* a red flag when a word of counsel disagrees with God's Word. God's Word is God's voice.
2. Is it in line with the counsel of those in authority over you? If godly counselors who are praying for God's will in your life do not feel that God is directing you to follow a certain path, it is best to ask God to bring more clarity to all of you, rather than move ahead impulsively.
3. Is the Holy Spirit confirming this word to you? Do you sense His conviction or comfort? If you feel cautious or confused . . . wait a bit longer for God to confirm His direction before proceeding.

Be discerning . . . every day.

## Give Back

*I will sacrifice a voluntary offering to you; I will praise your name,*
*O LORD, for it is good. For you have rescued me from my troubles*
*and helped me to triumph over my enemies.* PSALM 54:6-7

One of my favorite classic movies is *White Christmas*. It is the story of a soldier (an army private) who valiantly saves an officer's life by putting himself between a falling building and the officer. Though the private isn't seriously injured, the officer still feels obligated and indebted to him for the rest of his life. This harrowing experience knits them together, even after the war.

The psalmist expresses a similar gratitude toward God—who saved him numerous times. The psalmist's sense of indebtedness toward God became his passion and commitment. And in using the word *sacrifice*, the psalmist implies that his gift was not easy to give or without great cost.

Over your lifetime, you will have numerous opportunities to give an offering to the Lord. And unless you are careful, you may fall into the trap of giving back to God that which is either expected of you (a monthly tithe check) or in comparison to what others give. Instead, let the words of the psalmist remind you of the one or many days that God saved you from your enemies or spared your life. Allow the word *sacrifice* to cause you to reflect on the cost of sin Christ paid on the cross that you might have eternal life! Then prayerfully consider how you might give a voluntary offering to God. Make a list of all the possibilities, praying over each daily. Over the next sixty days, watch and see if small or large doors open, prompting you to turn one or more of those possibilities into reality.

# All-Powerful Jesus

*For a child is born to us, a son is given to us. The government will rest on his shoulders. And he will be called: Wonderful Counselor, Mighty God, Everlasting Father, Prince of Peace.* ISAIAH 9:6

Over two thousand years ago and today, Jesus' name is controversial and divisive. Yet those of us who call Him our God, who love Him and know Him, most affectionately call Him . . .

*Wonderful Counselor.* The greatest tangible experience that a believer has is the ability to talk to Jesus and listen to Him. Prayer is the free, available path of communication in which a believer of any age can come to God and receive counsel. Through the presence of God's Holy Spirit, Jesus comforts, advises, and corrects those who are His.

*Mighty God.* History reveals the God of all creation is also the personal God of men and women. We always have access to the all-powerful, all-knowing, ever-present Mighty God who is above all gods.

*Everlasting Father.* Jesus, the Only Son of the One True God, gave His life that we might call His Father our Father, and His God our God. That He provided a way for every man and woman to come to the Father through His death on the cross is beyond human reasoning.

*Prince of Peace.* The world will not know real peace until every knee bows at the name of Jesus. The Bible clearly states that no other name is given on earth or in heaven by which we can be saved (see Acts 4:12). Therefore, we wait in great expectation for the day when the Prince of Peace, Jesus Himself, will come again. . . .

# Old Sins

*Yes, I am afraid that when I come again, God will humble me in your presence. And I will be grieved because many of you have not given up your old sins. You have not repented of your impurity, sexual immorality, and eagerness for lustful pleasure.* 2 CORINTHIANS 12:21

Paul was obviously frustrated! And impurity, sexual immorality, and eagerness for lust are not just the tantalizing temptations of believers two thousand years ago—they are the *very same temptations* faced by today's average believer! We are barraged with images and invitations on our cell phones, televisions, computers, and movie screens to join in the sexual excitement of our culture. The common sins of the early church remain the constant sins of today's church.

I have seen sex lure Christians from two angles. (1) Christians who've stayed clear of sexual temptation mistakenly and naively think they could never be caught unaware—and they often get caught in compromising situations. (2) Christians who as nonbelievers were consumed by sexual sin find it incredibly difficult to abstain from lustful pleasures as Christians. They live in a relentless battle for their purity.

If this battle is yours, don't rationalize it or try to fight it alone. Get help. Spot it and blot it out of your heart and mind—*one temptation or decision at a time.* Think of it as a path or a doorway. Don't take one step down the path to it. Turn away from it. Kill any passion for it. Defy it, rather than letting it defy God in you.

Impurity, sexual immorality, or eagerness for lustful pleasure is actually easy to spot. So don't tolerate it in your friends, classmates, or leaders! Don't be silent. Say something. Do something.

# Drink Deeply

*In that day you will sing:"I will praise you, O LORD! You were angry with me, but not any more. Now you comfort me. See, God has come to save me. I will trust in him and not be afraid. The LORD GOD is my strength and my song; he has given me victory." With joy you will drink deeply from the fountain of salvation!* ISAIAH 12:1-3

I know so well the feeling of humility that comes over a person who is the recipient of God's willingness to forgive him or her over and over.

Because I've been so greatly and so often forgiven, I'll be the first to confess that forgiveness is almost intoxicating.

It comforts. It covers your body with warmth and healing.

It relieves fear. Lies are exposed and must flee away.

It removes guilt. The shame of sin is gone when you are forgiven.

It restores. That which was lost or seemed irretrievable is once again approachable.

It is refreshing. The fresh, cleansing waters of forgiveness wash over your repentant soul to purify you.

It is mind altering. When you are freely given another chance—when you are undeservedly redeemed—you are emotionally lifted from one frame of mind to another. Your past is now separate from your future.

Forgiveness must be understood and accepted in order for it to do its restorative, transforming work.

A friend of mine struggles with *feeling* forgiven. He thinks he must deserve it or pay someone back before he can receive it. I beg him to honestly confess his sin to God, accept His forgiveness, then drink deeply from the fountain of salvation!

# God's Approval

*Obviously, I'm not trying to win the approval of people, but of God.*
*If pleasing people were my goal, I would not be Christ's servant.*

GALATIANS 1:10

It is no easy thing to live for God's approval when your whole world revolves around your friends, job, or family. But *unless you set your heart and mind on doing all things to please God . . .* you'll most likely do all things to please yourself or others.

William Law, a seventeenth-century Anglican priest and author of *A Serious Call to a Devout and Holy Life*, wrote extensively on this very dilemma. He makes the point that pleasing God will always come into conflict with pleasing others or ourselves. Pleasing God is an ongoing decision each Christian must make. . . .

Though Law wrote these words over three hundred years ago, they sound as if they could be written to you and me!

> *If we can find any Christians that sincerely intend to please God in all their actions as the best and happiest thing in the world, whether they be young or old, single or married, men or women, if they have but this intention, it will be impossible for them to do otherwise.*
> *. . . I have chosen to explain this matter by appealing to this intention because it makes the case so plain, and because everyone that has a mind may see it in the clearest light and feel it in the strongest manner, only by looking into his own heart.*[3]

What you set your heart on, you will possess.
What you chase after, you will become.

If you will chase after the sacred with the same passion as you have chased after personal pleasure or man's approval, you will be amazed at the unexplainable satisfaction you receive from pleasing God with your life and choices.

# Each Morning

*As for me, I will sing about your power. Each morning I will sing with joy about your unfailing love. For you have been my refuge, a place of safety when I am in distress.* PSALM 59:16

Prayer . . .

It is a place of silence and solitude and safety, as well as singing.

It is the place in which you are shaped, not by the world, but by the breath of God.

It is a time of retreat. It is a time of reflection. It is a time of self-examination. It takes time.

It is the moment when soul meets Savior.

It is the place of anointing received, power imparted, wisdom divulged.

It is a time of waiting. It is a time of submitting.

It is a time of listening. It is a time to make decisions and commitments.

It is both a refuge and a school.

It is the place to shake off your addictions and compulsions, and expose the lies.

It is a moment—or hour—of truth.

It removes thirst and satisfies hunger.

It restores and nurtures your soul.

It is the place to find your healing.

It is where you receive hope for living and courage for dying.

He waits for you each morning. . . . Come and meet with the King.

# High Bar

*My old self has been crucified with Christ. It is no longer I who live, but Christ lives in me. So I live in this earthly body by trusting in the Son of God, who loved me and gave himself for me.* GALATIANS 2:20

As a young Christian woman and youth worker, I attended a conference where Elisabeth Elliot was the keynote speaker. Author of *Through Gates of Splendor* and wife of martyred missionary Jim Elliot, Elisabeth is an amazing testimony of a woman resolved to "live and die" for Christ.

Witnessing her passion for the Lord despite the incredibly difficult trials she faced as a young missionary, mother, and widow left an indelible impression upon me. She certainly raised the bar for those of us who complained about rather uncomfortable lives.

Her every lecture took my breath away. What she experienced in the name of Christ seemed so unfair, so impossible to overcome . . . yet she did so with God's power. Even after the loss of her second husband to cancer, she still had no complaints. She was not discouraged. Never did her love for God diminish.

Her goal over the weekend retreat was to challenge us to memorize Scripture. We learned Galatians 2:20—the theme verse of her life. By the end of the retreat, it was our desire and theme as well.

I have never forgotten the verse or forgotten the cost Elisabeth Elliot paid to live the Christian life. She showed me how to live for God and love Him at all times—not only when it is easy!

When Elisabeth told God that she would give her life to Him because He loved her and gave His life for her . . . she meant it and she did it.

You have set the bar high, Elisabeth.

SEPTEMBER 17

## Perfect Peace

*You will keep in perfect peace all who trust in you, all whose thoughts are fixed on you!* ISAIAH 26:3

One of the greatest benefits of knowing God is the immediate access you have to His presence, His power, and especially His peace. Isaiah spoke of it. Jesus spoke of it. (See John 14:27.) There is nothing like it. And no one else but God can deliver perfect peace.

Parents especially need the peace of God.

Because life with children is full of detours and decisions, a parent can easily lose God's peace if he or she gives in to worry!

After over twenty-eight years of experience as a parent, I am convinced that only prayer can bring immediate peace to a mother's soul and usher God's power into any situation. And not just prayer for what you want, but praying God's will for your children.

In fact, praying Scriptures for my son is the best way I know how to pray for God's will for his life!

In a favorite resource of mine, *Praying the Scriptures for Your Children* by Jodie Berndt,[4] there are special verses for any situation a child might face. This book has been a most valuable and practical guide, directing me to pray specific verses for my son's future, his relationships, and his character development.

Most importantly, when I pray God's Word, I receive that perfect, unshakeable peace, knowing that I can trust God—who loves my son even more than I do—to direct his steps.

So often, just ten minutes of praying the Scriptures for my child relieves my fear and fills me with hope and confidence!

Perfect peace comes when we consciously release our worries . . . and fix our thoughts on God and His life-changing Word.

# One Family

*There is no longer Jew or Gentile, slave or free, male and female. For you are all one in Christ Jesus.* GALATIANS 3:28

It is the most phenomenal experience to realize you've just become part of a new family when you ask Christ into your life. You immediately have a Father who loves you and all kinds of people you never knew before in your area who genuinely care about you. It is truly amazing to converse with people you've known only briefly and hear yourself spontaneously divulging some of your most intimate thoughts or personal flaws to them, even asking them to pray for you.

I can vividly remember how I felt when people of every race, age, and gender made me feel loved, not condemned; forgiven, not judged; free, not restricted—just because I was a follower of Christ! I also remember feeling nurtured by the surrogate mothers, fathers, sisters, and brothers who had entered my life.

It is so powerful to be loved when you don't deserve it, to be connected with mature Christians who don't judge you for your past, who welcome you with open arms, inviting you into their already busy lives!

I'm sure my early Christian experience is one of the reasons why I make it a point to talk to strangers to find out if they are in God's family, to see if they need something—a Bible, a church . . . anything! Even if they have complaints, I try to bring some type of godly counsel into their situations.

But if I find out that someone is not in the family of God, then I feel obligated to invite him or her to consider becoming a new member!

Are you in the family?

# Thirsty Soul

*O God, you are my God; I earnestly search for you. My soul thirsts for you;*
*my whole body longs for you in this parched and weary land where*
*there is no water.* PSALM 63:1

D o you love to pray? The Psalms clearly make known that heartfelt, passionate prayer happens when you are truly searching for God. If you are tentative, rebellious, or not willing to surrender yourself to God—prayer will be much less passionate and potent.

The psalmist shows us how to access God's presence—by asking for it! He teaches us to pray, "Lord, I'm seeking You today—Your counsel, thoughts, and love. My soul is thirsty for *only* You! I want to be near You."

Henrietta Mears, mentor to so many Christian leaders and young adults in the twentieth century, was widely known for the way she expressed herself to God in prayer. *Dream Big: The Henrietta Mears Story*, by Earl Roe, provides a vivid description of her prayer life.

She required all college leaders to attend a weekly 6 a.m. prayer meeting in which she "would already be on her knees as students trooped in to join her. . . . After reading the Word and with very little discussion, . . . she would then make a few brief remarks on the greatness of God and His willingness to answer believing prayers. Then down on their knees the group would go."

Roe's book also mentions, "To hear her pray in this intimate fellowship was an unforgettable experience. She climbed right to the bastions of heaven and threw the doors open for a fuller view of God. . . . The most prominent characteristic of her praying was her complete enthrallment with the person of Christ. She knew Him and He knew her."[5]

Do you know this kind of passionate prayer?

# Fruitful Life

*The Holy Spirit produces this kind of fruit in our lives: love, joy, peace, patience, kindness, goodness, faithfulness, gentleness, and self-control. There is no law against these things! Those who belong to Christ Jesus have nailed the passions and desires of their sinful nature to his cross and crucified them there.* GALATIANS 5:22-24

The standard by which to measure a Spirit-filled life is revealed for every believer within this short discourse. Contrasting the Spirit-filled life with the sinful life (see Galatians 5:19-21), Paul makes them both very identifiable! And yet, after defining the sinful nature, he gives the Christ-follower a mandate—to no longer follow the sinful nature, but instead "nail" those passions to the cross and crucify them. In other words, deny, even hate, all those things you used to love—which continue to tempt you.

You and I must make a decision to go from death to life, sinfulness to holiness, selfish to fruitful. We must chase the holy as passionately as we pursued the unholy.

The question is not "Which life do I now live?" but "Do I want to live the Spirit-filled life?"

The most practical way to live the Spirit-filled life is to conduct a daily "burial" of anything on the sin list. Each morning, identify any recurring thoughts that draw you back to your sinful nature. Expose them to the Lord. Tell them to leave. Every day say the words, "Holy Spirit of the living God, fill me up today—overflowing with an extra measure. I need more of You than I did yesterday!"

When the Spirit of God fills a man or woman of God, there is no room, no tolerance, no love for the sinful nature.

Do you want to live the Spirit-filled life?

## Must-Have Qualities

*Let's not get tired of doing what is good. At just the right time we will reap a harvest of blessing if we don't give up. Therefore, whenever we have the opportunity, we should do good to everyone—especially to those in the family of faith.* GALATIANS 6:9-10

The book of Galatians is packed with practical principles for biblical living. Endurance is one of them. It is a rare quality among the impatient, impulsive, fast-paced set. Paul refers to it as a "must-have" quality for the Christian.

What might the "must-have" quality of endurance look like in your life and mine? It might mean . . .

- never giving up praying for those who seem resistant, even rebellious, toward God
- never being too busy, too tired, or too lazy to read the Bible—ever
- never giving in to an old temptation . . . keeping your word, your commitments, and your promises, even when it is inconvenient or costly
- never shaming God's name—living intentionally in front of Him all day long
- always trusting God with your words and actions, even and especially when the situation is most difficult
- loving the unlovable
- forgiving an offense—over and over and over

Paul's letter to the Galatians challenges believers of every age to possess must-have qualities so that the name of God will be greatly glorified in our lives. . . .

Don't give up—even if it takes your whole life to reap the harvest of blessing assigned to you!

# Powerful Lord

*Those who trust in the LORD will find new strength. They will soar*
*high on wings like eagles. They will run and not grow weary.*
*They will walk and not faint.* ISAIAH 40:31

When our son was born, he had a little birthmark in the shape of an eagle on his forearm. That prompted us to choose a life Scripture for his baby dedication, reflecting the power and stamina of the eagle mentioned in the fortieth chapter of Isaiah.

When he was still a toddler, we taught him through these verses that God gives strength beyond what is humanly possible to those who trust in Him!

It is every parent's desire to see his or her children fulfill their dreams and achieve the purpose for which they were created.

Even so, very early in the life of a child, parents understand that their child *is not their own, but is God's child.* And though we'd like our children to do what *we* think is best for them, especially protecting them from making any mistakes . . . we must allow them to fly away. Our most important goal is to teach our children how to put their trust in the living, loving God all the days of their lives!

Isaiah reminds parents to tell their children that God is both their Creator and their Friend. He is their strength . . . He is always available. Tell them He can be seen in the power of nature and wants to live in the depths of their heart. Remind them that He knows them and loves them . . . and when they call on Him, He will supernaturally strengthen them. He will forever be there for them . . . and even when their parents fail them, He will not.

## Good Gift

*God saved you by his grace when you believed. And you can't take credit for this; it is a gift from God. Salvation is not a reward for the good things we have done, so none of us can boast about it. For we are God's masterpiece. He has created us anew in Christ Jesus, so we can do the good things he planned for us long ago.* EPHESIANS 2:8-10

Recently I shared my testimony with a group of high school athletes, many of whom were not necessarily looking for God and appeared unwilling to change their lives.

But when someone proves by his or her life that God is willing to love and change the most unlikely person, even the most rebellious, immoral addict, and offer that person the gift of salvation—it can be very convincing.

So when I presented the gospel to these athletes as an opportunity to start a new life and boldly asked them to leave their old lives behind in exchange for undeserved love and unlimited forgiveness—the response was overwhelming!

They—like so many others who are not familiar with the gospel—found it so amazing that salvation is not a reward for being a good person. It is a gift—a good gift.

That night, *the entire team* came forward, and one by one they asked Christ into their lives. Most had never heard the gospel, and each student seemed more grateful than the next to receive God's gift! Through tears and laughter we felt the joy of the Lord being released.

It is such a privilege to invite others to know God, to become part of His family, to receive forgiveness for sins and be filled with His Holy Spirit. I just love to share the Good News, the good gift of salvation. Do you?

## His Witness

*Do not tremble; do not be afraid. Did I not proclaim my purposes for you*
*long ago? You are my witnesses—is there any other God? No!*
*There is no other Rock—not one!* ISAIAH 44:8

A s a new believer, I was given a study series called *Know What You Believe* by Paul Little.[6]
Like many who have been raised in America, I went to church on Easter and Christmas, was baptized as a baby, and attended religion classes in middle school. Much of what I learned, memorized, or even remembered blended with other religions, philosophies, and popular culture by the time I was twenty-one.

So it was a wonderful opportunity for me, as a young Christian, to go through a basic Bible study, using ample Scriptures from both the New and Old Testaments in order to distinguish fact from fiction and biblical teaching from religious training.

The greatest benefit of knowing what I believed was being able to articulate my beliefs to others—to be God's witness who could accurately handle the Word of God and enthusiastically represent the living God. That was over thirty years ago! And for over two decades, I have continued to read the Bible daily, using the *Change Your Life Daily Bible*, a special edition of *The One Year Bible*. Today, my purpose for reading through the Bible every year from cover to cover is multifaceted:

- I hear God speak to me.
- I learn more about Him every day.
- I understand His ways more clearly.
- I proclaim more resolutely to others, "My God is the Rock! There is no one like Him!"

## Worthy of the Call

*Therefore I, a prisoner for serving the Lord, beg you to lead a life worthy
of your calling, for you have been called by God. Always be humble and
gentle. Be patient with each other, making allowance for each other's faults
because of your love. Make every effort to keep yourselves united in the
Spirit, binding yourselves together with peace.* EPHESIANS 4:1-3

**M**any of us struggle to expose the faults we see in others'
lives. But Paul is very direct in his counsel! He suggests
specific ways to lead lives that reflect the serious obliga-
tion that comes with calling ourselves Christian.

*Be humble and gentle.* Humility is such a defining characteristic.
The more a person genuinely loves God, the more humility he or
she exhibits. A humble person truly gives the impression that he or
she has been with Jesus!

*Be patient with each other.* So often anger—passive or aggressive—will undermine the love of God in our everyday lives! Don't
let the sun go down on your anger (see Ephesians 4:26). Count,
breathe . . . do whatever it takes to be patient with others. It
matters. What they think of you . . . gives them a picture of God.

*Make every effort to be united.* I am always surprised by Christian
groups who are critical of other Christian groups. It surely doesn't
look good to those outside the church, and doesn't feel good to
those inside the family of God. For the record, I've found that one
of the greatest avenues for creating unity among differing groups
and denominations is to pray together!

# Good Question

*Don't use foul or abusive language. Let everything you say be good
and helpful, so that your words will be an encouragement
to those who hear them.* EPHESIANS 4:29

I n the seventeenth century, William Law called abusive language
"common swearing." In fact he devoted an entire chapter of
his book *A Serious Call to a Devout and Holy Life* to the topic. He
wrote, "Now the reason of common swearing is this: it is because
men have not so much as the intention to please God in all their
actions. For let a man but have so much piety as to intend to please
God in all the actions of his life as the happiest and best thing in
the world, and then he will never swear more . . . as it is impossible for a man that intends to please his prince to go up and abuse
him to his face."[7]

As a non-Christian, I swore like few other women or men!
But the hour I became a Christian, my foul mouth was gone. The
only plausible explanation is that I became the residence of the
Holy Spirit.

That's why I have always thought it strange to hear a professing Christian swear profusely. In fact, it seems quite clear in
Scripture that using foul language is not to be the habit of God's
followers.

Yet whenever I express my thoughts on this matter, I rarely
find that I am preaching to the choir. More often by contending for
clean lips, I feel that I am considered legalistic or old-fashioned.

But should not all Christians represent the living, loving God
with their words and actions?

Today, simply ask yourself, *Do the words that come out of my
mouth at home, at work, on the sports field represent my Lord?* If not,
remove them from your vocabulary.

# Be Drunk!

*Don't be drunk with wine, because that will ruin your life. Instead,*
*be filled with the Holy Spirit, singing psalms and hymns and spiritual*
*songs among yourselves, and making music to the Lord in your hearts.*

EPHESIANS 5:18-19

The first time I drank, at age fifteen, I got drunk. In fact, every time I drank, I got drunk. I didn't know how to slow down nor did I have a limiting mechanism. Alcoholics . . . know how to be drunk! So when I asked God to fill me with His Holy Spirit, I got quite full!

Actually, I had never heard of the Holy Spirit when the person who led me to Christ asked me to invite Him into my life. Yet without any hesitation, I remember standing up, lifting my hands, and asking to be filled *to overflowing* with an extra measure of Him. . . .

Perhaps because I had so few inhibitions as a drinker, I had very few inhibitions in asking the Holy Spirit to fill me. I have always been one to want *more* . . . so when I became a Christian, I asked for more of God. In that first hour, He simultaneously filled me with His Holy Spirit and miraculously took away my desire for alcohol.

I found many similarities between being Spirit-filled and being drunk! I was happy, bubbly, and excited as a new Christian! And just like those who talk too much when they drink, I could not contain my enthusiasm for God around everyone I knew! I also love to sing and dance when I'm full of the Holy Spirit!

Over thirty years later, I can honestly say, "There is no better high than being completely sober, yet filled with the Holy Spirit. There is no greater joy than being happy in Jesus!"

## Evil Spirits

*We are not fighting against flesh-and-blood enemies, but against evil rulers and authorities of the unseen world, against mighty powers in this dark world, and against evil spirits in the heavenly places.* EPHESIANS 6:12

In the extremely practical resource titled *Fatal Attractions: Why Sex Sins Are Worse Than Others*, Jack Hayford discusses the continuum of sin in a person's life. Biblically and methodically he exposes the tactical approach in which demonic spirits urge Christians to "assault the pure lordship of Jesus Christ" in their lives, wooing Christians to worship immoral idols, rather than God.[8]

Do you seriously consider the evil that exists around you? How different would your life be if you truly believed what the Bible says about evil? Begin with Paul's advice. . . .

First, open your eyes to the *unseen* evil powers that fight against you.

Second, do not get distracted from seeing your real enemy by fighting with the human beings around you!

Third, clearly identify your invisible enemies . . .
- the voices that draw you away from God,
- the images that tempt you to sin,
- the half-truths that are actually very deceptive lies, and
- the thoughts that repeatedly and relentlessly draw you toward them.

Finally, acknowledge these voices, images, lies, and thoughts . . . as evil spirits that hate you *and* God. *You must hate them.*

# New Generation

*O God, you have taught me from my earliest childhood, and I constantly tell others about the wonderful things you do. Now that I am old and gray, do not abandon me, O God. Let me proclaim your power to this new generation, your mighty miracles to all who come after me.* PSALM 71:17-18

Y ou're never too old to tell the next generation about God, even if you think you are!

Though I had been a youth worker for over two decades, there came a day when I just stopped speaking to students—for a variety of reasons. Mostly, I convinced myself that . . .

- I'm not relevant to this new generation. . . .
- They don't want to hear what I have to say. . . .
- They'll tune me out like a parent. . . .

Then in the summer of 2000, I read an account of four people who determined to call the next generation to revival in 1947. And I got fired up! I began to imagine a young generation that loved God so much they would restore His famous name to its high place of honor in our nation.

From that moment, God fanned a little ember into a big flame in my heart. By the fall of 2004, I returned to college campuses with the Burning Hearts message—a call to prayer, purity, and purpose.

And in the past few years I've met many faith-filled, praying students who challenge me to know God better and make Him known! *I love them!* I love talking with them, hanging out with them, and listening to them.

What does every generation want to hear? The truth about God—that He is a mighty and powerful God. This new generation is no different than any other. Don't hesitate—proclaim God's power to them!

# Right On!

*God is working in you, giving you the desire and the power
to do what pleases him.* PHILIPPIANS 2:13

I got an e-mail from a student who recently heard me speak. She wrote that she had been lying to her parents about seeing a boy they didn't want her to see. She was also doing things with him that she didn't want to do, but . . . was doing anyway! She asked for advice on how to break up with him.

By the time people write to ask for my advice, they know what they'll get—God's Word. So you might wonder, *Why do they ask?*

I'm convinced it's because God's Word is what they really want!

The beauty of His Word is that it meets you right where you're at . . . no matter the century in which you're born, where you live, or how old you are. It is timelessly "right on." . . .

I immediately responded to this young woman, reflecting back on our time together. I wrote,

> *Remember . . . I talked about honoring God by obeying Him (and your parents), and not giving away the precious life God has given you— to hold on, to wait for the day you marry? It sounds like you know what to do—and that you truly want to do the right thing. It won't be easy, but here are a few practical suggestions. . . . You can do it!*

She responded,

> *Thank you sooo very much for taking the time to talk to me about this. It means so much to me that you care. I will definitely take your advice. This has been so heavy on my heart and I already feel so much better. God Bless!*

# He Waits

*I was ready to respond, but no one asked for help. I was ready to be found,*
*but no one was looking for me. I said, "Here I am, here I am!" to a nation*
*that did not call on my name.* ISAIAH 65:1

Can you imagine the almighty, all-powerful God waiting on His people, ready to respond—but no one asks for His help?

It's really not too hard to imagine, is it? Book after book in the Bible illustrates God's desire to visit, advise, and encourage His people.

As Isaiah records, *it is frustrating to God* to know what we need and seldom be consulted or trusted. He waits for us. But many times we rush around, too busy to meet with Him—except when we're in great need. Only then will we beg for help or quiet ourselves long enough to listen.

Dallas Willard, a professor of philosophy at the University of Southern California and the author of *Hearing God*, gives today's Christian a true picture of the God who waits. He writes, "Companionship with Jesus is the form that Christian spirituality, as practiced through the ages, takes. Spiritual people are not those who engage in certain spiritual practices; they are those who *draw their life from a conversational relationship with God.*"[1]

God tells us He is available. He has the answers we seek. He knows what we want. He knows the future. He waits for us to come to Him.

Today, not tomorrow, make an appointment with God. Put it on your calendar. Close the door. Turn off the computer, television, or radio. Talk to Him and listen to Him.

He waits.

## Press On

*I press on to reach the end of the race and receive the heavenly prize for
which God, through Christ Jesus, is calling us.* PHILIPPIANS 3:14

I am an avid sports fan. As a young girl, I was a competitive
athlete. At a time when my athletic abilities peaked, I entered
high school and immediately gave up my athletic pursuits for
other things . . . things that didn't require discipline or abstinence.

Perhaps that is why I am often moved to tears when athletes
win a hard-fought race or event. I wince and applaud their
achievements, knowing how hard they fought to accomplish their
goals. I wince because I am certain I missed many exhilarating
experiences when I was unwilling to discipline my body, focus
my mind, and endure to the end. I applaud, because I am inspired
to press on and give Jesus Christ all that I have—extra time and
effort, even sacrifice—to finish the race well and win the heavenly
prize to which He is calling me.

The Christian's race is not a sprint, but a marathon. For that
reason my friends at the Fellowship of Christian Athletes teach
believers the PRESS Method to discipline their bodies, minds, and
spirits for the race set before them:

> **P**ray—clear your mind and ask God to prepare you for the day.
> **R**ead—read at least a chapter from the Bible every day.
> **E**xamine—ask yourself daily, "Is there anything I must stop or
> start doing?"
> **S**ummarize—in a sentence or a word, summarize your daily
> reading.
> **S**hare—talk with God and another about what you read in the
> Bible.[2]

It takes daily effort over a sustained period of time to reach
the end and attain the victory. So press on!

# Start Marching

*"I knew you before I formed you in your mother's womb. Before you were*
*born I set you apart and appointed you as my prophet to the nations."*
*"O Sovereign LORD," I said, "I can't speak for you! I'm too young!" The LORD*
*replied, "Don't say, 'I'm too young,' for you must go wherever I send you and*
*say whatever I tell you. And don't be afraid of the people, for I will be with*
*you and will protect you. I, the LORD, have spoken!"*

JEREMIAH 1:5-8

I recall rereading these verses one summer when asked to
speak before twenty thousand students in the Washington
Convention Center. As much as I wanted to speak, I was truly
terrified to get up in front of so many students. I was fearful that
my message on prayer might be boring, or I might freeze and
forget to say something important.

As my fears grew, I felt physically and emotionally sick. I could
barely eat or sleep the day before I spoke. So I just kept repeating
these verses from Jeremiah, and soon I could almost hear God saying
to me, "I chose you to do this. Give the message I have asked you to
give. I don't care if anyone likes it."

If that wasn't enough admonition, the morning I was to speak,
I felt God give me a final challenge through the verses that follow
in Jeremiah 1:17: "Get up and prepare for action. Go out and tell
them everything I tell you to say. Do not be afraid of them, or I
will make you look foolish in front of them."

No matter your age, when God gives you His marching
orders . . . start marching!

## Changed Lives

*This same Good News that came to you is going out all over the world.
It is bearing fruit everywhere by changing lives, just as it changed
your lives from the day you first heard and understood the truth about
God's wonderful grace.* COLOSSIANS 1:6

Pastor and author A. W. Tozer defined revival as that which "changes the moral climate of a community."[3]

Recently, while voraciously reading books on revival, I uncovered two common threads that every revival leaves in its trail. The first is change—moral change, physical change, spiritual change—grand, sweeping change. Without change, without conversions, without the evidence of a supernatural outpouring of the Holy Spirit, there is no revival.

In an eye-opening observation written in 1909, James Burns touches on a second common thread of revival: resistance by the church!

> *To the church, a revival means humiliation, a bitter knowledge of unworthiness and an open humiliating confession of sin on the part of her ministers and people. . . . It comes to scorch before it heals; it comes to condemn ministers and people for their unfaithful witness, for their selfish living, for their neglect of the cross, and to call them to daily renunciation, to an evangelical poverty and to a deep and daily consecration. That is why a revival has ever been unpopular with large numbers within the church. . . . It accuses them of sin; it tells them they are dead; it calls them to awake, to renounce the world and to follow Christ.*[4]

The Good News is especially good news when you are desperate for change.

What is the Good News? God loves sinners. He sent His only Son to die a painful death on a cross so that we might receive the free gift of eternal life and worship Him forever.

# Personal Revival

*Just as you accepted Christ Jesus as your Lord, you must continue to follow*
*him. Let your roots grow down into him, and let your lives be built on him.*
*Then your faith will grow strong in the truth you were taught, and you*
*will overflow with thankfulness.* COLOSSIANS 2:6-7

I often meet Christians who cannot express their love for Jesus
in words. Rarely do their lives reflect His presence. And they
don't seem to know what the Bible says about . . . anything.
So I ask *when*, *where*, and *what* questions. . . .

When did you accept Christ Jesus as your Lord? Where were
you? How did He change your life?

Did following Christ look and feel different to you when you first
met Him compared to now? Explain the differences.

What efforts have you consistently made to grow closer to
God—to know Him better, to understand His teachings
and incorporate them into your life?

Do you attend a vibrant Christian fellowship? Are you
committed to weekly church attendance? If no . . . why not?

When did your faith take noticeable leaps? Where were you?

When was the first time you were challenged to give up
something for Christ? Did you immediately do it? If not,
why not? What has been the result of your hesitance or
disobedience?

If you are too busy to spend regular time with God and those
who deeply know and love Him, if you repeatedly ignore the
correction and discipline of God the Father, if you are resistant to
honest accountability relationships . . . the words *follow* and *grow*
will not characterize your life with God.

Is it time for personal revival?

# Honest Answers

*An honest answer is like a kiss of friendship.* PROVERBS 24:26

Do you have someone in your life with whom you can be honest—or more importantly, who can be honest with you? Small groups or "life" groups—where you regularly meet for fellowship and spiritual growth with other Christians— are popular in many circles. And though they provide great fellowship, very often they are not meeting the true accountability needs of twenty-first-century believers.

What makes an accountability group different than a fellowship or small group? Honest questions and answers.

For example, at weight-loss meetings, most people are required to weigh in weekly. With this simple activity, there is no hiding the truth. Though there may be sorrow expressed or excuses given, the truth about one's eating history is visible when one gets on the scale! And if weight gain is reported—firm, loving encouragement mixed with practical advice and the sting of backsliding motivate most people to new levels of success.

The same idea works for any area of life in which you need support: battling addictions like alcohol, drugs, pornography, overspending, gambling, or even anger or poor time management. Checking in weekly (sometimes daily) with caring, confidential Christians who ask tough, honest questions and *expect you to give honest answers* will produce change much more quickly than hiding, rationalizing, or attempting to change on your own.

The reason we don't like to receive honest answers is because they hurt us. But honest answers from true friends will improve our lives. They keep us from making the same or new mistakes, and add biblical perspective to our often self-centered lives.

Perhaps you might need to change your thinking about honest answers. Consider them as sweet as the kiss of a friend.

## God's Chosen

*Since God chose you to be the holy people he loves, you must clothe
yourselves with tenderhearted mercy, kindness, humility, gentleness, and
patience. . . .Wives, submit to your husbands, as is fitting for those who
belong to the Lord. Husbands, love your wives and never treat them harshly.*

COLOSSIANS 3:12, 18-19

I was a new Christian and intern with Youth for Christ when
I attended a Campus Life retreat with hundreds of kids and
dozens of staff. During that event, the director, Roger, broke
his eyeglasses chasing me in a football game.

Something special had been building between us—but during
the weekend that "something" escalated. After dropping a vanload
of kids off, Roger said, "I don't want to ruin our ministry relationship by dating."

I thought, *What does he mean? Is he asking me to date him . . . or is
there something more?*

He added, "We'll have to ask God for a Scripture and talk to
those in authority over us regarding our relationship."

The next morning, Roger asked me to go with him to buy a
new pair of glasses. At the first store, he tried on a pair that I really
liked. I looked for the numeric inscription inside the frame. It
read, *Col. 3.*

I said, "Roger, here's our Scripture—Colossians 3!" Neither
of us had a pocket Bible with us at the time, so I jotted down the
reference for later.

We headed to the only other eyeglass store in town. *As we
opened the door*, the owner said, "I'm a Gideon and would like to
give you each a Bible."

I flipped to the third chapter of Colossians, and read, "Dearly
beloved, chosen by God . . . wives . . . husbands . . ." That was just
the first of many signs.

We were married the following year!

# Devoted Life

*Devote yourselves to prayer with an alert mind and a thankful heart.*

COLOSSIANS 4:2

The *only way* I have found to pray for sustained amounts of time without getting distracted or falling asleep is to record my conversations with God in writing.

If you've never tried writing a letter to God, you must! It will give your prayer life an increased level of focus and intimacy.

- *Written prayer* takes your many thoughts and organizes them into topics (praise, requests, confessions, thanks) in which to talk with God.

- *Written prayer* forces you to be honest with your words. You can't say something you don't mean without revising or erasing. In other words, it "checks" your intentions!

- *Written prayer* takes conjecture out of prayer. When you ask God for something specific and receive a specific answer—*luck* and *chance* are eliminated from your vocabulary!

- *Written prayer* allows you to consistently pray for people by name. Forgetting to pray for someone is so easy! When you have a prayer list, it is impossible to forget to pray for others (though it is still possible to avoid or overlook the list).

- *Written prayer* is intentional, relational, and responsible! Telling God in writing that you will or won't do something increases your desire to keep your word.

If you are like me and have a wandering, lazy, or forgetful mind, stay alert in prayer by writing down your thoughts, feelings, and requests to God—and recording His answers!

## Your Life

*We loved you so much that we shared with you not only God's Good News*
*but our own lives, too.* 1 THESSALONIANS 2:8

P aul's words spur me to be a spiritual parent not only to
my own child, but to the many students God has recently
brought into my life.

It's uncanny. I have an overwhelming, all-encompassing,
protective mother's love for them—as if they were my own. Most
of all, I've been surprised at how happy I am to just sit and chat or
stay and pray with students! They pick me up at the airport and
we talk nonstop, no matter how long the drive. We stay up late
to get coffee or dessert and get up early to meet and pray. After I
leave, we regularly chat on the phone—no matter the time of day.
(Quite often they forget I live in a different time zone.)

When they visit me, I beg them to eat healthier, providing
organic food for them. I take them to my church and introduce
them to other "on fire" collegians. And we talk and talk and talk
about their prayer lives, dating lives, family lives . . . and futures.
I am compelled to preach the gospel to their hearts and souls
while caring for and praying deeply about every area of their lives.

Who has God given you to love, not only by sharing the Good
News with them, but by sharing your life?

# Love More

*May the Lord make your love for one another and for all people grow and overflow, just as our love for you overflows. May he, as a result, make your hearts strong, blameless, and holy as you stand before God our Father when our Lord Jesus comes again with all his holy people. Amen.*

1 THESSALONIANS 3:12-13

I recently received e-mails from two young women so desperate to go on a missions trip that they frustrated people around them with their impatience!

Reading their first reports from tough third world areas and knowing they risk their safety and health to be there has been incredibly inspiring! These women have exhibited more love, enthusiasm, and determination—amidst poverty and sickness—than I can recall seeing throughout my life!

One of the women visits an orphanage for hours each day just to hold and comfort babies dying of AIDS. At night she visits an unsafe district where prostitutes live. It is an area considered repulsive and dangerous to the locals, but not to her. She shares the gospel boldly, leading small groups of women to Christ.

The other woman sleeps on a church office floor because her living quarters are too unsafe at night. In her e-mail she explained that she was humbled by the love of two teenage orphans who volunteered to sleep by her side each night just to be near her. When informed by the pastor she had to leave because of the danger, she begged to stay, and her request was granted.

Will these strong, godly young women write books or preach sermons? I don't know. But they have lived out the New Testament mandate to exhibit God's unfathomable love to the most unlovely—stretching those who know them to love more.

OCTOBER 11

## Open Wide!

*Listen to me, O my people, while I give you stern warnings.*
*O Israel, if you would only listen to me! You must never have a foreign god;*
*you must not bow down before a false god. For it was I, the LORD your God,*
*who rescued you from the land of Egypt. Open your mouth wide,*
*and I will fill it with good things.* PSALM 81:8-10

God begs us to listen to His infinite wisdom and life-saving warnings. Still, many of us chase after false ideas and others' opinions, buying into religious traditions or cultural trends rather than listening exclusively to the counsel of God in the Bible.

Eventually, our misconceptions become our reality and we create a distorted set of rules regarding God's communication style, such as:

1. God is not a person, a Father, or a friend. He is impersonal.
2. God doesn't speak to imperfect people like me.
3. God's ways are so mystical, I could never understand them.
4. God is too busy to talk to me.

Opinions, excuses, or handed-down traditions will only keep you from the timeless truths in God's Word. Jerry Bridges, author of *The Pursuit of Holiness*, suggests four ways in which to hear God's voice:

1. Memorize key passages for immediate recall.
2. Listen for Scripture used in sermons that impact your life.
3. Study Scripture intently for special counsel.
4. Read the Bible regularly to know God's viewpoint in all aspects of life. [5]

God has *never* been reluctant to give His children good ideas, reveal great plans to them, or offer powerful protection. We need only open wide the Word of God and let Him fill us with His thoughts.

## Good Advice

*Always be joyful. Never stop praying. Be thankful in all circumstances, for this is God's will for you who belong to Christ Jesus. Do not stifle the Holy Spirit. Do not scoff at prophecies, but test everything that is said. Hold on to what is good. Stay away from every kind of evil.* 1 THESSALONIANS 5:16-22

In the history records of past revivals, there was a push-pull between those who led revivals and those who observed them, between those who eagerly attended and those who stubbornly refused to do so. The key points of the struggle were

- the outward manifestations of the Holy Spirit,
- prophetic words being uttered by nonclergy, and
- overt, emotional responses that occurred during extended hours of worship and prayer.

In the annals documenting revivals, communities reported a complete reversal in the moral climates of their cities. Additionally, those who had been touched by God remained deeply in love with Him for years to follow. From all that can be honestly observed and assessed, these meetings weren't evil; they were just different or more emotional than people were used to.

The Word of God gives us direction for understanding revival or prayer meetings that are intense or unusual.

- Are they joyful? There is nothing inherently wrong with powerful, loud praise—it will be the norm in heaven!
- Are they endless? Hosting or attending a never-ending prayer meeting is a bit out of the ordinary, but it is a common occurrence in revival times.

Don't scoff, but prayerfully consider and always test the Holy Spirit to see if He is not doing a great, new, and exciting work in your midst. If He is . . . watch in wonder!

## Prayerless Leader

*"What sorrow awaits the leaders of my people—the shepherds of my sheep—for they have destroyed and scattered the very ones they were expected to care for," says the LORD.* JEREMIAH 23:1

In his classic book *With Christ in the School of Prayer*, Andrew Murray, a nineteenth-century South African church leader, asserted that the very core of a leader's life—his or her holiness, ability to run the long race of faith, or willingness to submit to the Holy Spirit—is formed in prayer. He also believed that the devil works very strategically to *keep* a believer, especially the minister, from praying.

In February of 1984, I was an overworked youth worker who had no time for God. I read my Bible, not to hear His voice but to prepare a lesson. I didn't pray because I was too tired. I didn't even consider prayer a critical discipline in my life, primarily because I steered clear of most activities that required discipline!

These were startling realizations! I felt ashamed of myself. I had been given an awesome responsibility to shepherd hundreds of high school students—yet I rarely spent time in prayer with or for them.

These revelations prompted me to purchase a handful of Murray's books to glean more on prayer from one of the greatest Christian leaders of his century.

Murray was convinced that a prayerless leader is equally vulnerable to piety and perversion. He asserted that a prayerless leader cannot possess a robust, believing faith! And he was sure that no practice will reveal more of a person to God and more of God to that person than prayer.

In 1984, Murray convinced me, and I resolved to be a leader who prayed one hour a day for the rest of my life.

# Thank God!

*As for us, we can't help but thank God for you, dear brothers and sisters loved by the Lord.We are always thankful that God chose you to be among the first to experience salvation—a salvation that came through the Spirit who makes you holy and through your belief in the truth. He called you to salvation when we told you the Good News; now you can share in the glory of our Lord Jesus Christ.* 2 THESSALONIANS 2:13-14

For almost a decade, I was the cheerleading coach and Campus Life director at a large public high school in Ohio. It was exciting work, but the most rewarding aspect is the fruit that still remains.

One of my students, Steve, became a Christian at my kitchen table at the age of sixteen. Shortly after my husband and I left Ohio for California, Steve contacted us to tell us he was getting married and wanted to finish his college education in California. We encouraged him to move to our location—and at the end of his honeymoon, with trailer in tow, he and his bride arrived on our doorstep.

They got involved in our California youth ministry and became volunteers. Steve soon came onto our high school staff, as did his wife. He eventually graduated from college, took another full-time youth pastor position, and after leaving youth work to start his own company, became an elder at his church. We continue to meet weekly for prayer and accountability and still enjoy the holidays together.

We can't help but thank God regularly for the life Steve leads, the impact he continues to make on his peers and coworkers, and the love he has sustained for the Lord as a husband, father, son, businessman, and neighbor for over two decades!

## Food Addiction

*Do you like honey? Don't eat too much, or it will make you sick!*

PROVERBS 25:16

Food has become an addiction for millions of Americans. Providing weight-loss advice and remedies for those struggling to manage food in their lives is a billion-dollar industry.

For many, food provides comfort when they feel sad. It is an antidote for anxiety. For others, food has become the way to satisfy their emptiness. Many abuse food in some fashion. In addition to destroying their physical body, the abuse can cause intense guilt to build up and create an endless cycle of shame.

Food will never deeply comfort those who are sad; it is a temporary solution.

> *Only the Word of God* can replace our sorrow with lasting hope. "I weep with sorrow; encourage me by your word" (Psalm 119:28).
>
> *Only the Word of God* can satisfy our hunger for happiness. "Make me walk along the path of your commands, for that is where my happiness is found" (Psalm 119:35).
>
> *Only the Word of God* can relieve anxiety and give us emotional freedom. "Turn my eyes from worthless things, and give me life through your word" (Psalm 119:37).
>
> *And the Word of God* offers a healthy way of escape from our shameful habits. "Help me abandon my shameful ways; for your regulations are good" (Psalm 119:39).

When you need comfort, when you are anxious, when you cannot control that which is affecting your life, resist turning to food, *which is perishable*, to satisfy your soul. Instead, open the eternal Word of God.

# Shipwrecked Faith

*Cling to your faith in Christ, and keep your conscience clear. For some people have deliberately violated their consciences; as a result, their faith has been shipwrecked.* 1 TIMOTHY 1:19

In the past decade, I have attended churches where elders or pastors who committed adultery were brought in front of the congregation and their sin publicly exposed and confessed. Sadly, the wives and children were just as humiliated and devastated as the person who committed the sin.

The third time it happened, I couldn't even attend the service. I didn't want to watch. I didn't want to listen. I felt so sorry for the wife and children . . . so embarrassed for all of them. . . .

These men had shipwrecked their faith . . . their reputations, their family names, God's name, and their God-given ministries. It was as public as filming a ship's grounding for the evening news. In some cases, the news even made the front page of the morning papers.

For each person, the moral failure was very brief—he was not involved in an ongoing, illicit relationship. One mistake, one decision made in a fleeting moment of temptation was all it took to ruin a testimony.

In all three cases, the churches worked diligently with the leader to restore the marriage. Each has remained married, though his public ministry has been sidelined or diminished.

It's painful to learn of a man or woman who has shipwrecked his or her faith. It's painful for family, friends, and the church family who go through the reconciliation and restoration with this person.

Paul's warning to Timothy is a serious call to all Christians: *Take your life in Christ seriously*. Never forget that your daily or hourly choices affect more than yourself.

# Just Ask

*I urge you, first of all, to pray for all people. Ask God to help them;*
*intercede on their behalf, and give thanks for them.* 1 TIMOTHY 2:1

A missionary once scolded me for encouraging people to keep a daily prayer list. She said that in thirty years of ministry, she had never made such a list. In fact, she thought it lacked faith and irritated God.

It was difficult for me, as it would be for any Christian, to be reprimanded by someone who was older than me. But the standard by which we must pattern our life is not by another's walk or words, but by the Word of God. The first thing any believer must do is to know what the Word of God says . . . about everything . . . ridding ourselves of any misconceptions and discerning truth from opinion.

Fortunately I had previously looked up every verse in the Bible that contained the word *prayer.* Wow! The prayers and prayer teachings of Moses, David, Jehoshaphat, and Jesus allowed me to formulate prayer principles that gave me confidence, passion, and consistency in my prayer life, especially in intercessory prayer.

Thirty days after I challenged the missionary, she wrote a letter to me, which read, *Over the past month, I made 130 prayer requests of God and He answered 127 of them specifically!* She never told me *how* God answered her prayers, but her letter indicated that she was enormously encouraged by using a daily, detailed prayer list to record her requests to God and His answers!

Jesus taught us to *ask.* He said in Matthew 7:7, "Keep on asking, and you will receive what you ask for. Keep on seeking, and you will find. Keep on knocking, and the door will be opened to you."

*Just ask.*

# Grief Advice

*Singing cheerful songs to a person with a heavy heart is like taking someone's coat in cold weather or pouring vinegar in a wound.*

PROVERBS 25:20

What is the right thing to say or do when someone experiences loss or pain?

First, recognize that not everyone feels or thinks the way you do! Simply ask if there is anything practical you can do to help, then offer to meet his or her needs quietly, confidentially, and quickly.

Second, be there. Some people will tell you that they don't want to talk, but neither do they want to be alone while waiting for news, sitting in a hospital, or going through the stages of grief. Others might ask you to share their pain by listening to them, which helps their healing process to begin.

A newly married friend recently received a heart-wrenching letter from a first-time parent who delivered a stillborn daughter at thirty-seven and a half weeks. Her request to friends was eye opening:

> *We would ask that during this time you would keep us in your prayers. We will never "get over" this . . . but eventually we will move through it and be able to comfort others with the same comfort we have received. We ask that you would still write us and call us . . . we need you. Please don't pretend [our daughter] didn't exist . . . she does exist. We need to talk about her . . . and we need others to remember her too. She is an important part of our lives . . . and we hope and pray that her life will continue to touch other people's lives just as she has touched ours.*

God may call upon you to be a comforting friend in someone's time of need or grief. Pray, ask, listen, then respond.

## Young Leader

*Don't let anyone think less of you because you are young. Be an example to*
*all believers in what you say, in the way you live, in your love, your faith,*
*and your purity.* 1 TIMOTHY 4:12

I am profoundly inspired by the many young men and women I know who take their relationship with and responsibility toward the Lord very seriously.

One young woman started a twenty-four-hour prayer house on one of the largest universities in America in her sophomore year. She formed a board, registered as a nonprofit organization, and upon graduation, left an ongoing legacy of prayer on her campus.

A young man, as president of his senior class, traveled with a dozen underclassmen to build an orphanage in Thailand. He even raised the necessary funds from classmates and parents to purchase the building supplies.

One young woman took a semester off of college—just to pray. For six months she attended an intensive "school of prayer" in order to become a powerful intercessory-prayer missionary.

Another special young woman started a new ministry in her church for women who've had abortions. . . . Having known the pain of such a decision, she is making a powerful difference in others' lives.

And a favorite young friend was so determined to see a twenty-four-hour prayer room on his state school campus that he relentlessly petitioned the chancellor's office for nine months. He not only received permission for the prayer room, but also was given a temporary location in the very center of campus!

Youth are naturally equipped with fearlessness, courage, stamina, and persistence. . . . We should applaud, encourage, and move out of their way more often than standing in it!

## Stay Pure

*Never be in a hurry about appointing a church leader. Do not share in the sins of others. Keep yourself pure.* 1 TIMOTHY 5:22

W hat do you consider to be the most important qualifications of a leader? Would purity be on the top of your list?

Sadly leaders in every area of life no longer consider moral purity the path through which they gain influence. In fact, it is more often considered old-fashioned or irrelevant to be moral or clean-mouthed.

Author J. Oswald Sanders, a consulting director of Overseas Missionary Fellowship, addresses the practical, moral qualifications of the modern leader in *Spiritual Leadership*. He writes:

> *Moral principles common to the Christian life are under constant, subtle attack, and none more so than sexual faithfulness. . . . Faithfulness to one marriage partner is the biblical norm. The spiritual leader should be a man of unchallengeable morality. The spiritual leader must be temperate, not addicted to alcohol. To be drunk is to show a disorderly personal life. . . . A leader cannot allow a secret indulgence that would undermine public witness.* [6]

*Unchallengeable morality.* That's quite a description. Consider how many times in the last year you've read or heard about the questionable moral stance of a leader. Now consider how many times in the last year you've prayed for the leaders you know— that they will stay pure and focused on the Lord.

If you're in a position to choose a leader in your community—whether a pastor or civic leader—consider the criteria suggested by Paul and J. Oswald Sanders. Even if you aren't in a position to choose your leaders, you can still pray for them. Pray that God will remind them of His way of escape when they face temptation.

# Fight Hard

*But you, Timothy, are a man of God; so run from all these evil things.*
*Pursue righteousness and a godly life, along with faith, love, perseverance,*
*and gentleness. Fight the good fight for the true faith. Hold tightly to the*
*eternal life to which God has called you, which you have confessed so well*
*before many witnesses.* 1 TIMOTHY 6:11-12

I n a recent conversation with two young, married Christian men, they named a few men's magazines, considered by most to be harmless transporters of general information, as pornography disguised. As the conversation continued, our discussion turned to those in their circles whose marriages were in trouble—compromised by pornography, sexual misconduct, and even adultery.

Paul's counsel to Timothy provides a timeless challenge to every young follower of Christ.

First, if you *are* God's man, you must *be* God's man. Being God's man will always, always mean intentionally running from evil. There is no bubble, no protective shield that surrounds you when you become a Christian. In fact, you become more of a target. As Paul encouraged Timothy, run from evil . . . today, tomorrow, always.

Second, pursue that which is godly with such perseverance that you fight for your life all your life. The call to Christ is both now and forever . . . it is not to be discarded or diminished when you don't *feel* like living for Him anymore or when the temptations become too great. You must keep fighting, in part because you have told God and others that you would.

Fight hard for your life in Christ. Hold on tight to the living, loving God.

## Safe Place

*Those who live in the shelter of the Most High will find rest in the shadow of the Almighty. This I declare about the L*ORD*: He alone is my refuge, my place of safety; he is my God, and I trust him.* PSALM 91:1-2

I've lived such a fast-paced, telecommuter lifestyle for so many months that I didn't know if I could decompress during a much needed six-day vacation with my husband. Upon checking into my hotel room, I placed my cell phone, watch, and computer in the room safe . . . and locked it shut for six days. I expected to find perfection in paradise!

But within the first two hours, I actually felt like going back home! I could not believe how hard it was to physically and emotionally unwind! Even on a vacation, I had to repeatedly call on God's name, asking Him to dissolve the dreadful, irrational, and obsessive thoughts flooding me.

For the next five days, I maintained a simple routine of extended prayer, Bible reading, playing golf, briskly walking with my husband, and even going to bed early. Somewhere early in the process, I progressed from fighting off fear to consciously dwelling in the presence of the Lord, allowing Him to be my refuge, my safety, my peace giver, my counselor, my friend.

On the last morning, I opened the safe and pulled out its contents. I returned home incredibly refreshed. It's one of the first times I recall returning late at night after a long flight and not feeling exhausted or resentful that I was leaving paradise.

I learned God's shelter is my safe place of refuge amidst the busyness of daily life *and* in the relaxation of paradise. His protective love comes over me when I simply speak His name.

## Great Call

*If you keep yourself pure, you will be a special utensil for honorable use.
Your life will be clean, and you will be ready for the Master to use
you for every good work.* 2 TIMOTHY 2:21

I will never forget speaking to one particular audience that
seemed completely bored. I struggled for forty minutes to
engage them with every illustration and point in my talk. Not
only was I sweating under the lights, but the roof of my tongue
was so dry I could barely speak!

Despite the lack of response, I determined to do what I always
did—I called people to a closing time of prayer and confession.
Before I did, I felt compelled to quote 2 Timothy 2:21, reminding
them that remaining pure is not to impress others or attain favor
. . . but to be ready, clean, and special for God's use.

I closed in a prayer and said that I would be available for
prayer in the front row. I honestly thought it would be an early
evening . . . with little response, little prayer.

I hadn't been seated for more than a minute when a young
man approached me. He told me he was a leader who had been
struggling with lust since the age of ten. The closing Scripture had
absolutely convicted him.

He so desperately wanted to be used by God, but feared God
would not be able to use him because of his repeated sin. . . . He
got on his knees and made a sincere confession. He admitted that
he was no longer willing to risk being disqualified from the great
call, the exciting race God had set before him, *because of lust.*

How about you? Don't buy into the lie that purity is impossible! Be ready when the holy God calls on you.

# All Scripture

*All Scripture is inspired by God and is useful to teach us what is true and to make us realize what is wrong in our lives. It corrects us when we are wrong and teaches us to do what is right. God uses it to prepare and equip his people to do every good work.* 2 TIMOTHY 3:16-17

A newlywed shared with me how God got her attention shortly before she was married. She was seriously struggling with alcohol when she listened to an audio download of the Burning Heart message—a call to (1) give God no less than one hour a day in prayer and Bible reading, (2) live in complete purity and sobriety, and (3) fulfill her purpose.

Late that night, while alone in her apartment, she made a commitment to God. The next morning she told her fiancé how she had told God she would completely quit drinking *and* read the Bible and pray for one hour a day.

He said, "You don't have to . . ." She said, "Yes I do."

The habits of her life, even from the day before, dramatically changed. Prayer, Bible reading, and her newly sober life gave her increased joy and passion. People were amazed. A year later, they are still amazed!

The Word of God absolutely impacted her life. And it will radically impact your life—*if you will read it!*

The Bible is full of truth for every generation. It instantly reveals what is wrong in our lives. If you've never made a decision to read the Bible daily, I encourage you to do so today. It *will* change your life!

## The Message

*Preach the word of God. Be prepared, whether the time is favorable or not.*
*Patiently correct, rebuke, and encourage your people with good teaching.*
*For a time is coming when people will no longer listen to sound and*
*wholesome teaching. They will follow their own desires and will look for*
*teachers who will tell them whatever their itching ears want to hear. They*
*will reject the truth and chase after myths.* 2 TIMOTHY 4:2-4

There is a clear call by God, His prophets, His Son, and other biblical authors to live by the standards, principles, and teachings in the Bible.

The mandate in almost every chapter is to set your standards for living *by the Word of God*, allowing it to teach you so that you might call others to follow it. Repeatedly you are reminded to hold firm to the Word of God: to thirst for it and drink from it. You are warned not to deviate from it.

Paul's words to Timothy acknowledge that "the world" will never follow God's words. Instead, believers of every generation will be presented and tempted with myths that rival for their attention and affection.

Do you know what the Word of God says about every aspect of life? Do you know where God's standards differ from those of your culture? Is the Word of God the standard by which you live, speak, and act?

Your life preaches. . . . What is your message?

# Life Together

*This letter is from Paul, a slave of God and an apostle of Jesus Christ.*
*I have been sent to proclaim faith to those God has chosen and to teach*
*them to know the truth that shows them how to live godly lives.* TITUS 1:1

ietrich Bonhoeffer, author and seminary professor during
the Hitler regime, wrote extensively on the life of a
disciple. His classic works *The Cost of Discipleship* and *Life
Together* grasp the heart of every reader with such strength and
passion that upon the completion of his books, you cannot live in
the same manner as before unless you choose to reject his compelling teaching.

Like Paul, Bonhoeffer suggests that God has given us to each
other to proclaim truth that admonishes and encourages us. We are
indeed charged to call each other to live faithful, godly lives.

In *Life Together* he wrote:

> *But God has put this Word into the mouth of men in order that it
> may be communicated to other men. When one person is struck by
> the Word, he speaks it to others. God has willed that we should seek
> and find His living Word in the witness of a brother, in the mouth
> of man. Therefore, the Christian needs another Christian who speaks
> God's Word to him. He needs him again and again when he becomes
> uncertain and discouraged, for by himself he cannot help himself
> without belying the truth. He needs his brother man as a bearer and
> proclaimer of the divine word of salvation.[7]*

We are to speak the truth in God's Word, not only to the lost
but also to those closest to us—without fear or compromise.

## Totally Committed

*We are instructed to turn from godless living and sinful pleasures. We should live in this evil world with wisdom, righteousness, and devotion to God, while we look forward with hope to that wonderful day when the glory of our great God and Savior, Jesus Christ, will be revealed. He gave his life to free us from every kind of sin, to cleanse us, and to make us his very own people, totally committed to doing good deeds.* TITUS 2:12-14

If it seems there is a pattern in this devotional—the obsessive battle between the holy and unholy—it's because *it is* an overarching pattern in the Bible. God calls us to be His alone—a Sacred Obsession. *Everything else* calls us away from Him and toward satisfying our unholy passions.

There is no secret to turning from godless living and sinful pleasures. We cannot rationalize or negotiate with sin. It must immediately be denied access to our hearts and minds.

Dietrich Bonhoeffer wrote, not just for his generation, but to all Christians:

> *To follow Jesus means self-renunciation and absolute adherence to him, and therefore a will dominated by lust can never be allowed to do what it likes. Even momentary desire is a barrier to the following of Jesus. . . . Instead of trusting to the unseen, we prefer the tangible fruits of desire, and so we fall from the path of discipleship and lose touch with Jesus. . . . No sacrifice is too great if it enables us to conquer a lust which cuts us off from Jesus. . . . The gains of lust are trivial compared with the loss it brings.*[8]

## Continuous Love

*Shout with joy to the L*ORD*, all the earth! Worship the L*ORD *with gladness. Come before him, singing with joy. Acknowledge that the L*ORD *is God! He made us, and we are his. We are his people, the sheep of his pasture. Enter his gates with thanksgiving; go into his courts with praise. Give thanks to him and praise his name. For the L*ORD *is good. His unfailing love continues forever, and his faithfulness continues to each generation.* PSALM 100

As I walked into church one night, something was different. Forty children from Uganda filled the stage with beaming smiles and brightly colored gowns and headbands. The rhythmic stomping of their feet and staccato clapping ushered us into a new freedom of praise as they sang a familiar song with an exciting, youthful passion.

Tears immediately rushed to my eyes and choked in my throat. I was surprised by my instant, emotional response to their glorious praise. Their singing captured me—and I went with them!

When we sang the next selection *in their language*, the presence of the Holy Spirit came over us as we were greeted with the unexpected rapturous music that made us lift our hands to heaven!

The third song took me out completely. Slowly and clearly, words from angelic voices were sung to an old hymn, not allowing listeners to miss the intention of their meaning:

*I have a Father. He calls me His own.*
*He'll never leave me. No matter where I go.*
*He knows my name; He knows my every thought.*
*He sees each tear that falls; He hears me when I call.*

"Enter his gates with thanksgiving; go into his courts with praise. . . ."

## My Home

*I will be careful to live a blameless life—when will you come to help me?*
*I will lead a life of integrity in my own home.* PSALM 101:2

**M**y husband purchases more books and ancillary products online than anyone I know!

When a huge box appeared at our doorstep one day, I curiously watched as he unpacked its contents. I was shocked when he pulled out a doormat . . . with the Scripture Joshua 24:15: *But as for me and my family, we will serve the Lord.*

At first I laughed out loud and thought, *Who is this hokey-pokey guy I married?* I was immediately reminded of the man I met in 1976 who wore "Jesus" patches on his blue jeans and had Christian bumper stickers on his van.

Glancing closer at the felt-flower doormat, I had a second thought: *Everyone who approaches our home—from the UPS man to unsolicited visitors—will know* . . . if they don't already know . . . that we are followers of the Lord!

My mind began a quick search of my previous encounters with the neighbors to our left and right and those across the street. Did these words truly represent my recent interactions and conversations? I hardly knew my neighbors, and I'm quite certain most had no idea what Roger and I did for a living. So the doormat seemed most appropriate!

I looked at my husband and said, "Let's go for it, Mr. Hokey Pokey. Having this statement of faith at our front door will keep me on my toes!"

It has been our intention to live in our home with integrity and blamelessness all of our married lives—this little doormat gives me increased desire to honor the name of the Lord before everyone who may never enter our home but will stand at our door!

# Never Ending

*The faithful love of the LORD never ends! His mercies never cease. Great is his faithfulness; his mercies begin afresh each morning.*

LAMENTATIONS 3:22-23

Recently, the founding pastor of our church came back to preach to our congregation after five years away. He spent the past five years under the authority of a restoration team who helped him reconcile his marriage and restore his call to the ministry. He just celebrated his twelfth wedding anniversary and is now a recovery pastor in a large church, mentoring and ministering to men who struggle with addiction.

His message was about the *great* faithfulness of God. He honestly and vulnerably shared that though he both experienced and caused great pain, God never left him or his family. He shared how God's love was real and powerfully present every day during the last five years and would be there for them every day in the future.

Knowing so well how the average Christian more easily hides sin than relinquishes it, he challenged any of us who might be in places of great temptation or deep discouragement to never doubt the Lord's willingness to love, forgive, sustain, or heal us.

My former pastor is living proof that the Lord's mercies and faithful love are new every morning!

Remember to pray for your pastors and their families.

## Real Love

*He does not punish us for all our sins; he does not deal harshly with us,
as we deserve. For his unfailing love toward those who fear him is as great
as the height of the heavens above the earth. He has removed our sins
as far from us as the east is from the west.* PSALM 103:10-12

Whenever I am asked to explain how my life changed so powerfully on the day I asked Christ into my life, I can't point to a rousing message by a preacher, the soul-moving worship songs of a Spirit-filled band, or being mentored by a great leader.

What dramatically changed my life and gave me supernatural courage *to turn in an instant from the habits that I could not break for years* was the experience of being forgiven by a loving God *when I didn't deserve it.*

Being given a second chance at life, not being treated harshly by God, not suffering many of the consequences for my sins that I deserved . . . was so overwhelming that I fell irrationally, emotionally, and overtly in love with Him! Euphoric, I immediately turned my back on my old life, unwilling to hurt the God who loved and forgave me.

There is simply no other explanation for the complete freedom I felt from the sins that had so powerfully dominated me, except that God removed them so far away from me that they were no longer able to haunt or taunt me.

Have you experienced the tangible, undeserved, unfailing, forgiving love of God?

# One Day

*Be careful then, dear brothers and sisters. Make sure that your own hearts
are not evil and unbelieving, turning you away from the living God.
You must warn each other every day, while it is still "today," so that none
of you will be deceived by sin and hardened against God. For if we are
faithful to the end, trusting God just as firmly as when we first believed,
we will share in all that belongs to Christ.* HEBREWS 3:12-14

Whenever I tell my testimony, I never hold back on the
ugly details of my addiction or the shame it caused in
my life. I know there is power to change a person's
life when he or she hears how God can take the most rebellious
life and turn it around.

After a recent talk, I sat on the stage to pray with people.
Before I'd even unhooked my microphone, a muscular guy in his
thirties with a hoop earring, surfer shorts, and a T-shirt came
running down the center of the aisle and landed on his knees,
sobbing with his face planted in his hands. He was crying so loud,
the people in the first row stopped their worship to look at him.
Through tears he said, "From the moment you began to speak,
I started to cry and couldn't stop. I have five months of sobriety
and your story gave me so much hope I cannot stop crying."

People want hope to change for good! They want to believe it
is possible.

When I came to Christ, I didn't know what trusting God or
belonging to Him would entail. But I started on the journey over
10,950 days ago . . . and "one day at a time" I'm still here, trusting Him with the same (or even more) passion than the day I first
believed!

## Daily Read

*The word of God is alive and powerful. It is sharper than the sharpest two-edged sword, cutting between soul and spirit, between joint and marrow. It exposes our innermost thoughts and desires.*   HEBREWS 4:12

I t's not official, but I am guessing that I have read through the Bible over twenty times . . . in twenty years. The formula that has made this discipline so manageable and accessible is the *Change Your Life Daily Bible* (a special edition of *The One Year Bible*).

Knowing that I can daily open the Bible to each day's date and read consecutive passages from the Old and New Testaments was exactly what I needed to overcome my previous weaknesses of procrastination or indecision on when or where to read in the Bible.

But I have more than a reading plan. The Word of God is His voice to me. It is as real, vibrant, significant, and powerful as the voice of the wisest counselor, the most brilliant professor, or the gentlest parent.

The Word of God surgically slices into the most hidden recesses of my heart and mind to expose what isn't right, what is festering, or what threatens to choke or smother the plans God has for me.

As I open God's Word daily, I say, "Speak to me, Lord." And it never fails. The Lord makes Himself and His standards very clear to me. His Word prompts and asks me not to think or ponder—but to obey. It is convicting, intriguing, impressive, comforting, inspiring, and touching.

His voice keeps me coming back day after day.

# Solid Food

*You have been believers so long now that you ought to be teaching others.*
*Instead, you need someone to teach you again the basic things about God's*
*word. You are like babies who need milk and cannot eat solid food.*

HEBREWS 5:12

Are you a baby believer who still needs milk—or are you hungry for solid food? To find out, ask yourself these questions. Are you convinced that

- the Word of God is as essential to your daily life as food is to your body?
- God *requires*, if not *demands*, holiness of those who call Him Lord?
- your body is the temple of His Holy Spirit?
- the Holy Spirit lives in you and is your ongoing, available source of supernatural power and comfort?
- sin will continue to tempt you all your Christian life?
- you have been given a spiritual gift to use for God's glory?
- you've been given an assignment to fulfill the Great Commission?
- you can hurt God if you are careless?
- God loves you—and nothing can separate you from His love?
- if you love God, you will obey Him?
- love is the language by which God's disciples are recognized?

If anything on this list is foreign to your thinking or of no concern . . . it is time to begin a search to find the biblical reference behind each of these concepts and grow in your knowledge and hunger for God. And if you are familiar with them, determine to teach them to others by starting a neighborhood, apartment, workplace, or dorm Bible study.

# God Speaks

*The Spirit of the LORD came upon me, and he told me to say, "This is what the LORD says to the people of Israel: I know what you are saying, for I know every thought that comes into your minds."* EZEKIEL 11:5

Ｇod spoke to Ezekiel.

And God speaks to you and me. He speaks through His Word and through those in authority over us, preachers, teachers, and His Holy Spirit. God speaks through circumstances, in whispers, and in storms. God will even speak through strangers.

Shortly after becoming a Christian, I felt God wanted me to leave California and return to Ohio. The feeling grew stronger every day as I read my Bible, listened to sermons, and talked with my new Christian friends.

My listening skills were certainly tested when a used-car salesman came into the car dealership where I was working for his monthly visit. When I told him I had become a Christian, he was shocked. Only the previous month, I was a foulmouthed, chain-smoking, hungover twenty-one-year-old. He could hardly believe that I was suddenly a sober, nonswearing Christian. If that weren't enough, I boldly added, "And God wants me to return home to Cleveland." He poked fun at me, asking, "Yeah, and how is God going to get you home?"

I answered, "God will find a way." He laughed in my face.

The very next day he returned saying, "My friend owns a car dealership outside of Cleveland. He also owns a twenty-nine-foot motor home that is stuck in Oakland, California. He offered to pay you (and for the gas) to drive the motor home to Cleveland. And when you get there, he'll give you a job at his dealership!"

I laughed and said, "I told you God would find a way!"

## Confession Session

*Some of the leaders of Israel visited me, and while they were sitting with me, this message came to me from the LORD: "Son of man, these leaders have set up idols in their hearts. They have embraced things that will make them fall into sin. Why should I listen to their requests? . . . Therefore, tell the people of Israel, 'This is what the Sovereign LORD says: Repent and turn away from your idols, and stop all your detestable sins.'"* EZEKIEL 14:1-3, 6

I used to think confession was a form of prayer primarily meant for unbelieving souls. In fact, I still remember my first confession session with the person who led me to Christ . . . the tears, the renunciation of specific sins, and the clean feeling that came over me when I had finished confessing every known sin I could think of . . .

But in the past few years, God has prompted me *at every meeting* to call Christians to confession. At the close of every message—whether delivered to parents, students, or Christian leaders—I ask all to examine their hearts for any known sin. I ask if they are struggling with sexual immorality, pornography, addiction, greed, lust, prejudice, pride, or unforgiveness. I beg them not to leave the meeting without renouncing, confessing, and *immediately* taking steps to remove specific sins from their lives.

I am especially surprised at how many leaders come forward to confess very serious sins.

It's as if God Himself is calling leaders out, confronting them with thoughts and words directly from Him. *I believe God is speaking to many hearts*, saying, "I see your sin and I hate it. I beg you to hate it and chase after *Me*. Make *Me* your *most sacred obsession*."

## Sick Heart

*You have prostituted yourself with the Assyrians, too. It seems you can never find enough new lovers! And after your prostitution there, you still were not satisfied. You added to your lovers by embracing Babylonia, the land of merchants, but you still weren't satisfied. What a sick heart you have, says the Sovereign LORD, to do such things as these, acting like a shameless prostitute.* EZEKIEL 16:28-30

*You can never find enough new lovers.*
   *After your prostitution . . . you still weren't satisfied.*

*You added to your lovers . . . and you still weren't satisfied.*
   *With a sick heart . . . you act like a shameless prostitute.*

Frankly, this sounds like an accusation made toward someone who is addicted to pornography!

Later, in Ezekiel 20:7-8, God's anger again emotes: "Then I said to them, 'Each of you, get rid of the vile images you are so obsessed with. Do not defile yourselves with the idols of Egypt, for I am the LORD your God.' But they rebelled against me and would not listen. They did not get rid of the vile images they were obsessed with."

Pornography is a billion-dollar industry. The dictionary defines *pornography* as "sexually explicit material intended to cause arousal." It is an insidious, hateful, evil, destructive form of prostitution that chases after men and women. It distorts. It creates false expectations from unrealistic and vile images. It is rebellion against God. It is idol worship. It is destructive to one's soul. It is exceedingly shameless and completely temporary.

Ultimately, it steals your ability to have true intimacy with God and your spouse.

If you are stuck in pornography, God says your heart is sick. Get help right now for your heart. There are sexual addiction groups in every community, most churches, and even on the Internet.

# Heartfelt Counsel

*The heartfelt counsel of a friend is as sweet as perfume and incense.*

PROVERBS 27:9

Though I'm not a counselor, I've had the opportunity to mentor, and more recently, act as a life coach for quite a few people over the past few years.

I find a great deal gets accomplished quite quickly when a person follows a three-prong system for admitting struggles, overcoming addictions (to food, alcohol, drugs, or gambling), and improving relationships:

1. *Expose the lies.* We all have blind spots. Most of us can't see *at all* what others can see clearly. An objective accountability partner—with whom you feel safe—can help identify the truth from the lies and won't be afraid to tell you so!

2. *Form new habits.* No matter what area of your life you want to change, I am convinced that the best and most strategic way to form new habits (whether you need to overcome, let go, or start fresh) is through a daily, rigorous habit of prayer and Bible reading. You must bring the presence of God, His Word, and the Holy Spirit into your difficulties if you want to see permanent change.

3. *Make firm decisions.* I always ask those I coach to make their decisions verbally and in writing. Whether they are making commitments to weight loss, sobriety, prayer, or sexual purity, telling me and God what they promise to do— or no longer do—makes a lasting impression.

If you don't have a friend who is able to inspire you to make desired spiritual, physical, emotional, financial, or relationship changes in your life, then perhaps it is time to join a support or prayer group, see a counselor, or hire a personal trainer or life coach.

## Passionate Heart

*Put all your rebellion behind you, and find yourselves a new heart and
a new spirit. For why should you die, O people of Israel? I don't want you
to die, says the Sovereign LORD. Turn back and live!* EZEKIEL 18:31-32

Ezekiel repeatedly spoke on God's behalf to the people of
Israel, begging them to put away anything that kept them
from giving their whole heart to Him.

Over the centuries, God has used messengers to reach out,
call out, and even beg His people to turn their hearts—with real
emotion—toward Him and find true love and everlasting life.

Henri Nouwen, priest and author, captured the dilemma of
one who longs to be devoted to God. In *A Cry for Mercy*, he writes,
"You are my Lord, Lord of my heart, mind, and soul. . . . Why do
I keep relating to you as one of my many relationships, instead
of my only relationship? Why do I keep looking for popularity,
respect from others, success, acclaim, and sensual pleasures? Why,
Lord, is it so hard for me to make you the only one? Why do I
keep hesitating to surrender myself totally to you?"[1]

God knows the heart of man. It can soar, chase, reach . . . and
reject.

God does not want you to love Him with words or duty
alone. He wants you to love Him with a passionate heart.

Oswald Chambers, a student of Charles Spurgeon and author
of *My Utmost for His Highest*, gave us the path to find a heart of
passion and love for the Lord. Simply he said, "Get into the habit
of saying, 'Speak, LORD,' and life will become a romance."[2]

# Fatherly Advice

*Be wise, my child, and make my heart glad. Then I will be able to answer my critics.* PROVERBS 27:11

**M**y husband, who is the oldest pastor among a young church staff, was asked to speak for weekend services from the book of Proverbs—written *by* the wise *for* the instruction of the young.

Roger accepted the invitation as any pastor might do, but couldn't shake the idea that he should deliver his message not as a pastor or preacher, but as a father speaking to his children.

After thirty-five years of full-time ministry—from youth to recovery to premarital and marriage counseling—Roger has watched young men and women struggle to navigate the Christian life with each passing decade.

As he began speaking, he asked, "How many of you heard *the sex talk* from your father?" He then proceeded to share from the Word of God—and from the heart of both a father and a counselor—about the damage and self-destruction he sees. Using Proverbs and other Bible verses, he begged young adults to pay attention to, grasp tightly, and try to understand—rather than avoid—the biblical principles for healthy relationships.

So he gave *the sex talk*—like a wise father who didn't want to see his children hurt God or themselves any longer. He suggested boundaries—asking young adults in every service if they would be willing to make a decision *not* to look at or touch another person's private parts until marriage. At the fourth service, full to capacity with over a thousand college students who had returned to the area for classes after a summer away, he received a round of applause—and we don't clap after sermons at our church.

The fatherly advice hit home in their hearts!

## God Search

*I looked for someone who might rebuild the wall of righteousness that guards the land. I searched for someone to stand in the gap in the wall so I wouldn't have to destroy the land, but I found no one.* EZEKIEL 22:30

G od is *still* looking for people to firmly stand for His righteous Word!

God is *still* searching, calling desperately for people to stand in the gap. . . .

A few years ago, I had the impression that God was calling me to go back and speak on college campuses. At first I was amused by the idea, then I grew terrified.

Soon it became more than a thought. God began to burn something into my heart. It was a message and a passion that wouldn't go away until I obeyed.

The first time I spoke to students, I trembled. The next time, I yelled like a preacher! (And I had never done that before!) The next time, I took only a half sheet of paper with a few "God thoughts" up to the podium. It was perhaps the most concise, clear message I've given to date. The next time, I cried and prayed with students for hours after the message.

Now I just get on the plane. I know why I go. And I have a pretty good idea what is going to happen when I get there. I will stand in the gap . . . the widening gap between a holy God and His children. I will tell the prodigals—those who have been away—that He loves them and wants them to come home. And I will call the lost to the One who finds and forgives and heals and loves. And they will come.

Are *you* called to stand in the gap?

# Deliberate Sinning

*Dear friends, if we deliberately continue sinning after we have received knowledge of the truth, there is no longer any sacrifice that will cover these sins.* HEBREWS 10:26

well-read friend gave me numerous religious classics. I found they illuminated the obvious: Men and women of every century and nation and culture have a "sin" problem! He gave me books by William Wilberforce, John Owen, and Jonathan Edwards. They gave sin a persona, which in turn made it much more visible! By adding Charles Spurgeon and Charles Finney to my reading stack, I found all the revivalists and preachers to agree on this: *Deliberate sin is an indicator of trouble in one's soul!*

William Wilberforce, politician and honored Englishman, wrote extensively on the contrast between a Christian who is holy and one who deliberately sins, calling the latter a nominal or bad Christian! He argued, "The true Christian . . . knows therefore that this holiness is not to *precede* his reconciliation with God, and be its *cause*; but to follow it, and be its *effect*. That, in short, it is by faith in Christ only. . . . Faith, where genuine, is always accompanied with repentance."[3]

About a half century later, Charles Spurgeon gave his very riveting explanation for ridding oneself of ongoing, deliberate sin, saying, "Oh, that you would run away from your old master tonight, without giving him a minute's notice. If you give him any notice, he will hold you. Run to Jesus, and say, 'Here is a poor runaway slave! My Lord, I still wear the chains upon my wrists. Will You set me free, and make me Your own?'"[4]

Convinced, I too give sin a persona. If you can see it, you can run from it.

## Confident Faith

*It is impossible to please God without faith. Anyone who wants to
come to him must believe that God exists and that he rewards those
who sincerely seek him.* HEBREWS 11:6

In 1897, A. B. Simpson, the founder of the Christian and
Missionary Alliance denomination, said, "God chooses people
He can depend upon. . . . God is looking for people on whom
He can place the weight of His entire love, power, and faithful
promises."[5]

The eleventh chapter of Hebrews captures just a small number
of those men and women on whom God placed the entire weight of
His promises. And they believed!

God asked Noah to build a boat on dry land, fill it with animals,
and expect rain to cover the earth. Noah obeyed God and saved his
family—the only human beings spared in the great Flood.

God asked Abraham and Sarah to believe He would give
them a child when it was humanly impossible. They were past
their childbearing years, yet they still believed. And indeed they
received the promise.

God asked Moses to cross the Red Sea *as if it were dry ground*,
with two million of His people, all the while with an army of
Egyptians on their heels. They crossed safely and the Egyptians
drowned.

God gave Joseph a dream when he was a young man. Joseph
held on to that dream, and though first a slave and then a prisoner,
he became a ruler in a foreign land and saved his family from famine.

What about Daniel, Esther, King Jehoshaphat, or Anna and
Simeon? What about Nehemiah, Ezra, Joshua, or Caleb?

The common denominator of these men and women was
*courage to believe the God they couldn't see* while being ridiculed by
observers, mocked by opponents, even shunned by their families.

Do you exhibit such confident faith?

## Praise Report

*How amazing are the deeds of the L*ORD*! All who delight in him*
*should ponder them. Everything he does reveals his glory and majesty.*
*His righteousness never fails.* PSALM 111:2-3

We shouldn't have to be reminded, but so often we consider others' experiences with God so amazing that we lose sight of how often, how much, and how deeply God cares for us. As often as He protects, provides, and promises—we complain, envy, or wallow.

*If I only took time to thank Him for my relationships . . .*

My husband . . . I can't begin to list the many ways that God meets the needs of my heart through this man.

My son . . . being a mother has taught me more about God's unfailing love than any other earthly relationship.

My mom . . . I can't explain how inspired I am by her life—after eighty-five years she still enthusiastically loves God and others.

*But there is so much more. . . .*

My church . . . it is so vibrant, so "on fire" for the Lord, and has such great teaching, so many incredibly talented musicians, teachers, and artists.

My work . . . over thirty years ago, I answered God's call to reconcile others to Him. I look back amazed. I look forward expectantly.

For some of us, a grateful heart has to be encouraged. I, for one, need the practical tool of a daily, written thank-you note to God to lift me out of pity or pride in order to recognize and record the wonderfully delightful ways my God and King is working around me today.

Give Him *your* praise and thanks!

## Faith Race

*Therefore, since we are surrounded by such a huge crowd of witnesses
to the life of faith, let us strip off every weight that slows us down,
especially the sin that so easily trips us up. And let us run with
endurance the race God has set before us.* HEBREWS 12:1

How do you run the faith race and not get weary after three months or three years or even after thirty years? Hebrews 12:2 says, "We do this by keeping our eyes on Jesus, the champion who initiates and perfects our faith. Because of the joy awaiting him, he endured the cross, disregarding its shame. Now he is seated in the place of honor beside God's throne."

Hebrews reminds us:

1. Be encouraged that others who've run their race *are watching yours!* Athletes will tell you that one of the most motivating factors of competition is the cheering crowd. The galleries exhilarate them, giving them adrenaline to keep going when their storehouses of energy are depleted.

2. Cut ties quickly with those things or persons that stall or stop your forward movement. This seems *so* practical, but is *so* difficult. Your best tactic is immediacy. Once you discover unnecessary extra weight, quickly throw it overboard or strip it off. It has only one purpose: to slow you down or make you lose your race.

3. Emulate your leader, your Champion, Jesus Christ. He ran His race, knowing it would include suffering and difficulty. He ran it anyway . . . to please His Father. For the joy set before Him, He endured the cross.

Don't forget that your biggest fan, Jesus, is one of the many witnesses who cheer you on.

## Satisfied Soul

*Just as Death and Destruction are never satisfied, so human desire is never satisfied.* PROVERBS 27:20

J ames Allen captured the nature of our hearts concisely in *As a Man Thinketh*, saying, "You will always gravitate toward that which you, secretly, most love."[6]

The heart is never satisfied. It longs to be filled with unfailing, endless love. But the love that the world offers is only counterfeit and temporary.

Those of us who have chased hard and long to satisfy our insatiable "love" appetite with alcohol, food, drugs, or relationships often make a great impact on those still chasing after those things. Those of us who've spiraled so far down the hole, chasing that which will never satisfy, can prove with our broken lives how destructive that is.

I was like a zombie. I was caught in a cycle of self-destruction. I refused to see reality—the possibility of pregnancy, the shame I was extending to my family name, the talent and money I was throwing away. I could not admit that what I chased—over and over and over—was never going to satisfy my soul. I came to the brink of suicide.

Sometimes I still choke up when telling an audience how ashamed I am of my past sexual immorality and alcoholic binges. Those experiences are still incredibly humiliating to me. But I share them because I just wish someone had had the guts to take me aside when I was a teenager and say, "Becky, you can't tell me that being sexually active with different men, getting drunk every night, smoking dope and cigarettes, and swearing profusely *makes you happy* or fills your deepest emotional and spiritual needs. Becky, only Jesus can satisfy your soul. . . ."

That is why I can't stay silent. I have to ask: . . . *Is it well with your soul?*

## Your Obedience

*Now, son of man, I am making you a watchman for the people of Israel.*
*Therefore, listen to what I say and warn them for me. If I announce that*
*some wicked people are sure to die and you fail to tell them to change their*
*ways, then they will die in their sins, and I will hold you responsible for*
*their deaths. But if you warn them to repent and they don't repent, they*
*will die in their sins, but you will have saved yourself.* EZEKIEL 33:7-9

Two weeks after I had spoken at a college chapel service, a faculty member called me. He asked me to come back to campus and give a longer presentation to a smaller group of students who were very interested in learning more about prayer. He suggested a date, not even a week later. I hesitated. I was leaving for a trip the morning after his proposed date and I felt it would be inconvenient to make the long drive and speak for three hours the night before a trip. He was so persistent I told him I would prayerfully consider his invitation, but I was fairly sure I would not do it.

At the time (November), the book of Ezekiel was scheduled for my daily Old Testament readings. Not once, but twice, I felt God warning me as I read the words in Ezekiel, "If you don't go where and when I ask you to go, and take My message of prayer, confession, and repentance to them, their lives will be at risk— and so will yours! Now go."

I called the faculty member back the next morning and said, "I'll be there."

It isn't about someone else's obedience, it's about your own!

## New Heart

*I will sprinkle clean water on you, and you will be clean. Your filth will*
*be washed away, and you will no longer worship idols. And I will give*
*you a new heart, and I will put a new spirit in you. I will take out*
*your stony, stubborn heart and give you a tender, responsive heart.*
*And I will put my Spirit in you so that you will follow my decrees*
*and be careful to obey my regulations.* EZEKIEL 36:25-27

This Old Testament picture perfectly illustrates the New
Testament conversion that takes place when God forgives
a sinner because of Jesus' blood sacrifice.

First, God must clean the filth away. A common barrier that
keeps people from surrendering their lives to God is pride. They
simply refuse to admit they are sinners. Unfortunately, this can
keep them far from God for a long time. And over time, they
risk becoming insensitive to God's Holy Spirit. They find it easy
to resist God's truth, His promptings, His messengers. And their
hearts become like stone.

Second, God requires that they give up all other gods—any
idols that have stolen the love and loyalty due to Him. Again, this
becomes a "deal breaker" for many. Immediately giving up, letting
go . . . is not an option for them. They want more time; they negotiate. God will have none of that. It is all or nothing with Him.

Finally, if they will come clean and relinquish all other gods,
He will then give them *all* they need to follow and obey Him.
He puts His powerful Holy Spirit into their hearts, giving them
indomitable power to live new lives.

Is your heart *stony and stubborn* or *tender and responsive* to the
Lord?

The good news is that God's heart-replacement methods
haven't changed.

NOVEMBER 18

## Do It

*Don't just listen to God's word. You must do what it says. Otherwise, you are only fooling yourselves.* JAMES 1:22

One of the most powerful phrases available to the mind and mouth of a believer is *I will*.

In contrast, the phrases *I'll try*, *I hope to*, *I want to*, *I should*, *I need to*, *I wish*, *I'd like to* all reserve the right to fail! They do not engage your heart, mind, and body with conviction; they allow room for relapse, laziness, and haphazardness.

When I speak, I always ask people to make decisions about what they believe God is asking of them. I almost always quote Oswald Chambers near the end of my speaking engagements: "When a truth of God is brought home to your soul, never allow it to pass without acting on it internally in your will, not necessarily externally in your physical life. Record it with ink and with blood—work it into your life."[7]

Most often, I hear God's marching orders during my quiet time. Because I already am in the habit of writing my thoughts and prayers, I am positioned to respond to God by making decisions *in ink!* This is why written prayer is so powerful! It is convicting to write down what you *think or feel* God is asking you to do. When you tell Him in writing what *you will* do, you take your relationship with God to another level. Your word to Him is no longer good intention—it is a commitment.

I find I have the most courage and motivation to obey God when I *don't hesitate*, when I make quick decisions and step out immediately.

Has God been asking you to do (or not do) something? Don't debate or negotiate with yourself or Him. Just do it. Do it now.

## Victory Song

*The LORD is my strength and my song; he has given me victory.*

PSALM 118:14

Y ou know you've really reached the climax of a live concert when the audience and artist become one; tens of thousands of whooping and hollering fans are waving their arms, swaying their bodies, and singing the lyrics in complete unison!

While in an arena for a meeting, I could hear quite a loud noise. So I poked my head into a doorway to hear a favorite worship band firing up the crowd. Even if you didn't know their songs, you could pick up the chorus and feel as if you were part of one loud voice bringing heaven down!

The band was so compelling, I slowly moved from the mezzanine entrance to an aisle of the lower grandstand. I wasn't dressed appropriately for the concert like everyone else. While they were casual and layered, I wore high-heeled boots, long wool pants, and a thick wool turtleneck sweater.

All of sudden, the worship leader instructed us to put our arms around each other's necks and waist and—jump! Jump? I didn't want to be included at that point—but it was too late! A huge football player in the row below me threw his big forearm and hand around my waist and the girl next to me grabbed my neck—and started jumping up and down, each to a different beat of the music. I knew instinctively if I didn't jump hard and high, I'd be launched from the steel benches into the hockey banner above.

It was an unforgettable experience of praising, worship, and laughing, and loving Jesus.

Now when I'm home alone, I turn on those worship songs and *jump*! I want to relive that exhilarating feeling as often as possible!

## Humble Yourself

*Humble yourselves before God. Resist the devil, and he will flee from you.*
*Come close to God, and God will come close to you. Wash your hands,*
*you sinners; purify your hearts, for your loyalty is divided between*
*God and the world.* JAMES 4:7-8

The Bible tells us that humility is the character trait that will combat and defeat the devil, and force him to leave you alone.

I get a vivid picture when I read this verse. . . .

*I am a believer barraged and assailed all day long by my enemy, as*
*well as by my own silly, sad charades. I am so easily and consistently*
*distracted by my emotions, circumstances, and thoughts.*

*Then, I walk into a room and unexpectedly see Jesus.*
*Suddenly, everything becomes clear.*

*First I am humbled—because of who He is and who I am.*
*I immediately regard Him with the awe and respect He deserves.*
*I offer no excuses for myself. I am not proud or arrogant in front*
*of Him, but keenly aware of my propensity toward sin, lust, and*
*temptation.*

*I realize how negligent I have been in watching over my soul.*
*I am humbled again, realizing I must be much more empathetic and*
*patient with others. I know—I do not need to be told—that only*
*those with clean hands and pure hearts will remain in the company*
*of a holy God.*

*I kneel, bow, and confess that I must more diligently harness my*
*individual personality and give it to Him in complete and undivided*
*loyalty, for only then will I have wisdom, courage, and discernment to*
*live each day close to Him.*

What is the picture *you* see when you read these verses?

# Effective Prayer

*The earnest prayer of a righteous person has great power and produces*
*wonderful results. Elijah was as human as we are, and yet when he prayed*
*earnestly that no rain would fall, none fell for three and a half years!*
*Then, when he prayed again, the sky sent down rain and the earth*
*began to yield its crops.* JAMES 5:16-18

I can't say it enough: Prayer is incredibly essential to a believer's life. It is your instant access to God's power, comfort, direction, warning. It is your weapon. You protect yourself and others when you launch offensives at your enemy using God's name!

Prayer is the source of *continual, ongoing* strength.

Jesus taught His disciples often and much about prayer. He modeled it daily, nightly, in crisis, and as a lifestyle. In prayer, He knew He would receive courage from His Father to keep going; He would be given answers to His questions and would be sustained in waiting.

The most compelling aspect of these James verses is that they give you and me the impression—and the permission—that anyone can become a powerful and effective pray-er.

People who act upon the biblical principles of prayer do so because they trust them. They believe that if they apply these principles to their lives, they *will see* the promises of God fulfilled in their lives. George Müller did it. Hudson Taylor did it. Corrie ten Boom did it. Hannah Whitall Smith did it. You and I can do it!

I remember the answer Anne Graham Lotz gave to the question "What does it feel like being the child of Billy Graham?" She replied, "Not everyone can be the child of Billy Graham, but anyone can *be* a Billy Graham!"

No more excuses. . . . Go and be, make, do . . . believe!

# Settle It

*You love him even though you have never seen him. Though you do not see*
*him now, you trust him; and you rejoice with a glorious, inexpressible joy.*

1 PETER 1:8

I love the story found in the classic devotional *Streams in the
Desert*, of a dutiful church man who confessed he had never
experienced the emotional love of God.

Then it happened. During a regular church service following
a sermon, the preacher closed in a simple prayer that changed his
entire perspective of God. The prayer was, "Oh Lord, Thou know-
est we can trust the Man who died for us."

The church man said:

> *I pondered deeply all that consecration might mean to my life—
> and I was afraid. . . . I reached home . . . and there upon my knees
> I saw my past life. I had been a Christian, an officer in the church,
> a Sunday School superintendent, but had never definitely yielded
> my life to God. Yet as I thought of the daring plans which might be
> baffled, of the cherished hopes to be surrendered, and the chosen
> profession I might be called to abandon—I was afraid. . . .*
>
> *I did not see the better things God had for me, so my soul was
> shrinking back; and then for the last time with a swift rush of convict-
> ing power, came to my innermost heart that searching message: "My
> child, you can trust the Man that died for you. If you cannot trust
> Him whom can you trust?" That settled it for me, for in a flash I saw
> that the Man who so loved me as to die for me could be absolutely
> trusted with all the concerns of the life He had saved.*[8]

Duty does not settle it; devotion does. Is it settled in your life?

# Happy Hour

*So think clearly and exercise self-control. Look forward to the gracious
salvation that will come to you when Jesus Christ is revealed to the world.
So you must live as God's obedient children. Don't slip back into your old
ways of living to satisfy your own desires. You didn't know any better then.*

1 PETER 1:13-14

The first smell—and taste—of alcohol was always enticing to me. But as the hours progressed, the smell got stale, and the taste became dull. It was not an exaggeration to say that I drank myself into oblivion every night. I either fell asleep right where I was sitting—with my head on a table, waking up hours later to drive myself home—or someone just carried me out and drove me home or to his or her house. Many mornings I woke up at friends' homes . . . until the morning I woke up next to a stranger.

A few weeks later, I became a Christian and received a miracle—at least it was to me. God took away the desire to drink that had consumed me, my father, and his father. From that moment, I hated the smell of alcohol. I considered it poison. I knew if I continued to drink, it would steal my new life in Christ. I knew it was critical to quit completely or I'd slip back. I had no option but to cut loose my friends and never touch liquor. It took only a few setbacks, then I made one last decision to hate what I once had loved—and never have another drink.

That which I had formerly loved and had thought I so desperately needed became my enemy. I've been sober over thirty years. . . . I believe that decision saved my life and gave me a faith-filled marriage and ministry.

# Lifestyle

*People who conceal their sins will not prosper, but if they confess and turn from them, they will receive mercy.* PROVERBS 28:13

Our natural tendency is to hide, rationalize, or even under-estimate the pursuit of our old favorite—but deadly—sins. John Owen, in his extensive treatise *Sin and Temptation*, discusses the power of lingering sin in a believer's life. He suggests that sin must *never* be tolerated. He writes, "To let sin alone in our lives is to permit sin to grow until it chokes and blinds the conscience."[9]

Owen contended that if you put up with them—even in a weak-ened state in your life—or allow them to remain like wounded prey healing their injuries, they will recover strength to use against you!

A Christian simply cannot conceal his or her sins *and expect* to have victory over them. If we have such expectation, we are only fooling ourselves. There is a way to obtain freedom from them and mercy for them:

*First, confess.* Through confession, more than forgiveness is available. There is healing power released in public confession. James 5:16 says, "Confess your sins to each other and pray for each other *so that you may be healed*" (emphasis added).

*Second, turn.* Be active, not passive. Do you need to write a letter or make a call? Recovery ministries refer to this activity as "making amends." What does it take to keep a clean slate with God and others? It requires that we take consistent, personal inventto-ries of all areas of life and make adjustments, apologies, and resti-tution wherever and whenever necessary.

*Third, receive.* Mercy is God's supernatural provision. Mercy from God gives us the courage to change, to do and say what was previously impossible, uncomfortable, or even unfathomable.

Consider making this pattern of "confess, turn, and receive" a daily lifestyle habit!

# Not Ashamed!

*You must worship Christ as Lord of your life. And if someone asks about your Christian hope, always be ready to explain it. But do this in a gentle and respectful way. Keep your conscience clear. Then if people speak against you, they will be ashamed when they see what a good life you live because you belong to Christ.* 1 PETER 3:15-16

In 1995, I returned to Monterey, California, to attend an evangelism seminar. Earl Palmer, a fabulous theologian, was the guest speaker. On the first morning, he delivered an unforgettable message on the power of the gospel, saying, "Over time the gospel, which is the good news that Jesus loves us and died for us, *will* vindicate itself."

Nineteen years earlier, I had become a Christian in Monterey. At the time, no one seemed excited about my dramatic spiritual and moral changes. My boyfriend was especially afraid I was changing for the worse. He hoped it would be a passing fad. It wasn't. . . .

Sitting in the conference, I reflected on how productive, fulfilling, and healthy my life had truly become because of Christ.

That afternoon, I took a ride through my old neighborhood and headed to my aunt and uncle's house, not far from the conference hotel. They, especially, had been skeptical of my professed faith in Christ many years earlier—but I was excited to see them.

As if on cue, while driving through the wharf area of downtown Monterey, my old boyfriend randomly ran across the street in front of my car. We hadn't spoken in nineteen years. . . . I stopped the car and jumped out. At first he didn't even recognize me! Then he asked, "Beck, what are you doing here?"

I was not ashamed to say that I was still captivated by the One who had won my heart years ago!

## Enemy Alert

*Stay alert! Watch out for your great enemy, the devil. He prowls around like a roaring lion, looking for someone to devour. Stand firm against him, and be strong in your faith. Remember that your Christian brothers and sisters all over the world are going through the same kind of suffering you are.*

1 PETER 5:8-9

Y ou know you have an enemy—but are you aware of him in your daily life? Can you discern his presence, tactics, or intervention in any situation?

When I was five years old, I was chased and attacked by a neighbor's cat. Forced into a crouched position at my front door, I was scratched in the face and even had to get stitches. I've *never* forgotten the experience. In fact, I've never really liked cats since then. (Imagine how concerned you would be if you had a loose lion roaming your neighborhood, as they do in the hills of Southern California!) To this day, I'm cautious and aware of the presence of a cat, always keeping it in my peripheral vision. I don't trust them.

Peter's words come to life for me because of that childhood experience.

Staying alert and watching out for your *great enemy, the devil* is not optional for a believer. You must not be careless or uneducated about his presence in your life because *he is* prowling around you like a roaring lion (not a neighborhood cat) looking to devour (not scratch) you!

Do you understand this concept—or have you minimized the impact and destruction that your enemy desires to cause in your life?

Peter begs you and me to be alert and stand firm against our great enemy, the devil. How? Start by keeping him in your peripheral vision at all times.

# Your Testimony

*King Nebuchadnezzar sent this message to the people of every race and nation and language throughout the world: "Peace and prosperity to you! I want you all to know about the miraculous signs and wonders the Most High God has performed for me. How great are his signs, how powerful his wonders! His kingdom will last forever, his rule through all generations."*

DANIEL 4:1-3

How amazing it must have been for Daniel to record that a king who previously did not know or follow God became so convinced of His power and fame that he proclaimed it for the world to know!

Proclaiming the power of God is the privilege and responsibility of every believer. If you know God, you are to proclaim the miraculous signs and wonders He has performed for *you*!

Your testimony never ends. How God drew you to Him, how He is working in your life today, and what you believe He is going to do in your life in the future *is how others will come to know Him*!

Your testimony is the ongoing story of God's power displayed in your life. As God changes your life, He will show others that He has the power to change their lives too! When He changes your attitude, actions, even your plans . . . nonbelievers will be amazed and challenged to put their trust *in your God*! It doesn't matter if you are a world leader or a high school student—when God works in your life, there is a ripple effect as you speak out about what He has done for you.

Don't hesitate to look for opportunities to tell the amazing story of God's ever-present work in your life. Give God credit for opening a door, answering a specific prayer, improving your situation, or healing a relationship.

## Your Hope

*You are my refuge and my shield; your word is my source of hope.*

PSALM 119:114

L ife is difficult.

Whether you are a new believer and you can barely see out of a hole you've dug, or you're a middle-aged father whose children are in college (and you're terribly concerned about each one of them), life is difficult.

I, frankly, don't know how you can "do" life without being in a personal relationship with the living, loving God!

To know that God is your friend—that He cares, sees, and knows . . . can make the worst day manageable.

To know that God loves you just the way you are, especially on those days when everyone around you does not love you . . . keeps you going.

To know that God forgives you when you don't deserve it, when you've surpassed seventy times seven . . . allows you to sleep at night.

To know that God offers you protection, whether it is unseen or visible . . . gives you courage to rise above your fears.

To know that God can give you hope, real emotional relief in stressful situations . . . is priceless if your life is consumed with unrelentingly stressful situations.

You must truly *know* God to believe that He is your refuge and shield.

You can know God better by reading His Word. His Word is your greatest source of hope. Do not neglect receiving the hope He longs to give you daily. Let the psalmist's words in Psalm 119:116-117 become your prayer today: "Lord, sustain me as you promised, that I may live! Do not let my hope be crushed. Sustain me, and I will be rescued; then I will meditate continually on your decrees."

# Quality Character

*The other administrators and high officers began searching for some fault in the way Daniel was handling government affairs, but they couldn't find anything to criticize or condemn. He was faithful, always responsible, and completely trustworthy.* DANIEL 6:4

This current generation is particularly bent on living life to the fullest. Their personal happiness conveniently fits into their theology until something happens that rocks their world or redefines their purpose.

For each of us, character-building experiences are not usually sought after, but are found when we step over a line or get caught doing something wrong.

We can talk about character until we're blue in the face, but when we do something that is unfaithful, irresponsible, or untrustworthy . . . life takes on a new perspective.

As believers, there must come a day when we see ourselves not as our own person or our parent's child, but as God's representative, His ambassador.

Daniel had his relationship with God firmly in perspective at a very young age. He was willing to defy culture in order to please and honor his God (see Daniel 1). He was such a fine example of a young person who grew stronger in his love and devotion for God, even as his position in a godless government grew more prominent.

Daniel's life serves as a model for anyone of any age who lives in a godless culture. To make a lasting impact with our lives, we must have godly character. We must realize that every choice we make reflects not only upon us, but more importantly, upon the God we serve and profess.

# Jesus Concealed

*As my vision continued that night, I saw someone like a son of man coming with the clouds of heaven. He approached the Ancient One and was led into his presence. He was given authority, honor, and sovereignty over all the nations of the world, so that people of every race and nation and language would obey him. His rule is eternal—it will never end. His kingdom will never be destroyed.* DANIEL 7:13-14

Daniel received a vision of Jesus. He saw the "son of man" approaching the presence of God as no unholy human being could do. Daniel understood that this "son" was given the authority and power to rule over all the nations of the world. He saw every race and every nation obeying the "son." He saw His kingdom as never ending and indestructible.

Daniel received this vision—and recorded it—hundreds of years before Christ came to earth.

The Old Testament reveals Jesus, and the New Testament is Jesus revealed.

What is your understanding of the prophecies found in the Bible? Are you uncertain about Bible prophecy and avoid it or do you dig in to better understand it?

Prophecy in the Bible is not meant to confuse us, nor is it to be ignored.

Old Testament books of the Bible, such as Daniel, and New Testament books, such as Revelation, are in the inspired Word of God. They are in the Bible so that we might know God better, clearly hear His voice, and understand His work among His people in the past and in the future.

Take care to read and understand the entire Bible, not limiting yourself to those books that are more comfortable to read or easier to understand.

# Constant Craving

*Do not love this world nor the things it offers you, for when you love the world, you do not have the love of the Father in you. For the world offers only a craving for physical pleasure, a craving for everything we see, and pride in our achievements and possessions. These are not from the Father, but are from this world. And this world is fading away, along with everything that people crave. But anyone who does what pleases God will live forever.* 1 JOHN 2:15-17

It begins when you're young. You want something you can't have or can't afford. You want it anyway. . . . You're convinced that if you get it, it will satisfy you.

Sex especially becomes a constant craving for many. But there are other obsessions . . . more money, a better house, the best car. Whatever you don't have becomes what you must have. Those cravings never end.

John's counsel certainly didn't take into consideration the pop-psychology advice that suggests that phrases beginning with *do not* will not motivate people. But perhaps "motivating people" was not his intent?

John met the Son of God. He knew there is only one God, one love, one truth, one hope. He knew there was only One who could satisfy the constant cravings of our bodies, minds, and souls. Only One.

He was telling the truth—explaining the difference between love and lust. He knew that chasing after physical or visual gratification or material possessions would never satisfy, because they were fading, temporary pleasures and man was created for an eternal relationship with the living, loving God!

He wasn't asking us to agree with him. He was telling us what he knew to be true—if we will live to please God, it will change *what we crave* and *how we love*.

# Humble Pray-er

*He explained to me, "Daniel, I have come here to give you insight and
understanding. The moment you began praying, a command was given. And
now I am here to tell you what it was, for you are very precious to God.
Listen carefully so that you can understand the meaning of your vision."*

DANIEL 9:22-23

Daniel was an amazing man of prayer. What made him
special was his intimacy with God and lifelong humility
toward Him. Whenever he was afraid or concerned, or
wanted to move God's heart, Daniel would fast and pray for long
periods of time. The prayer that prompted an angel to be sent to
him is recorded in the ninth chapter of Daniel, giving us great
insight into the heart of this humble pray-er.

> Daniel began with a proclamation of God's faithfulness,
> telling Him He was great and awesome and thanking Him
> for always fulfilling His promises.
>
> He immediately confessed the specific—not general—
> sins of God's people, including his own sins.
>
> Next Daniel begged God to turn His anger away from
> them, to have mercy on them . . . even to smile on them!
> He knew they didn't deserve such compassionate treat-
> ment, but Daniel gave valid reason for his demand—God
> was known as a forgiving God. It was in His nature to be
> merciful.
>
> He finally pleaded with God to lean down and listen to him,
> to come close to him and not delay sending an answer.

Daniel teaches us how to humble ourselves in prayer—to
proclaim His greatness, to confess any known sin, and to ask Him to
listen, *not because we deserve to be heard, but because it is in God's nature to
mercifully answer us.*

# Bold Confidence

*Dear friends, if we don't feel guilty, we can come to God with bold confidence.* 1 JOHN 3:21

Irst John 3:7-22 contains a very concise to-do list of those things that will make your life bold in prayer and powerful in witness.

John first warns those in God's family not to keep sinning (verses 7-10). He goes so far as to say, if you keep sinning, you're not really in the family of God. (Surely those words riled up some folks then and still do today, but he was not hesitant to make his point clear and strong.)

John then talks about love between believers. He calls those who don't love their Christian brothers and sisters *murderers at heart* (verses 11-15)! (John is a "no mess around" communicator. I doubt he would be preaching in a megachurch with this text!)

He also must have seen too much greed and hypocrisy, because he goes right after those who have "enough money to live well" (verse 17) but who show no compassion to those in need; he questions whether God's love is even in them (verse 16-20)!

If John is hard on them, it appears there is a real purpose behind his admonition. In sharing these apparent, glaring traits of his fellow believers, John encourages them to live in right relationship with God and others so they might experience great boldness and confidence in prayer (verse 21). He concludes in 1 John 3:22, "And we will receive from him whatever we ask because we obey him and do the things that please him."

Bold confidence and great power in prayer are the promised results of a believer who has a clean heart, gives generously, and loves genuinely.

## Greatest Story

*God showed how much he loved us by sending his one and only Son into the world so that we might have eternal life through him. This is real love—not that we loved God, but that he loved us and sent his Son as a sacrifice to take away our sins.* 1 JOHN 4:9-10

Blaise Pascal, seventeenth-century French mathematician and philosopher, concluded, "There is a God shaped vacuum in the heart of every man which cannot be filled by any created thing, but only by God, the Creator, made known through Jesus."[1]

If you know Jesus, you've been commissioned to tell the world that He lives, He loves, and He forgives. It is the greatest story. He is the answer to the emptiness in every heart.

Perhaps that is why I cannot keep myself from sharing the gospel, most especially with strangers. I've shared Jesus with hotel cleaning staff, flight attendants, waiters, counter clerks, grocers, bank tellers, mail carriers, manicurists, hairstylists, radio and television producers, politicians, maintenance workers, and garbage men. I've given them Bibles, invited them to church, written letters, and sent them books, *because I am convinced that every one of them was searching to fill the hole in their hearts with God's love!*

Charles Spurgeon, the "Prince of Preachers," called the art of sharing the gospel "soulwinning." In *The Soulwinner* he wrote, "Soul winning is the chief business of the Christian; indeed it should be the main pursuit of every true believer." He added, "We should bring men to Christ, not to our own particular views of Christianity."[2]

When you have only a short amount of time to share the greatest story in the world with someone you barely know . . . remember, first and foremost, it is a love story between a Father and Son—and us!

# Holy Affection

*Dear children, keep away from anything that might take God's place in your hearts.* 1 JOHN 5:21

I t is normal to be excited about someone you love.

It is normal to be passionate.

It is abnormal, perhaps even a sign of trouble, if you are passive, bored, or unenthusiastic about your true love.

So why, here on earth, should your holy affection for the living, loving God *ever* fade or remain unexpressed? Who would it benefit for you to be reserved, unenthusiastic, or passionless about the most sacred obsession of your life? In fact, isn't that what everyone is searching for and chasing after—endless love, overwhelming joy, undeserved forgiveness, eternal life?

God is not passive in His love toward you. I see no reason, whatsoever, to be passive in your love toward Him. If you chase after Him, He will not only reveal Himself to you as the object of your deepest longing and heart's desire, but He will fill up to overflowing every emptiness! He will fall all over you with His love and presence. He loves you deeply. He will light your inner fire. He will warm your heart. He will quench your thirst. He will fill your hunger with Himself. He will immediately infuse you with all you need to exhibit discipline and courage. *He will enable you to do what you could not do before.*

You choose or refuse the Sacred Obsession.
You chase or neglect the Sacred Obsession.
You invite or ignore the Sacred Obsession.
You embrace or avoid the Sacred Obsession.
You become what you chase after.

## Tipping Point

*Hear the word of the LORD, O people of Israel! The LORD has brought charges against you, saying:"There is no faithfulness, no kindness, no knowledge of God in your land." HOSEA 4:1*

Hosea, a prophet of God, delivered the following charges against God's people for their unfaithfulness toward Him.

*You make vows and break them . . . commit[ting] adultery. There is violence everywhere. . . . Even the wild animals, the birds of the sky . . . are disappearing. Don't point your finger at someone else. . . . My complaint . . . is with you. . . . My people are being destroyed because they don't know me. . . . You have forgotten the laws of your God. . . . The more priests there are, the more they sin against me. They have exchanged the glory of God for the shame of idols. . . . Wine has robbed my people of their understanding. They ask a piece of wood for advice! . . . Longing after idols has made them foolish. They have played the prostitute, serving other gods and deserting their God. (Hosea 4:2-12)*

God, who is completely fed up with them, declares His tipping point:

*When they come with their flocks and herds to offer sacrifices to the LORD, they will not find him, because he has withdrawn from them. They have betrayed the honor of the LORD. . . . Sound the alarm. . . . I will be like a lion to Israel. . . . I will carry them off, and no one will be left to rescue them. Then I will return to my place until they admit their guilt and turn to me. For as soon as trouble comes, they will earnestly search for me. (Hosea 5:6-15)*

The book of Hosea still speaks. . . .

## Storytellers

*When the LORD brought back his exiles to Jerusalem, it was like a dream!
We were filled with laughter, and we sang for joy. And the other nations
said,"What amazing things the LORD has done for them."Yes, the LORD has
done amazing things for us! What joy!* PSALM 126:1-3

For every season of illness, or those times when you feel abandoned or rejected, during self-imposed hibernation, or after extended periods of God's mysterious silence—you must hold on to the hope that God desires to restore you.

Were you once imprisoned and now set free?
Were you once addicted and now sober?
Were you once terrified and now fearless?
Were you once humiliated and now unashamed?
Were you once consumed with worry and now full of faith?
Were you once distressed and now overflowing with peace?
Were you once humiliated and now restored?
Were you once intimidated and now strong?
Were you once infirm and now healed?

People are watching. They are hopeless, defeated, confused. When you tell the story of your healing or restoration, they receive hope to believe God will do the same for them. When you tell the story of how God did the impossible, the unbelievable, or even the unusual in or for you, those who need great intervention will be compelled to call on your God for help.

If the Lord has released you from bondage, set your soul free, removed your shame, healed your body, answered your prayer, defeated your enemy, or restored your fortunes . . . tell the story so others might come to know the God of the Bible and put their trust in Him.

# Revival Fire

*You, dear friends, must build each other up in your most holy faith, pray in the power of the Holy Spirit, and await the mercy of our Lord Jesus Christ, who will bring you eternal life. In this way, you will keep yourselves safe in God's love.* JUDE 1:20-21

D
r. Wesley Duewel, former president of OMS International and missionary to India for almost twenty-five years, is a renowned historian of the work of the Holy Spirit over the centuries. His accounts of revival in *Revival Fire* and *Ablaze for God* will set your heart on fire as you witness the flame of revival crossing the globe, which reveals the presence and power of the Holy Spirit in almost every culture and generation.

Duewel found the prevailing characteristics of every revival included

- prolonged periods of intercessory prayer
- a call to holiness
- a new hunger for and obedience toward the Word of God
- consecutive days of anointed and powerful preaching
- a great harvest of souls being saved
- tearful, public confessions resulting in citywide moral change

To each new generation, revival preachers delivered the same, unchanging message that released the same revival results: The same Holy Spirit power and fire that came down at Pentecost also fell down on them! Those in attendance indeed experienced an overwhelming conviction of sin, a desire for holiness, endurance to pray for long hours, assurance of salvation, miraculous healing, restoration of broken relationships, and such an outpouring of the Holy Spirit that praise and worship singing went on for hours.

Keep your eyes and ears open to the work of the Holy Spirit and the return to revival in your church, campus, or community—most especially in your heart!

## God's Version

*That is why the LORD says, "Turn to me now, while there is time. Give me your hearts. Come with fasting, weeping, and mourning. Don't tear your clothing in your grief, but tear your hearts instead." Return to the LORD your God, for he is merciful and compassionate, slow to get angry and filled with unfailing love. He is eager to relent and not punish.*

JOEL 2:12-13

My husband recently reminded me, "People love the Jesus who forgives. They just aren't as excited about the Jesus who says, 'Go and sin no more!'" We must preach the full gospel, not leaving out the parts that make us uncomfortable.

He asks us to turn to Him while there is time. He asks us to fast and weep and mourn over our sin.

We cannot underestimate or undermine the power of confession to a holy God.

He wants our hearts. He is a jealous God. He is a holy God. We cannot pretend to know what He is doing in another's life. We must only honestly and truthfully present who He is to another.

His mercy and power are beyond our understanding. At any time, He can perform a miracle, forgive a sinner, or heal one who is sick.

There is no one like God. No one loves like God. We cannot compare Him to anyone. Yet, when we present Him to others, we must not deliver our opinions. We must deliver Him to others in His own words.

# Think First

*There is more hope for a fool than for someone who speaks without thinking.*

PROVERBS 29:20

This proverb is for everyone who doesn't want the reputation of a fool.

*If you're a parent* and want to maintain communication with your children through all seasons of their lives—when they need you, like you, don't like you, and need you again—you must know when to hold your tongue, when to pray instead of speaking, and when to speak the truth in love. Consider the long-term effects of uncontrolled tongue lashing *before speaking*. Determine to treat your children as God's treasured possessions.

*If you're a boss* and want to retain the respect of your coworkers, don't entertain an impulsive, abusive, fiery, demeaning style of communication. It will only lead to turnover. Think first before speaking.

*If you're a child* (of any age), disrespectful retorts dishonor your parents and in fact break one of the Ten Commandments. Make every effort to be empathetic with your parents, and if all else fails, treat them with the same respect as you would an older, ornery neighbor.

*If you're a member of a church*, you'll always see things that can be done differently, perhaps even more efficiently. But since you don't know *everything* that is going on behind the scenes, consider offering your services or money before offering your criticism!

*If you're a husband or wife*, there should be no one you speak to more courteously and respectfully than your spouse. Not only are your children watching, but your greatest fan and most trustworthy friend *should* be your spouse. If your marriage is based on daily, healthy communication, your home will be a safe place for every family member.

Think before you speak, and save your reputation!

## Great Expectation

*I am counting on the LORD; yes, I am counting on him. I have put my hope in his word. I long for the Lord more than sentries long for the dawn, yes, more than sentries long for the dawn.* PSALM 130:5-6

s today the day? Is now the time?

One of the greatest struggles and inevitabilities of the Christian life is waiting on God, hoping in His Word, counting on Him to come to you.

Over thirty years ago, the janitor who led me to Christ laid hands on me and prayed over me. He said, "You will be an evangelist throughout the world." He didn't see me as I was; instead, he breathed a word from God into my heart that has never gone away.

The most astonishing thing about his words is that I believed him and immediately began looking for ways to be an evangelist—something I wasn't trained to do and had no previous aspirations for doing! Yet within three months of praying with the janitor, I became a volunteer with Youth for Christ (an evangelism and discipleship ministry for students). That following summer, I became an intern with YFC . . . and I have been in full-time ministry ever since.

In *Visioneering*, a book about waiting on God, author and pastor Andy Stanley wrote, "A man with a vision from God is a man on a mission."[3] I am—daily— intent on fulfilling the mission God put in my heart thirty years ago to be an evangelist throughout the world. I wake up daily and look with longing for the Lord to fulfill this dream.

How about you? What is the dream that God has put in your heart that won't go away?

*(right margin, vertical)* DECEMBER 11

345

### Your Friend

*Look! I stand at the door and knock. If you hear my voice and open the door, I will come in, and we will share a meal together as friends. Those who are victorious will sit with me on my throne, just as I was victorious and sat with my Father on his throne.* REVELATION 3:20-21

God gives us many images of Himself in the book of Revelation. But "our friend" is a picture that anyone of any age in any culture can understand.

As a friend, He doesn't force His way into our lives. He knocks on the door of our hearts and asks if we will open our lives to Him. Then He waits for our answer.

*The moment before* I asked Jesus to come into my heart, I had a very vivid thought: If I do this, it is going to change *everything* about my life. I knew instinctively that His entrance into my heart would be pervasive; it would require many other things to leave. I knew that if I asked Jesus to come into my heart, there would not be room for both Him and my other loves. . . .

Once we decide to invite Him in . . . He offers to share a meal together with us *as our friend!*

The disciples knew Jesus as their Lord and Savior, but He also went fishing with them, ate breakfast with them, enjoyed wedding celebrations with them, and ate the Passover meal with them.

When we open the door to Jesus, He becomes our friend and we become a part of His family forever.

Never lose perspective of the friend you have in Jesus. . . .

# Trusting God

*Fearing people is a dangerous trap, but trusting the LORD means safety.*

PROVERBS 29:25

D aniel was a young man who somehow gathered enough courage to trust His invisible God—when it could have cost him not only power and position, but even his life. We see a similar fearlessness in Esther, Moses, Joseph, Amos, Ezra, and Nehemiah. They each chose to trust the *invisible* God instead of obeying the strong, intimidating voices of other people in their lives.

Because their successes were so compelling, we must seriously consider what it practically means to trust God.

*First*, you must be able to recognize His voice, especially when everyone else's voice is louder! Charles Spurgeon said, "Daniel sustained the energy of his outward profession by constant secret communication with God."[4] Time alone with God is not an option for a believer, especially a leader. Through two-way conversations with God, you receive clear direction from heaven.

*Second*, you must willingly obey what you hear God say. Most often, obedience to God will cost something, if not everything. Yet obedience is the one response that builds indomitable trust between you and the unseen God.

*Third*, you must follow God even in the dark, even when alone. The ultimate test of trusting God is the belief that *no matter what*, He knows best. He is with you. He is trustworthy.

Trusting the Lord is a lifelong process. When does it start? Whenever you're ready.

## Get Up!

*The LORD spoke to Jonah a second time:"Get up and go to the great city of Nineveh, and deliver the message I have given you." This time Jonah obeyed the LORD's command and went to Nineveh, a city so large that it took three days to see it all. On the day Jonah entered the city, he shouted to the crowds:"Forty days from now Nineveh will be destroyed!" The people of Nineveh believed God's message, and from the greatest to the least, they declared a fast and put on burlap to show their sorrow.* JONAH 3:1-5

There is much to learn from Jonah.

- We are God's messengers to a lost, sinful, dying world. We cannot hesitate (or refuse) to take the message of salvation to the large cities full of lost, unbelieving souls. They are hungry for the gospel. We must overcome our arrogance or sense of inconvenience and speak out.
- We can't be overwhelmed by the size of the task. We can begin with the people we know who do not know the Lord by making a list of their names and praying for them daily, asking God how to introduce them to Him.
- We must be expectant that God's Holy Spirit goes before us to convict others to believe. We must not entertain excuses, speculating why others *might* resist the gospel. We must respond to God's promptings whenever and wherever.

Now is the time for you to boldly proclaim the gospel. Make your list of unsaved friends and family. Sign up for a missions trip. Get up and go!

## Praise Him

*Oh, praise the LORD, all you servants of the LORD, you who serve at night in the house of the LORD. Lift up holy hands in prayer, and praise the LORD. May the LORD, who made heaven and earth, bless you from Jerusalem.* PSALM 134

Busy, tired, lazy, overworked, overwhelmed, afraid, discouraged, stressed, even oppressed . . .

The psalmist gives us the solution for eliminating stress, overcoming oppression, and refusing to be discouraged despite our workload or unchanging situations: *We must praise the Lord!* One way to instantly find new resolve or new strength is to look up and into the eyes of the One who knows the present and the future and praise His name!

The psalmists didn't minimize their struggles. They revealed the constant pressures in their lives to God in prayer. They lifted their complaints to God, not to others. They asked Him for immediate help. They told God they were counting on His abilities to rescue them. And most importantly, they continued to serve Him night or day, despite their troubles.

The *purpose* of praise is to honor God with our lips by engaging our hearts to trust Him.

The *power* of praise is to lift us out of our moment of despair and into the ever-present, very real arms of God . . . until we *feel* His arms around us, carrying us, comforting us.

The *pattern* of praise is always to take our eyes off of ourselves or our circumstances and put them on the living, loving God.

Wherever you find yourself today, lift up your hands, praise His name, then tell Him you love Him and need Him. Go ahead . . . just praise the Lord!

# Micah's Message

*O people, the L*ORD *has told you what is good, and this is what he requires of you: to do what is right, to love mercy, and to walk humbly with your God.*

MICAH 6:8

Y ou don't have to be a theologian to understand that the message Micah received from the Lord was filled with relevant words for every generation who reads them. The greater concern is, "Will we heed God's Word any more diligently than the people who heard it in Micah's time?"

What did Micah say the Lord requires of His people?

*Do what is right.* As a mentor to students, I listen intently to their very real concerns or struggles. Then I always ask the question, "What is the *Lord* asking you to do?" Almost every time I receive a very honest, "right to the point" answer. Most people know the right thing to do. It is *doing* what is right that proves we have surrendered our will and heart to God.

*Love mercy.* When we actively pursue ways to exhibit more of Jesus' unfailing love, we become His hands in our community and throughout the world. But an equally merciful experience unfolds when we extend forgiveness to someone who has repented and turned back to God. Be God's messengers of mercy to strangers and your family!

*Walk humbly.* The most godly—and perhaps most difficult—characteristic to maintain over one's lifetime is humility. Life experiences take us through peaks and valleys, prosperity and poverty, success and failure. The ability to walk daily in front of God and others without pride or arrogance is God's request of His people.

What does the Lord require of you and me? Do what is right, love mercy, and walk humbly with Him.

# Jealous God

*The LORD is slow to get angry, but his power is great, and he never lets the guilty go unpunished.* NAHUM 1:3

I n *The Pulpit Commentary*, expositor W. J. Deane details the vision of Nahum, the prophet burdened by a message from God for the city of Nineveh. Deane writes, "Jonah had preached repentance to Nineveh, and the people had hearkened to his voice, but had soon relapsed into their old sins; and now Nahum pronounces their sentence."[5]

Chapters 1–3 of Nahum use word pictures to expose God's sentence to the people who have exalted themselves against Him:

> *The LORD is good, a strong refuge when trouble comes. He is close to those who trust in him. But he will sweep away his enemies in an overwhelming flood. He will pursue his foes into the darkness of night. (1:7-8)*

> *"I am your enemy!" says the LORD of Heaven's Armies. (2:13)*

> *What sorrow awaits Nineveh, the city of murder and lies! She is crammed with wealth and is never without victims. (3:1)*

> *There is no healing for your wound; your injury is fatal. (3:19)*

Deane concludes, "Their pride, oppression, idolatry, and especially their defiance of God's sovereignty, are severely rebuked, and the certain and complete destruction of the nation is plainly announced."[6]

Isn't it amazing that the salvation message the Ninevites previously received from Jonah was so quickly discarded and they eventually turned away from God and back to their old ways? Nahum 1:2 records, "The LORD is a jealous God, filled with vengeance and rage. He takes revenge on all who oppose him and continues to rage against his enemies!"

Clearly God is a jealous God.

## Written Instruction

*I will climb up to my watchtower and stand at my guardpost. There I will
wait to see what the LORD says and how he will answer my complaint. Then
the LORD said to me, "Write my answer plainly on tablets, so that a runner
can carry the correct message to others."* HABAKKUK 2:1-2

I f you are an author, this passage in Habakkuk is particularly
interesting. If you, like me, are a person who has recorded
your conversations with God in writing daily for many years,
it is even more compelling. It certainly invites you to learn more
about Habakkuk!

In *The Pulpit Commentary*, the book of Habakkuk is described
as a two-way conversation in prayer between God and Habakkuk.
While conversing with God, Habakkuk receives and records the
warning God has for Judah: He is about to allow another great
empire to attack them because of their great unfaithfulness toward
Him!

In his exposition, W. J. Deane writes, "Habakkuk speaks with
himself, and . . . waits for the communication which he confidently expects. . . . As a watchman goes to a high place to see all
around and discern what is coming, so the prophet places himself
apart from men, perhaps in some secluded height, in readiness to
hear the voice of God and seize the meaning of the coming event.
. . . He watches for the inward revelation which God makes to his
soul. . . . He watches till he hears God's voice within him."[7]

This description of prayer rings so true to me. I truly believe
that God wants us to write down what He says to us in prayer. He
will not only encourage us through our two-way conversations
with Him, but God might well use *us* to instruct or warn others
with His words.

# Mighty Savior

*For the LORD your God is living among you. He is a mighty savior. He will
take delight in you with gladness. With his love, he will calm all your fears.
He will rejoice over you with joyful songs.* ZEPHANIAH 3:17

I am often teased, even by my own husband, for those times
when I actually feel or think God is near me, or has done or
changed something specifically for me, or when I suggest that
He is present . . . meaning right here, right now in the same room
with me.

I can't help it! From the first day I met Christ, I talked out
loud to Him—as if He was right there—and I still talk out loud
to Him over thirty years later! I often think I feel His arm on my
shoulder or hear His whisper in my ear. And those small, gentle,
warm breezes that cross my face make me smile; they prompt me
to talk to God or listen to Him.

Even in my nightmares, when I am afraid, I wake up calling
out His name!

Whom do we have but the Lord of Heaven's Armies to fight
our battles?

For as difficult as life is (or I am for others), I do feel the
continuous delight of the Lord upon my life. I think He laughs
with me (and sometimes at me). I can feel His love calm my fears.
And I love to sing worship songs, especially when a blanket of
God's presence comes over the whole room—there is no place
I'd rather be!

Zephaniah's words are comforting to me, if not confirming.
I feel just as certain as he did, just as he penned . . . the Lord *is*
living among us, and He is a mighty Savior.

## Among Us

*Now the LORD says: Be strong, Zerubbabel. Be strong, Jeshua son of Jehozadak, the high priest. Be strong, all you people still left in the land. And now get to work, for I am with you, says the LORD of Heaven's Armies. My Spirit remains among you, just as I promised when you came out of Egypt. So do not be afraid.* HAGGAI 2:4-5

There is so much work to do. The harvest is so plentiful that more of us must get involved with His work.

I believe God is calling you. He is asking you—whatever you are currently doing—to add *His* work to *your* workload! It is time for *you* to bring in the harvest and fulfill His Great Commission.

Hear the Lord say to you, businessperson, "Start a Bible study or a noon-hour prayer meeting at your workplace."

Hear the Lord say to you, parent, "Start a Friday or Saturday night gathering in your home. . . . Kids will go where there is food and fun and family."

Hear the Lord say to you, single men and women, "Give time to your church's youth ministry. They need godly volunteers who will give a little love and attention each week to elementary, junior high, and high school students. And you just might find your future spouse there!"

Hear the Lord say to you, empty nesters, "Become mentors to young married couples in your church or neighborhood. Marriage is hard. Mentors who pray for, care about, and meet with newly-weds might well save a marriage."

Get to work. Remain strong. Be filled with His Holy Spirit. Don't be afraid.

## Their Testimony

*They have defeated him by the blood of the Lamb and by their testimony.
And they did not love their lives so much that they were afraid to die.*

REVELATION 12:11

D ietrich Bonhoeffer first published *The Cost of Discipleship* under the title *Nachfolge* in 1937. He spoke in great earnestness about the power of a believer's testimony, giving believers reason and courage to speak boldly of Christ, saying, "Neither failure nor hostility can weaken the messenger's conviction that he has been sent by Jesus."[8]

In his chapter titled "The Suffering of the Messengers," he reminded Christians they might be persecuted for sharing the gospel, saying, "The Lord promises them his abiding presence. . . . Nothing can happen to them without Jesus knowing of it."[9] He wrote honestly about the temptation to desert Jesus, begging believers to testify for Christ, to endure persecution and even hatred in His name. Bonhoeffer suffered the fate he wrote about and was hanged in April of 1945 in a Nazi concentration camp.

Bonhoeffer became a twentieth-century martyr who encouraged those who call themselves Christian to remain courageously loyal to Jesus all the days of their lives, to hold fast to the Word of God, and even to expect persecution for their testimony.

Perhaps the greater, more imposing challenge to those of us in the twenty-first century, especially in Western cultures, is not that we will suffer physical death for identifying ourselves with Jesus, but that we must suffer the loss of "self-love." We must be unafraid to let go of our entitlements, our worldly pleasures, and our selfishness.

Bonhoeffer's life and words will not leave me alone. . . .

DECEMBER 21

# The Accuser

*The angel showed me Jeshua the high priest standing before the angel of
the LORD. The Accuser, Satan, was there at the angel's right hand, making
accusations against Jeshua. And the LORD said to Satan, "I, the LORD, reject
your accusations, Satan. Yes, the LORD, who has chosen Jerusalem, rebukes you."*

ZECHARIAH 3:1-2

This is not the first time Satan is called the accuser of the
brethren. It is his reputation throughout the Bible—from
Job to Jesus.

My husband often teaches that our battle, as Paul says in
Ephesians, is not against flesh and blood, but against demonic
forces that tempt us to accuse those closest to us, even God!

Therefore, when you hear a voice accusing you or tempting
you to accuse others, you must identify and reject that voice.

Accusations divert attention from the truth. Accusations are
often half-truths sprinkled with lies. Accusations are designed to
discourage, demean, and destroy confidence or trust. Accusations
are not spoken in love; they fuel anger or promote arrogance.

You must speak back to these voices, rebuking and rejecting
them in the name of the Lord Jesus Christ!

When you hear a voice or receive a thought that wants you to

- deny God's power,
- ridicule a brother or
  sister in the Lord,
- dwell on negative or
  harmful thoughts,

- rationalize your sin,
- avoid or ignore truth,
- lie or cheat
- steal,
- use or abuse . . .

you must immediately stand up to these thoughts or voices and
simply say, "In the name of Jesus, get out of here." *Say it as often as
necessary* until the thoughts, temptations, or threats are gone.

If the accuser came to Jesus, surely he will not hesitate to
come to you and me.

# My Spirit

*He said to me, "This is what the LORD says to Zerubbabel: It is not by force
nor by strength, but by my Spirit, says the LORD of Heaven's Armies."*

ZECHARIAH 4:6

Every one of us has been created for a purpose; we've been
given a job to do by the living, loving God. Yes, it will take
much effort and creativity, persistence and teamwork,
money, supplies, time, and courage. But above all, if God has
something specific for you to do, it will come with these marching
orders: *"It is not by force nor by strength, but by my Spirit, says the LORD
of Heaven's Armies"* that you will

win the battle,

achieve the goal,

perform the work,

complete the job, or

succeed in your mission.

The Lord has assigned a specific work to you. Without His
presence, advice, or encouragement—*without His intervention*—
you are limited in power.

The Holy Spirit is man's supernatural power source. One
of the most critical appointments in your day is to connect with
God's power! When you spend time alone—talking to God and
listening to Him—you receive His instructions and the next steps
in the plan He has for your life. In prayer, you distinguish between
"other" voices of counsel and God's direction. During time alone
with God, you are given strength to restrain yourself from moving
impulsively ahead of Him.

What is the plan God has for your life? It is *never* too late to
begin the job or finish the work God has destined for you.

Complete it—not by your own might, but by God's powerful,
supernatural Spirit working in and through you!

# God's Word

*They were singing the song of Moses, the servant of God, and the song of the Lamb:"Great and marvelous are your works, O Lord God, the Almighty. Just and true are your ways, O King of the nations. Who will not fear you, Lord, and glorify your name? For you alone are holy. All nations will come and worship before you, for your righteous deeds have been revealed."*

REVELATION 15:3-4

From Genesis to Revelation, the voice and person of God is made known.

Though I've read the entire Bible yearly for many years, I am still profoundly amazed when the prophecies and prayers depicting Jesus Christ, concealed in the Old Testament, are revealed in the New Testament.

And each year, I grow more committed to knowing God better and more compelled to make Him known to more people. This objective becomes easier when I consider the Bible as the best instruction available to those who are searching for Him or have misconceptions about Him.

To date, I have been responsible for getting at least thirty thousand copies of the Bible into people's hands. I tell you this not because I am a scholar of the Bible, nor a theologian, but because I am convinced that if I can get the Word of God into the hands of those who have questions about Him, *He can get into their hearts*.

I encourage you to give Bibles away this coming year—at least one a month, maybe even one a week or one a day! Order a reserve stock for home and office. Put a few in your car and an extra one in your travel bag. If you have Bibles on hand, you'll give them away—He'll even show you to whom!

## With You

*Many peoples and powerful nations will come to Jerusalem to seek the LORD of Heaven's Armies and to ask for his blessing. This is what the LORD of Heaven's Armies says: In those days ten men from different nations and languages of the world will clutch at the sleeve of one Jew. And they will say, "Please let us walk with you, for we have heard that God is with you."*

ZECHARIAH 8:22-23

Immanuel. God with you!

What an interesting picture in the book of Zechariah. It is the image of a God who walks with His people!

Though an Old Testament reference, it could easily describe the relationship between Jesus and the disciples.

*Surely* the disciples who walked with Jesus enjoyed being with Him . . . truly they enjoyed the spontaneity of His miracles, sharing meals, fishing, listening to His revolutionary teaching, and spending time in prayer together. And *surely* when others encountered Jesus' disciples, they had to ask . . . "You know Jesus, don't you? Tell us about Him—what is He really like? We've heard that He is with you!"

Immanuel. God with you!

It should be no different today.

*Surely* those who know us should see Him—Immanuel, God with us—in our homes, in our office suites, in our classrooms, in our conversations, in our daily choices . . . the admiration for Him spilling out of our hearts and mouths.

*God is with you.* Walk with Him in such a personal and powerful way that others beg you to introduce them to Him!

# Praying Mother

*Let each generation tell its children of your mighty acts; let them proclaim your power.* PSALM 145:4

When my son, Jake, was a college student, I prayed daily that his passion for a particular style of music would diminish—and I told him so! I prayed and prayed. One day, I received a long distance phone call from Jake that began with, "Mom, you won't believe what happened." He continued, "I fell asleep on a train. My backpack was locked to my seat, but someone cut it off and stole it! It had my passport, airline tickets, travel cash, and . . . stacks of my music! When I figured out what happened, I started searching the train and found the backpack dumped in the trash. The money, tickets, passport . . . were all there! The only thing missing was my entire library of music!" As he relayed the story, I went from dread to laughter! I said, "Jake, I've been praying for God to take away your desire for that music—I didn't think He'd just . . . *take it*."

Because I believe that every child needs a regular investment of prayer and fasting over his or her life, no matter how old he or she is, I continued to pray for Jake—specifically for a breakthrough. Just recently, at the end of a twenty-four-hour fast, I received another phone call. The news made me stop everything and call my son. The breakthrough I had been praying for . . . happened that afternoon!

My friends at Moms in Touch International, a network of praying mothers, ask this challenging question—and I pass it along to you: "What could God do with an entire generation of children that has been prayed for?"

## Decision Time

*"All the nations have fallen because of the wine of [Babylon's] passionate immorality. The kings of the world have committed adultery with her. Because of her desires for extravagant luxury, the merchants of the world have grown rich." Then I heard another voice calling from heaven, "Come away from her, my people. Do not take part in her sins, or you will be punished with her."* REVELATION 18:3-4

When God says, "Come away with Me," it most often means come away *from* something or someone else. Oswald Chambers wrote of this great surrender, saying, "Not often, but every once in a while, God brings us to a major turning point—a great crossroads in our life. From that point we either go toward a more and more slow, lazy, and useless Christian life, or we become more and more on fire."[10]

Is this a "decision time" in your life? Have you come to this year's end with unfulfilled dreams? Have you allowed indulgence or lust or laziness to steal your true passion? Is this the day to determine to no longer take part in something unholy or unhealthy and instead, chase after the Sacred Obsession?

Oswald Chambers wrote that the battle for our souls—much like the one described in Revelation—is fought in our wills. He said, "Our battles are first won or lost in the secret places of our will in God's presence, never in full view of the world. The Spirit of God seizes me and I am compelled to get alone with God and fight the battle before Him. Until I do this, I will lose every time."[11]

Today, get alone with God. Take a journal, a Bible, and a pen. Fight and win the battle; make your decision in writing.

He calls, "Come away. . . ."

# Spiritual Kingdom

*I heard again what sounded like the shout of a vast crowd or the roar of mighty ocean waves or the crash of loud thunder:"Praise the LORD! For the Lord our God, the Almighty, reigns. Let us be glad and rejoice, and let us give honor to him. For the time has come for the wedding feast of the Lamb, and his bride has prepared herself."* REVELATION 19:6-7

When it all passes away—the earth and life as we know it—the Word of God says there will be a vast crowd of God's holy people singing praises in such loud chorus that it will surpass any sound ever heard on earth.

In *The Pursuit of God*, A. W. Tozer describes the very real dilemma that human beings have in understanding the God who reigns in heaven. He wrote, "Faith enables our spiritual sense to function. Where faith is defective the result will be inward insensibility and numbness toward spiritual things. A spiritual kingdom lies all about us, enclosing, embracing us, altogether within reach of our inner selves, waiting for us to recognize it. God Himself is here waiting our response to His presence. This eternal world will come alive to us the moment we begin to reckon upon its reality."[12]

My understanding of heaven is stretched by the book of Revelation's detailed images of what is to come; things I've never seen. But the riveting testimony of the angelic beings, the heavenly worshippers, and the elders in heaven—moves me most. Their worship honors Him for His sacrifice, for defeating the great enemy of our souls, for saving us from eternal separation.

This I can understand: worshipping the Risen Lamb, the Holy Son of God, the One who died for me. . . .

Let your worship begin now for all eternity!

## Name Written

*Anyone whose name was not found recorded in the Book of Life was thrown into the lake of fire.* REVELATION 20:15

**M**y older sister is quite accomplished. She is highly educated and both an avid student and a wonderful teacher. She is—and always has been—incredibly compassionate. Volunteering has always been a part of her life. She was always religious . . . and eventually took a very spiritual path, but it led her far away from the God of the Bible.

As time passed, our ability to discuss God, the Bible—and especially Jesus—became very difficult. Our differences were vast; our relationship became very strained.

My entire family continued to pray for my sister. How could she be reached with the truth when she resisted it so completely? Years of daily prayer had accumulated on her behalf . . . but we could not see any change or openness.

Then two years ago, my sister needed to come to Southern California for an extended visit while her son underwent a very serious operation. My mother invited my sister to her "purpose-driven" church called Saddleback. The timing was right . . . at the end of Rick Warren's message, my sister said a simple prayer and went to the information table and picked up a Bible.

Within two months, my sister moved permanently to Southern California, joined the church, was baptized, and attended new-believer classes. She has already been to Africa *twice* as a lay missionary!

Last night we were talking on the phone about her assigned reading in Randy Alcorn's book *Heaven* for her small group at church. She said, "I'm so glad my name is in the Book of Life!"

So are we!

# Heavenly Home

*He will wipe every tear from their eyes, and there will be no more death or*
*sorrow or crying or pain. All these things are gone forever.*

REVELATION 21:4

The final chapters in the book of Revelation deliver incredibly vivid pictures of the end of time, including a stunning holy city in heaven and the pit of a fiery hell. Many of the details seem vastly outside our understanding, uncommon to our earthly experiences. . . .

But when John says he heard a loud shout from the throne of heaven saying, "He will wipe every tear from their eyes," these words are compelling. If given the option, every one of us would wish never to undergo excruciating pain or the finality of separation that occurs when someone we love dies.

Dr. Randy Alcorn, in his book *Heaven*, narrows down chapters 21 and 22 in the book of Revelation as those which depict the most incredible details of what heaven will be like![13] Sin will forever be removed. There will be no more death. God will dwell face-to-face with humans. There will be ongoing corporate worship, no more shame, and no more tears. These expressions of heaven are *surely* experiences we can understand!

But the Bible says there is more! There will be abundant food and water, unlimited access to Paradise, fertile gardens, and complete harmony between man and animals!

So often we ignore the book of Revelation. In so doing, we risk missing out on the full understanding of the eternal hope God has for us!

# Jesus Calls

*The Spirit and the bride say, "Come." Let anyone who hears this say,*
*"Come." Let anyone who is thirsty come. Let anyone who desires drink*
*freely from the water of life.* REVELATION 22:17

J esus calls, "Come."

In *The Pursuit of God*, A. W. Tozer, a twentieth-century pastor and author, makes a powerful case for apprehending God. In 1948, he was a forlorn theologian, saddened by the state of a lifeless, passionless body of believers. He wrote, "I want deliberately to encourage this mighty longing after God. The stiff and wooden quality about our religious lives is a result of our lack of holy desire. Complacency is a deadly foe of all spiritual growth. Acute desire must be present. . . . He waits to be wanted."[14]

Tozer is adamant about passionately chasing after God. He begs men and women to burn with zeal for God; never to squelch the fiery urges that would drive us into the heart of God. He pleads with us never to relent, always to push forward, to love God with our emotions and feelings and personality . . . to follow *hard* after Him. At the very least, Tozer wants us to admire the freedom of others to chase after, lift their hands up to, and dance with the living, loving God.

Oh, won't you abandon your soul to the pursuit
of the holy One?

Oh, won't you love Him with an outrageous passion,
an extreme intensity to know Him more deeply,
and an unrelenting fervor to remain true to Him
above all others?

If you will chase after the sacred in this very hour, I am absolutely convinced you will both *discover* and *possess* the most unimaginable, overwhelming love and joy-filled passion you have ever felt.

Jesus calls, "Come."

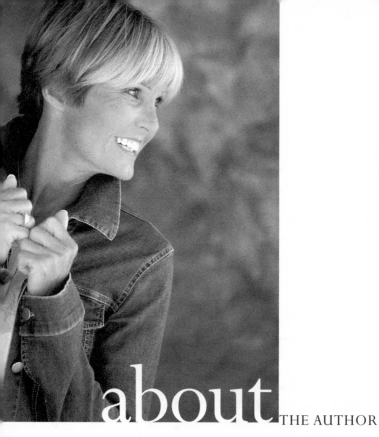

# about THE AUTHOR

BECKY TIRABASSI has been sharing her story at conferences, churches, and colleges since 1976. After almost two decades as a writer and speaker in youth work, Becky began a multimedia corporation, Becky Tirabassi Change Your Life, Inc. In 1996, she began to reach men, women, and students with her life-changing message through radio, television, resources, and events. Her many opportunities to reach people include having been a guest contributor on CBS's *The Early Show*, the host of the *Change Your Life Daily Radio Minute*, an occasional guest on *Focus on the Family* with Dr. Dobson, and a speaker with Women of Faith and Youth

Specialties, as well as sharing her story in her hometown at the 1994 Greater Cleveland Billy Graham Crusade.

In 2005, Becky Tirabassi founded a student organization, Burning Hearts, Inc. Surprisingly, after almost a decade away, she has returned to speaking to students across America, as well as adults, and she is passionate about calling them to be sold out to prayer, set apart in purity, and sent out with purpose.

*To reach Becky Tirabassi or for more information on events or resources, contact*

BECKY TIRABASSI CHANGE YOUR LIFE, INC.

BOX 9672

NEWPORT BEACH, CA 92660

1-800-444-6189

WWW.CHANGEYOURLIFEDAILY.COM

*or*

BURNING HEARTS, INC.

BOX 10926

NEWPORT BEACH, CA 92658

1-949-644-7466

WWW.THEBURNINGHEARTCONTRACT.COM

# *Notes*

## January

1. Corrie ten Boom, quoted in Awake and Go! Kingdom Quotes, http://www.watchword.org//index.php?option=com_content&task= view&id=5&Itemid=23.
2. Dietrich Bonhoeffer, *Life Together* (New York: HarperCollins, 1954), 13.
3. Rosalind Rinker, *Prayer: Conversing with God* (Grand Rapids: Zondervan, 1959), 23.
4. Hannah Whitall Smith, *The Christian's Secret of a Happy Life* (Whitefish, MT: Kessinger Publishing, 2003), 113.
5. Earl O. Roe, *Dream Big: The Henrietta Mears Story* (Ventura, CA: Regal Books, 1990).
6. Charles G. Finney, *Lectures on Revival*, ed. Helen Wessel (Minneapolis: Bethany House Publishers, 1977), 15.
7. J. Oswald Sanders, *Spiritual Leadership* (Chicago: Moody Press, 1994), 51.

## February

1. Oswald Chambers, *My Utmost for His Highest* (Grand Rapids: Discovery House, 1995), February 22.
2. Michael Richardson, *Amazing Faith: The Authorized Biography of Bill Bright* (Colorado Springs: WaterBrook, 2000), 37–38.
3. Helmut Thielicke, *Encounter with Spurgeon* (Philadelphia: Fortress Press, 1963), 93.
4. Steve Sherbondy, *Changing Your Child's Heart* (Wheaton, IL: Tyndale House, 1998), 27.
5. H. D. M. Spence and Joseph S. Exell, eds., *The Pulpit Commentary*, (New York: Funk and Wagnalls Company, 189-?), 4:187.
6. Jerry Bridges, *The Pursuit of Holiness* (Colorado Springs, CO: NavPress, 1978), 19.

## March

1. Smith, *Christian's Secret*, 114.
2. George Barna, *Revolution* (Carol Stream: Tyndale, 2005), 31.
3. Chambers, *Highest*, June 2.
4. Ibid., February 22.
5. Catherine Marshall, ed., *The Prayers of Peter Marshall* (New York: McGraw-Hill, 1954), quoted in Rueben P. Job and Norman Shawchuck, *A Guide to Prayer for Ministers and Other Servants* (Nashville: The Upper Room, 1983), 297.

6. Chambers, *Highest*, July 11.

7. Barna, *Revolution*, 17.

# April

1. Samuel Shoemaker, "I Stand by the Door," quoted in Job and Shaw-chuck, *Guide to Prayer*, 305.

2. Medical Research News, "New Research Suggests College Students Who Regularly Get Drunk Have a Higher Risk of Injuries," News-Medical .Net, May 23, 2005, http://www.news-medical.net/?id=10344.

3. National Institute on Alcohol Abuse and Alcoholism, *What Parents Need to Know about College Drinking*, April 2002, http://www .collegedrinkingprevention.gov/media/FINALParents.pdf.

4. Andrew Murray, *With Christ in the School of Prayer* (New Kensington, PA: Whitaker House, 1981), 89, 92–93.

5. Julie Rawe and Kathleen Kingsbury, "When Colleges Go on Suicide Watch," *Time*, May 22, 2006.

6. Theophan the Recluse, quoted in Job and Shawchuck, *Guide to Prayer*, 378.

# May

1. Chambers, *Highest*, June 16.

2. Sanders, *Spiritual Leadership*, 29.

3. Ibid., 31, 33.

4. A. T. Pierson, *George Müller of Bristol* (Old Tappan, NJ: Fleming Revell, 1899), 179–81.

5. Leonard Ravenhill, *Revival Praying* (Minneapolis: Bethany House Publishers, 1962), 105.

6. Samuel Chadwick, quoted in Becky Tirabassi, *Let Prayer Change Your Life* (Nashville, TN: Thomas Nelson, 2000), 10.

7. Billy Graham, *The Holy Spirit* (Waco: Word Publishers, 1978), 94.

8. Henri J. M. Nouwen, *The Way of the Heart* (San Francisco: HarperSanFrancisco, 1991), 31.

9. Matthew Bramlett and William Mosher, National Center for Health Statis-tics, "First Marriage Dissolution, Divorce, and Remarriage: United States," Advance Data from Vital and Health Statistics, no. 323 (May 24, 2001): 21.

10. Sanders, *Spiritual Leadership*, 82.

11. Ibid.

12. Luis Palau, *Heart After God* (Portland, OR: Multnomah, 1982), quoted in Tirabassi, *Let Prayer*, 80.

13. William Clement Stone, quoted in Tirabassi, *Let Prayer*, 43.

14. Ravenhill, *Revival Praying*, 105.

15. O. Hallesby, quoted in Tirabassi, *Let Prayer*, 43.

## June

1. Dr. and Mrs. Howard Taylor, *Hudson Taylor's Spiritual Secret* (Chicago: Moody Press, 1989), 156.
2. Charles Haddon Spurgeon, *The Soulwinner* (New Kensington, PA: Whitaker House, 1995), 42.
3. Ibid., 43.
4. Florence Littauer, *Personality Plus* (Old Tappan, NJ: Fleming H. Revell, 1983).
5. Bridges, *Holiness*.
6. Richardson, *Amazing Faith*, 26.
7. J. B. Phillips, *Letters to Young Churches* (New York: MacMillan, 1952), xiv.
8. Spence and Exell, *The Pulpit Commentary*, 9:339–340.
9. Jack Hayford, *Fatal Attractions: Why Sex Sins Are Worse Than Others* (Ventura, CA: Regal Books, 2004), 95–96.
10. Ibid., 97.
11. Sanders, *Spiritual Leadership*, 133.

## July

1. Murray, *School of Prayer*, 89.
2. Charles G. Finney, *The Autobiography of Charles G. Finney*, ed. Helen Wessel (Minneapolis: Bethany House Publishers, 1977), 70.
3. Ibid.
4. Spurgeon, *The Soulwinner*, 18–19.
5. Catherine Marshall, *A Man Called Peter* (New York: Avon Books, 1951), 302–3.
6. John Owen, *Sin and Temptation: The Challenge to Personal Godliness*, ed. James M. Houston (Minneapolis: Bethany House Publishers: 1996), 18–19.
7. Nikos Kazantzakis, *The Saviors of God: Spiritual Exercises*, quoted in Job and Shawchuck, *Guide to Prayer*, 116.
8. Bramlett and Mosher, "First Marriage," 21.
9. Owen, *Sin and Temptation*, 45–48.
10. Ibid., 47–48.
11. Chambers, *Highest*, May 20.
12. Ibid.
13. Mother Teresa, *A Gift for God*, quoted in Job and Shawchuck, *Guide to Prayer*, 216.
14. Dietrich Bonhoeffer, *The Cost of Discipleship* (New York: Simon and Schuster, 1959), 44.

# August

1. Jonathan Edwards, *Religious Affections: A Christian's Character before God*, ed. James Houston (Portland, OR: Multnomah Press, 1984), 10–11.
2. Bonhoeffer, *Discipleship*, 55.
3. C. S. Lewis, *The Screwtape Letters* (London: Geoffrey Bles, 1942), 9.
4. Bonhoeffer, *Discipleship*, 89.
5. Vigen Guroian, "Dorm Brothel," *Christianity Today*, February 2005.
6. A. W. Tozer, *Keys to the Deeper Life* (Grand Rapids: Zondervan, 1988), 77–78.
7. Lance Wubbels, ed., *Charles Spurgeon on Prayer: A 30-Day Devotional Treasury* (Lynwood, WA: Emerald Books, 2002), 94–95.
8. Zig Ziglar, *Over the Top*, rev. ed. (Nashville: Thomas Nelson, 1997), 183.

# September

1. The Barna Group, "Twentysomethings Struggle to Find Their Place in Christian Churches," The Barna Update, September 24, 2003, http://www.barna.org/FlexPage.aspx?Page=BarnaUpdate&BarnaUpdateID=149.
2. Andrew Murray, *Holy in Christ*, quoted in *Andrew Murray on Holiness: A 30-Day Devotional Treasury*, ed. Lance Wubbels (Lynwood WA: Emerald Books, 1998), Day 13.
3. William Law, *A Serious Call to a Devout and Holy Life* (San Francisco: HarperSanFrancisco, 2005), 21–22.
4. Jodie Berndt, *Praying the Scriptures for Your Children* (Grand Rapids: Zondervan, 2001).
5. Roe, *Dream Big*, 218–19.
6. Paul E. Little, *Know What You Believe* (Colorado Springs: Chariot Victor Publishing, 1999).
7. Law, *A Serious Call*, 15–16.
8. Hayford, *Fatal Attractions*, 114.

# October

1. Dallas Willard, *Hearing God* (Downers Grove, IL: InterVarsity, 1999), 222.
2. Fellowship of Christian Athletes, *Heart of an Athlete* (Ventura, CA: Regal Books, 2005), 15–16.
3. A. W. Tozer, quoted in Winkie Pratney, *Revival*, (Lafayette, LA: Huntington House, 1994), 17.
4. James Burns, *Revivals, Their Laws and Leaders*, quoted in Pratney, *Revival*, 24–25.
5. Bridges, *Holiness*, 102.
6. Sanders, *Spiritual Leadership*, 41.

7. Bonhoeffer, *Life Together*, 22–23.
8. Bonhoeffer, *Discipleship*, 131–32.

## November

1. Henri Nouwen, *A Cry for Mercy* (New York: Doubleday, 2002), 33.
2. Chambers, *Highest*, January 30.
3. William Wilberforce, *Practical View of the Prevailing Religious System of Professed Christians in the Higher and Middle Classes in this Country Contrasted with Real Christianity* (Whitefish, MT: Kessinger Publishing, 2004), 255.
4. Spurgeon, *The Soulwinner*, 280.
5. A. B. Simpson, quoted in L. B. Cowman, *Streams in the Desert*, ed. James Reimann (Grand Rapids: Zondervan, 1997), 426.
6. James Allen, *As a Man Thinketh* (Camarillo, CA: DeVorss and Co., 1979), quoted in Job and Shawchuck, *Guide to Prayer*, 272.
7. Chambers, *Highest*, November 4.
8. Cowman, *Streams in the Desert*, 294–5.
9. Owen, *Sin and Temptation*, 21.

## December

1. Blaise Pascal, quoted at http://en.thinkexist.com/quotes/blaise_pascal/.
2. Spurgeon, *The Soulwinner*, 9–10.
3. Andy Stanley, *Visioneering* (Sisters, OR: Multnomah Publishers, 1999), 86.
4. Wubbels, *Charles Spurgeon on Prayer*, 48.
5. W. J. Deane, introduction to Nahum in Spence and Exell, *The Pulpit Commentary*, 32:i.
6. Ibid.
7. Deane, introduction to Habakkuk in Spence and Exell, *The Pulpit Commentary*, 32:22.
8. Bonhoeffer, *Discipleship*, 213.
9. Ibid., 214.
10. Chambers, *Highest*, December 27.
11. Ibid.
12. A. W. Tozer, *The Pursuit of God* (Camp Hill, PA: Christian Publications, 1993), 47–48.
13. Randy Alcorn, *Heaven* (Carol Stream: Tyndale House, 2004).
14. Tozer, *Pursuit*, 17.

# download

## FREE AUDIO CLIPS
## OF BECKY SPEAKING

www.changeyourlifedaily.com

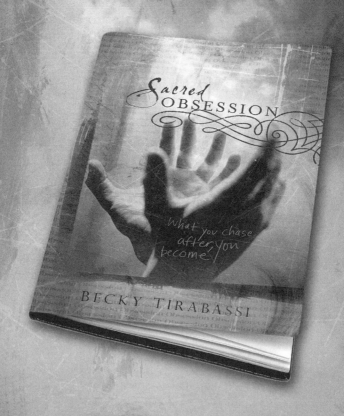

**What You Chase After, You Become....**

CHASE THE *Sacred*

**Available now at bookstores or online**

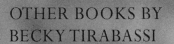

OTHER BOOKS BY
BECKY TIRABASSI

**AVAILABLE NOW AT
BOOKSTORES OR ONLINE**

## Sacred Obsession

## Change Your Life Daily Bible

### Change Your Life Daily Journal

## Keep the Change

### Let Prayer Change Your Life

### The Burning Heart Contract

### My Prayer Partner Notebook

## Transform Your Game *(with Roger Tirabassi)*

### The Front Nine *(with Roger Tirabassi)*

# Keep your
# Devotional Time
*fresh*
## with these
## popular

# devotionals.

## For Men

The One Year® Book of
Devotions for Men
by Stuart Briscoe

The One Year® Book of
Devotions for Men
on the Go by Stephen
Arterburn and Bill Farrel

## For Women

The One Year® Book of
Devotions for Women
by Jill Briscoe

The One Year® Book of
Devotions for Women
on the Go by Stephen
Arterburn and Pam Farrel

## For Youth

*The One Year® Book of Devotions for Kids*

*The One Year® Book of Devotions for Boys*

*The One Year® Book of Devotions for Girls*

*The One Year® Devos for Teens by Susie Shellenberger*

## For Family

*The One Year® Book of Family Devotions*

*The One Year® Book of Josh McDowell's Family Devotions*

## For Couples

*The One Year® Book of Devotions for Couples by David and Teresa Ferguson*

## General

*The One Year® Great Songs of Faith*

*One Year® through the Bible*

*The One Year® Book of Praying through the Bible by Cheri Fuller*

If You Need a
# Quick Moment of
*refreshment*
during Your **Busy Day,**
Try These

**MINI Gift Devotionals.**

**The One Year Mini for Women**
helps women connect with God through several
Scripture verses and a devotional thought.
Perfect for use anytime and anywhere between
regular devotion times. Hardcover

**The One Year Mini for Men**
helps men connect with God anytime,
anywhere, between their regular devotion
times, through Scripture quotations and a
related devotional thought. Hardcover

**The One Year Mini for Students** offers
students from high school through college
a quick devotional connection with God,
anytime and anywhere. Stay grounded
through the ups and downs of a busy student
lifestyle. Hardcover

**The One Year Mini for Moms**
provides moms with encouragement and
affirmation for those moments during a
mom's busy day when she needs to be
reminded of the high value of her role.
Hardcover